£ 3.25

LEARNING. services

01209 616259

680 JEN

Cornwall College Camborne
Learning Centre - FE

This resource is to be returned on or before the last date stamped below. To renew items please contact the Centre

Three Week Loan

Traditional
Country Craftsmen

Traditional Country Craftsmen

J. Geraint Jenkins

Drawings by Winifred Mumford

Routledge & Kegan Paul
London, Henley and Boston

First published in 1965
Revised edition published in 1978
by Routledge & Kegan Paul Ltd
39 Store Street,
London WC1E 7DD,
Broadway House, Newtown Road,
Henley-on-Thames, Oxon RG9 1EN and
9 Park Street,
Boston, Mass. 02108, USA
Set in 11 on 12pt Baskerville by
Kelly & Wright, Bradford-on-Avon, Wiltshire
and printed in Great Britain by
Redwood Burn Ltd
Trowbridge and Esher

British Library Cataloguing in Publication Data

Jenkins, John Geraint
Traditional country craftsmen.
–2nd ed.
1. Handicraft – Great Britain
2. Country life – Great Britain
I. Title
680   TT57   77–30381
ISBN 0 7100 8726 8

Contents

v

List of Figures

List of Plates

xiii

THE WOOLLEN WORKER

THE ROPE MAKER

THE TANNER

THE CURRIER

THE SADDLER

THE BOOT MAKER

THE CLOGMAKER

ACKNOWLEDGEMENTS

Grateful acknowledgements are made to the following for the use of photographs:
W. T. Jones: Plates 40–3, 74–5, 83, 97–8, 117, 119, 120–3, 169, 175–6; C. F. Snow: Plates 22–5, 28–36, 38, 44–7, 68–9, 100–7, 109, 111, 114–17, 158, 160, 162–4; M. L. Wight: Plates 12–14, 21, 26–7, 37, 146; B. W. Kinsey: Plate 39; D. J. Stanbury: Plate 113; G. Herbert: Plates 138–41; A. Fenton: Plate 161; J. W. Waterer: Plate 170; J. H. Thornton: Plates 178–81; The Leather Institute: Plates 167–8; City of Gloucester Museum: Plates 148–9; University of Leeds, Folk Life Survey: Plates 143–5, 159; Rural Industries Bureau: Plates 91, 96, 108, 110, 118, 132–3, 135–6, 142; National Museum of Wales, Welsh Folk Museum: Plates 2–3, 48–51, 56–61, 92–5, 99, 112, 115, 116, 124–7, 137, 150–7, 165–6, 171–4, 177; University of Reading, Museum of English Rural Life: Plates 1, 4–11, 15–20, 52–5, 62–7, 70–3, 76–82, 84–91, 130–1, 134, 182–5; National Museum of Wales, Department of Geology: Plate 147; Luton Museum: Plates 128–9.

I

Introduction

THE CRAFTSMAN CAME INTO BEING in order to fulfil society's needs for a specialist who could supply it with its day to day requirements. Although in the past a great deal of equipment for the farm and home could be made by the farmers and non-specialists, there was a great deal of work that they could not undertake without the assistance of a specialist who was proficient in a particular trade. For example, in the Pennines in the nineteenth century, many farmers in the more isolated parts built the wheel-less sledges that they used for harvesting sloping fields from the timber growing in their own farms. All they required was a saw, a hammer and a few nails and they could produce a perfectly efficient vehicle. But if a farmer required a more sophisticated vehicle, a two-wheeled cart or a four-wheeled wagon to undertake transport on his farm, then he would have to call on the services of a highly specialised and proficient craftsman – the local wheelwright.

Since the dawn of civilisation, the craftsman has been an essential member of society throughout the world and the history of crafts is as old as the history of mankind itself. 'Without these', said an Old Testament prophet, 'can not cities be built, nor inhabited nor occupied . . . they maintain the state of the world and their desire is concerning their work and occupation.' Until recent times the craft element in British communities was as essential as it was in ancient Israel. Most rural communities were almost self-sufficient and only on rare occasions did the countryman find it necessary to

venture far outside his own community and locality to search
for the means of life.

Most of the inhabitants of a country district were born,
lived and died within the narrow confines of their own localities
or villages and most realised their ambitions within their own
communities, to which they were tied by ties of blood, family
and neighbourliness. But the rural neighbourhood or country
village was something far more than a social entity; it was an
economic entity as well, for most of the day to day needs of the
community could be met by members of that community
itself. Most of the food required could be produced locally; the
countryman had animals that could supply him with milk,
meat, skins and wool; he had fields, gardens and orchards
that supplied him with cereals, root crops, fruit and vegetables.
In most parts of the country, at least until the end of the
nineteenth century, farming depended very heavily on a large
labour force and the co-operative effort of relatives and
neighbours during busy periods of the farming year and on a
wide range of hand tools and horse-drawn implements, many
of them produced by the numerous bands of craftsmen that
lived in each locality. Until recently, such tasks as baking
bread, making butter and cheese, brewing beer and cider
making were very much a part of the household routine of
rural homes. Pigs were killed and salted in most districts and
many products of the farm, corn, wool and animal skins could
be taken to a local mill for processing. The products of those
mills – flour, oatmeal or blankets, could be used directly in the
home, while other products, such as cloth or leather could be
used by one of the many local craftsmen to make some essential.
In some parts of the country, the craftsmen who processed
farm produce were not paid in cash at all, but were allowed to
keep a proportion of the produce as payment. Corn millers
were allowed to keep a bushel or two of corn for their own use,
while woollen manufacturers in parts of Wales were allowed to
keep a tenth of all the work brought to their mills by farmers
for processing, as payment. For example, Isaac Williams of the
Esgair Moel Mill, Llanwrtyd, Powys, whose mill is now at the
Welsh Folk Museum, St Fagans, in processing wool for local
farmers and supplying them with knitting yarn, cloth and

blankets, always kept a proportion of the fleeces as payment. This he made up into cloth which he sold on his market stall in Builth Wells.

Craftsmen were responsible too for such tasks as producing tools and equipment for the farm and home, and essentials, ranging from field gates to horse shoes and from ploughs to shovels could be produced locally by hosts of wheelwrights, blacksmiths and carpenters. Since each craftsman was concerned specifically with farm tools for his own locality and made them to suit local conditions of soil and topography, considerable variation in tool design came into being. Take, for instance, one simple farm tool, the billhook, described by Richard Jeffreys as 'the national weapon of the English labourer'. In the past, billhooks, like other farm tools, were made by village blacksmiths for the farming population of their own districts and, since each tool was designed for dealing with a specific type of vegetation and local conditions, many hundreds of different patterns of billhook came into existence. On the Suffolk coast, for example, billhooks made by blacksmiths at such places as Orford and Woodbridge were designed primarily for cutting banks and edges that were mostly below the level of the worker's hands. Consequently the blades were heavier at the front and each tool was equipped with a long, rounded handle. To deal with rough sedge, rushes and woody roots, the Suffolk billhook had a slightly convex blade with a short straight bite at the end for dealing with those roots. The billhooks of Brecknock on the other hand were designed primarily for laying hedges of straight willow, hazel and thorn and consequently the tool had an almost straight blade. The shape of the handle and the method of hafting also varied from district to district. In some places, such as parts of Dyfed where briar and thorn predominate, long, turned handles which kept the worker's hand well clear of the prickles were preferred.

A craftsman's response to environmental conditions could also be seen in large farm implements. Thus, for example, an all-wooden plough from the Vale of Pewsey that was still being made to a three-hundred-year-old pattern in the 1930's was specifically designed for heavy clay land. Country wheelwrights produced farm wagons that were well suited to local conditions of geology and topography[1] so that it was possible to distinguish regional types of four-wheeled vehicle. For example, take the county of Gloucester, where the wheelwrights' art was very highly developed. A wheelwright producing wagons for the heavy pasture land of the Vale of Berkeley provided his blue-painted vehicle with greatly dished, double-straked wheels as befitted a clay land district. He provided them with nearly upright fore and tail ladders to carry the heavy hay crops of this dairying region and since the roads and lanes of the district are generally straight, the locking capacity of wagons was not a first consideration. The yellow-painted Cotswold wagons, on the other hand, were quite different (Plate 1). Here, the wheelwrights built their wagons as light as possible as befitted a region with many changes of slope. Lock was very important in a country of winding lanes, and small, nearly horizontal end ladders were fitted. These were designed to carry corn sheaves rather than hay and the whole vehicle with its wide track was designed for a rolling countryside, where sheep raising and cereal cultivation forms the basis of the economy. In the land beyond the Severn in west Gloucestershire, the Forest of Dean wagon was quite different. Here a heavy box-like vehicle with broad wheels and a deep body predominated. It had a poor lock and the vehicle was designed not only to carry hay and corn, but also to carry apples from the cider orchards, gravel, sand, stone and root crops. Consequently body planks were much thicker than for a purely harvesting wagon and the metal body standards were very thick and strong so as to support heavy loads in bulk. Undoubtedly country wheelwrights, in providing the day-to-day requirements of the farming population, contributed in no small measure to the personality and character of the various regions of Britain.

But country craftsmen were responsible for far more than the production of farm tools and implements. It was local craftsmen who provided furniture for the home, wearing apparel, boots, clogs, utensils for the kitchen and dairy; indeed everything that a countryman required could be produced locally. But even if a locality did not possess all the essential craftsmen, then there were always travelling dressmakers, travelling

4

saddlers, travelling brick makers and other intinerant craftsmen who could pay visits even to the remotest country district.

Since the 1920's, but especially since 1945, great changes have taken place in rural Britain, for no longer does the countryman look towards his own locality for the means of life. The craftsman has lost his place as an essential member of the rural community, for the products of the industrial regions are within reach of even the remotest farmhouse in the hills. The newspapers and television are constantly encouraging the countryman to buy goods and articles that are exactly the same in all quarters of the globe, while ever-improving means of transport carry these standardised products with ever-increasing efficiency to the heart of the countryside. The crafts-man is therefore less essential than he has ever been. In this book we shall be concerned with the skill and artistry of ordinary people who were concerned with supplying the day to day needs of ordinary people. Many of the craftsmen concerned were still practising their trade in the early 1960's; many were the last representatives of a tradition that went back for thousands of years; many have disappeared within the last few years.

II

What is craftsmanship? Why is it that the craftsman was such a respected member of society the world over? Why did an Old Testament prophet sing his praises; why did the Welsh medieval court give the blacksmith and his fellows a special place of honour in its hierarchy?[2] How indeed does the craftsman differ from the ordinary worker in a factory?

There are three characteristics inherent in craftsmanship.

1. The craftsman is able to marry beauty and utility. He is able to combine good taste and usefulness.
2. The true craftsman does not depend on complex mach-inery and equipment to complete his work.
3. The true craftsman is not only able to work in an ancient tradition, but he is able to build on the foundation of history. The past provides a solid basis for his work.

5

1. Craftsmanship. A combination of utility and good taste

The craftsman came into being in order to supply the community with its day-to-day necessities. If a farmer required a plough then a plough was made; if his wife required a butter churn, then the local cooper made one; if the daughter required a dresser as part of her dowry, then the local carpenter built one. The craftsman's chief quality is his ability to make these simple things; to make something useful and durable without any unnecessary adornments and decorations. In the wake of this utilitarian purpose, there follows pride, the true craftsman's pride in creating something useful, but creating it with beauty and good taste. In the material history of Britain, it is surprising what taste and beauty is often exhibited in the ordinary things of the farm and home. A four-wheeled farm wagon, for example, is a very ordinary piece of equipment designed for carrying the harvest to the shelter of the farmstead. Strictly speaking a large box on four wheels would do the work quite as well, but the country wheelwright's pride of craftsmanship, the traditional workmanship of his region dictated that he had to curve the sideboards over the rear wheels as gracefully as possible; it dictated that he had to cut delicate chamfers, to cut down weight wherever possible; it dictated, too, that he had to paint his vehicle in delicate colours, not only to keep out the rain but so that people could say on seeing his product, 'This was indeed craftsmanship'.

For as long as the country craftsman clung to the idea that his whole purpose in life was to make something that could be used, then more often than not beauty and good taste followed. But far too often, especially in recent times, we find country craftsmen being led astray by their imagination, adding decoration upon decoration to no purpose. In every case this shows a deterioration of craftsmanship.

For example, one of the oldest Welsh potteries is that at Ewenni, near Bridgend in Glamorgan. In the past, the Ewenni pottery like all others was concerned with producing ordinary utilitarian commodities – water pitchers and drinking mugs, butter churns and butter crocks, washing tubs and cooking dishes; simple things designed for use. For as long as these potters stuck to the idea that their main purpose in life was to make ordinary utilitarian things, for as long as they continued to work in the tradition of centuries then true craftsmanship was inherent in their work. But in many cases as soon as they departed from that tradition degeneration of style set in. Compare the excellence of the ordinary butter churn (Plate 2) and the grotesqueness of the vase (Plate 3). Yet, while the first utensil was made for use and its simplicity of line displays a certain beauty and good taste, the vase with its uninspired decoration was made as a wedding present for King George V and Queen Mary on their marriage in 1893. To the craftsman, this, and not his day-to-day work was the zenith of achievement, his greatest work; a piece of pottery far removed from the traditional products of this Welsh craftsman. Today, where a vast proportion of the products of the Welsh pottery are aimed at the tourist trade, the design, style and craftsmanship of those pieces is far below the standard of workmanship displayed in the eighteenth and nineteenth centuries, when the potter was an essential member of the community.

2. Craftsmanship and Hand Work

In the heart of the countryside today, craftsmen are still found who employ the same techniques of manufacture, the same tools as have been used for many hundreds of years. For example, in the craft of barrel making, the modern cooper uses tools that are not dissimilar to those used by craftsmen in Roman times; today's maker of gold leaf uses techniques that were well known in ancient Egypt, while the twentieth-century wheelwright uses exactly the same method of tireing a wooden wheel as was used in Iron Age Europe. Yet, even today, in an age of mass production, there are craftsmen turning out by hand, objects of such quality that no machine can equal.

The basic difference between a true craftsman and the factory worker is the fact that the final result of a craftsman's effort is entirely in his own hands. It is he and no one else who determines the speed at which he works; the world of production schedules, of demarcation disputes and strikes is very far away indeed from the isolated workshops of rural Britain. However complex a machine may be, it can after all, only accomplish a pre-determined task. A machine cannot think, it cannot design and it cannot express its character in what it does or creates. But give a man a piece of stone or wood, give him a few simple tools, give him practice, add to this a love and understanding of his medium and a highly developed sense of taste, and the craftsman's technique, however simple, becomes unsurpassable. Today, hand-made furniture, hand-made shoes, and even hand-made bricks are greatly valued, and, as in medieval times, there is a premium on skilful hands and a pride in the ability of ordinary men to supply ordinary needs.

3. Craftsmanship and the Persistence of Tradition

In many rural industries there has been a continuity of tradition over many years, and modern craftsmen still depend on techniques and styles that have been well-known for hundreds of years. In the Welsh bowl turning industry, for example, prehistoric patterns persisted until recent times while in the chair making industry in the Chilterns pieces of equipment similar to those excavated from Iron Age sites were used very recently. A village rake maker in Berkshire has not changed his techniques of manufacture, nor the tools of his trade, since his ancestor established the workshop over four hundred years ago, while his neighbour, a wattle hurdle weaver, uses the same methods as were used for making building wattle in prehistoric times. In one of the most modern furniture factories in High Wycombe there is a museum containing hundreds of chairs made by the Buckinghamshire craftsmen in the past. The main purpose of this vast collection is to provide inspiration for the modern designers of the company, who in designing modern furniture gain inspiration from the traditional workmanship of the district; the past providing a solid basis for the future of a competitive industry.

Furthermore, the persistence of ancient traditions is expressed in a spectacular way in the tools and implements manufactured by modern industry in the urban centres of Britain. For example, in the past every district in the land had its own peculiar type of farm tool made by the craftsmen of those districts. A tool that varied tremendously from one district to the other was, as has been said, the billhook, a simple but valuable farm tool that dates back to prehistoric times. In the past these were made by village blacksmiths, but in the late nineteenth century the blacksmiths were disappearing very rapidly and their work was being taken over by the large-scale manufacturers. But not only did these manufacturers take over the work as such, but they also took over the old patterns of the country blacksmiths, and at the present time they still make the great variety of billhook that custom and tradition had said were best for a particular region.

III

The country crafts of Britain may be divided into three broad categories.

(i) The processing crafts where the craftsman is concerned with processing some raw material.

(ii) The service crafts where the craftsman is concerned with the repair and renovation of equipment.

(iii) The creative crafts where the craftsman takes a raw material and converts it into a finished product.

These creative crafts themselves can be divided into three distinct groups:

a. Those that owed their location to the presence of raw materials.

b. Those that came into existence to meet a local demand.

c. Home crafts, including the leisure crafts.

(i). The Processing Crafts

Processing craftsmen are concerned with converting a raw material so that it can be used on the farm and home or by another craftsman. The corn miller, for example, is concerned with processing grain, so that it can be used by the baker or housewife, while the maltster was concerned with the processing of barley by moistening and artificially drying grain, ready for use by domestic and commercial brewers. Tanners were concerned with treating animal skins by long immersion in a series of tan pits containing mixtures of varying strengths of oak bark and water, which acted as a tanning agent. In turn, the leather, if it was to be used for making horse harness or boot uppers, had to be passed on to another processing craftsman, the currier or leather dresser who prepared the tanned leather for the saddlers and bootmakers by adding oil and grease to its surface and polishing it with glass, stone, mahogany and steel polishers.

In most processing crafts a great deal of immovable equipment was required, and since in most cases water power was required for driving machinery and often for treating the product itself, the processing industries were carried out in small factories or mills, located on the banks of streams. For the process of tannery, for example, the following equipment was necessary.

A water-driven mill wheel and a mill for grinding bark.
A plentiful supply of clean water for initial washing of hides.
At least three lime pits for initial immersion of hides before fleshing and unhairing.
Two or three mastering pits containing a mixture of hen or pigeon manure or dog dung and water for treating calf skins.
A pit for fleshings and other waste products.
Up to fifty tan pits containing oak bark and water in varying strengths for the actual tanning of hides.
Beams to act as work benches for fleshing and unhairing.
Unhairing and fleshing knives. Scudding knives for removal of lime.
A rounding table (wood) and knives for cutting up hides into six or eight parts before tanning.
Hooks and long-handled tongs for handling hides in pits.
Plungers for mixing oak bark. Bark baskets and bark barrows.

A heavy brass roller for rolling tanned hides on a zinc rolling platform.

After rolling, sole leather did not require further treatment before it could be used, but harness and boot upper leather had to be dressed by the currier. The currier's craft did not depend on water power or any large, complex machinery, for dexterity in the use of hand tools was the main requirement. Nevertheless it was an advantage for the currier to locate his workshop either in or near the source of supply – that is, the local tannery.

A woollen mill preserved at the Welsh Folk Museum, St Fagans, near Cardiff, to quote an other example of a processing plant, contains the following equipment:

A pair of dye vats, one equipped with windlass.
A devil or willy for intermixing and disentangling wool.
A carding engine.
A spinning jack of eighty spindles.
A twister.
A warping wall.
Three hand looms.
A cutting machine.
A press.
Fulling stocks.
A rowing frame.
A tenter frame, twenty yards long.
A water wheel.
A washing trough and tubs.

Rural paper mills accommodated a number of heavy, water-driven beaters, and a plentiful supply of water was essential for driving these, and clean pure water was essential in the paper-making process itself. This particular craft became located in surprising places such as in the remote valley of the Grwyne in south-east Powys. It developed there because there was a never-failing supply of pure, soft water which, since it had run over limestone, was very suitable for paper making.

(ii). The Service Crafts

The service craftsman is concerned with the repair and renovation of farm and domestic equipment. For example, the joiner is concerned with repairing buildings; the cobbler is concerned with boot and shoe repairs and the agricultural engineer is concerned with the repair of farm equipment. Within recent years, many craftsmen who were in the past creative craftsmen have, due to changing circumstances, become service workers. For example, in the past every locality in Britain had its blacksmith, a creative craftsman responsible for making a great variety of goods for the farm and home. Within recent years, however, the blacksmiths have become much rarer and in many cases they have ceased to be creative craftsmen, becoming mechanics and agricultural engineers instead. A blacksmith in a certain Oxfordshire village began his three-year apprenticeship in 1910, working for twelve hours or more every day until he became fully competent in his craft. After another year as a journeyman blacksmith he took over his present workshop in 1914. At that time he was but one of a large number of blacksmiths in the region, but by the end of the 1930's he was the only one practising the trade within a radius of ten miles. In the 30's, the smith's work was very much a creative one; he built gates, ploughs and harrows, he tired wheels, undertook decorative wrought iron work and shod horses, all these tasks being done with the minimum of machinery. The forge fire had to be blown by hand, iron had to be drilled, welded and filed by hand and the craftsman had to work a twelve-hour day and a six-day week in order to make ends meet. Today machinery has replaced hand work: the forge fire is blown with an electric fan, and the smith has electric drills, electric grinders, oxy-acetylene welders and a great deal of other equipment that has made his life much less strenuous than in the past. The character of the work has also changed, for no longer is the blacksmith concerned with making farm and domestic equipment but is primarily concerned with the maintenance and repair of factory-made commodities.

late-nineteenth-century plunger churn by
Jenkins of Ewenni, Glamorgan.

1. A Cotswold farm wagon.

3. A vase of 1893 by Jenkins of Ewenni.

4. The beechwoods of Hampden, Buckinghamshire with the bodger's hut.

5. Owen Dean, the last of the Chilter
chair bodgers, cutting beech logs with
beetle and wedge.

THE CHAIR BODGER

6. Trimming billets with a side axe.

7. Shaping beech pieces on a shaving hors

Turning a chair leg on the pole lathe.

9. The pole lathe, a piece of portable, home-made equipment.

THE CHAIR BODGER

10. The pole, the driving power for the lathe.

11. A 'hedgehog' of seasoning chair legs awaiting collection.

12. Seasoning clog soles ready for transport to the clogmaking factories of the North of England.

13. Jonah Webb at work in the alder groves of Gwent in the early 1930s.

14. A pair of cloggers at work in South Wales in the 1930s.

15. Weaving on a wattle mould.

THE WATTLE WEAVER

16. S. F. Cox of Tadley, Hampshire, trimming a hazel sail to length on the gallows.

17. Close-up of weave.

18. (*Top left*) Finishing.

19. (*Top right*) Trimmi
finished hurdle with t
trimming knife.

THE WATTLE
WEAVER

20. (*Left*) The complet
hurdle.

21. (*Below*) A shepherd
the Vale of the White Hor

22. A Sussex hoop maker splitting rods on a brake.

23. Shaving a hoop on the upright horse

THE HOOP MAKER

24. Coiling.

25. Stacking finished hoops.

26. Charcoal burning in the Wyre Forest of Worcestershire, *circa* 1910.

THE CHARCOAL BURNER

27. Charcoal burner's hut, Worcestershire.

28. Modern charcoal burners using retorts, in the Weald of Sussex.

29. (*Top left*) An Oxfordshire spar maker splitting hazel rods with a hook.

30. (*Top right*) Shaping spar gadd.

THE THATCHING SPAR MAKER

31. Pointing spars.

32. Planting withy in the Thames Valley in Berkshire.

33. Harvesting withy stools

THE OSIER
BASKET MAKER

34. Making white willow by inserting bundles in water pits.

35. Drying white willow at Baughurst, Hampshire.

36. (*Above*) Stripping willow.

37. (*Left*) Boiler for making brown willow.

THE OSIER BASKET MAKER (continued).

38. (*Below left*) Sandford of Baughurst making a basket on a lap board.

39. Gwilym Jones of Ffostrasol, Dyfed, making a traditional potato basket—the *gwyntell*.

40. (*Top left*) Alfred Birch, Wyre Hill, Worcestershire, removes a log ready for splitting from the boiler.

41. (*Top right*) Weaving strips of cleft oak on to the frame.

THE SPALE
BASKET MAKER

42. (*Right*) Weaving chissies.

43. (*Below*) Trimming a completed five peck scuttle.

44. (*Top right*) A member of the Smith family of Hurstmonceaux, Sussex, selecting chestnut rods for the trug frame.

45. (*Top left*) Shaping the trug rim.

THE TRUGGER

46. (*Below left*) Shaping the frame.

47. (*Below*) Bending trug boards in the setting brake.

49. (*Above*) William Rees of Henllan, Dyfed, with
stall at Carmarthen market place in the 1930s.

48. (*Left*) John Davies, the last of the Abercuch, Dyfe
bowl turners at work in 1960.

THE BOWL TURNER

50. (*Below left*) Gwyndaf Breeze of the Welsh F
Museum using the pole lathe.

51. (*Below*) Examples of Breeze's work.

52. (*Top left*) George Lailey of Bucklebury Common, Berkshire, at work in the 1920s.

53. (*Top right*) The pole lathe used by Lailey until 1956.

THE BOWL TURNER (continued).

54. (*Left*) Examples of Lailey's elm bowls.

55. (*Below*) The bowl turner's hut at Turner's Green, Bucklebury Common.

THE SPOON CARVER

56. (*Top left*) W. R. Evans of the Welsh Folk Museum, St. Fagans, near Cardiff, splitting a sycamore log. 57. (*Top right*) Shaping handle. 58. (*Middle left*) Shaping shoulders. 59. (*Middle right*) Scooping with a crooked knife. 60. (*Bottom left*) Smoothing with a spokeshave. 61. (*Bottom right*) Finishing with a hand knife.

(iii). Creative Crafts

Crafts that owe their existence to the presence of raw materials. For example chair-leg making in the Chilterns came into existence because of the availability of beech in the area; indeed the existence of the furniture industry in High Wycombe can be traced back directly to the presence of a suitable raw material. Basket making in Sedgemoor, turnery in the Teifi Valley and besom making in northern Hampshire are all examples of rural industry that developed because of the existence of a suitable raw material in the region.

Crafts that came into existence to meet local demand. These were the crafts and industries essential to every self-sufficing community and ranged from saddlery to iron founding. It is craftsmen belonging to this class that have disappeared more than any other. In 1831, for example, the Ceredigion district of Dyfed had 28 saddlers, 1 whip maker, 12 printers, 15 tin smiths, 17 clock makers, 275 blacksmiths, 6 basket makers, 33 wheelwrights and millwrights, 393 tailors, 523 carpenters, 8 thatchers and 334 stone masons. At that time, too, it had specialised craftsmen who met the local demand of the maritime communities. In 1831 the Ceredigion district of Dyfed had 5 sail makers, 13 rope makers, and 43 shipwrights.

The advent of mass production, mass advertising and mass transport has meant the death of numerous creative craftsmen, who were dependent on a local market. Within the last fifty years craftsmen such as wheelwrights, white coopers and clogmakers have virtually disappeared.

Leisure and Home Crafts. In this category are crafts such as butter and cheese making, lipwork and needlework carried out by the craftsman to supply a local or even a family demand. Once again mass production has led to a marked decrease in the homecrafts. Within this category, too, fall such leisure crafts as basket making, woodcarving, quilting and lace making carried out by amateurs in their spare time. The advent of mass entertainment has to a great extent killed the leisure crafts.

II

Woodland Craftsmen

THE TRADITION of itinerant woodland craftsmanship is a dying one, for today only a few workers practise a trade that is essentially seasonal, in the solitude of a coppice or glade. 'Bodging' as itinerant craftsmanship is called in some parts of the country, survived in isolated pockets of woodland until recent times and the Chilterns, Furness, the Weald and Wyre Forest were particularly well known as the haunt of these picturesque workers. It survived to a later date in those trades where there is a great deal of wastage of raw material, as in clog sole making. It survived, too, in those crafts such as charcoal burning and hoop shaving, where the finished product is considerably lighter than the raw material, a vital factor when many woodland workers obtain their materials from isolated forests and glades. Bodging survives, too, in those trades where the tools and equipment of a craft are few in number and easily transportable. A thatching spar maker, for example, needs nothing more than a billhook to complete his work.

A number of well-known crafts such as birch besom making in Hampshire, heather broom making in East Yorkshire and spale basket making in the Wyre Forest and Furness were, in the past, important woodland crafts. In more recent times, the tradition of bodging in those trades gave place to working in permanent workshops and as such they must be regarded as village trades. There are others, such as wattle hurdle making, that are in some parts of the country carried out in the woodlands, while in others they are carried out in village workshops. Only a few itinerant crafts have persisted, the most notable

14

being thatching spar making and wattle weaving. Others like chair bodging have become extinct within the last few years, while others like clogging ceased to exist in the 1930's. Some woodland crafts like bundling hazel for drainage purposes and making spile and wire fencing are relatively simple and demand the minimum of skill in the use of hand tools. Others like hoop shaving and clog sole making demand considerable knowledge of raw materials and dexterity in the use of hand tools. Some of the products, like chair legs and tent pegs, can be made very quickly, others like wattle hurdles demand hours of work, a thorough understanding of the materials, skill in the use of hand tools, together with a good eye and judgement.

In the past, a vast number of products were made by itinerant craftsmen, but in this chapter only those more complex trades that persisted until recent times will be described. Well-known, but simple trades like tent peg making and split chestnut fencing will not be considered. In the case of many of the crafts, the traditional products have been replaced by more modern materials. Thus the virtual extinction of the dry coopering trade has meant the disappearance of hoop shavers, while the disappearance of the clog as a piece of footwear has meant the extinction of the travelling clogger. In other trades such as chair bodging, factory methods and modern machinery have replaced traditional techniques, with the result that all the men engaged in the trades a few years ago have been forced to give up work.

The virtual disappearance of vegetable tanning has meant the end of the crafts of oak bark extraction, practised until recently in many forested districts.

1. The Chair Bodger

A chair bodger is an itinerant craftsman who moves from one place to the other in the woods making nothing but the legs and stretchers of Windsor chairs. The craft of chair making is concentrated in the High Wycombe district of Buckinghamshire and, in that town and the surrounding countryside, all the evolutionary stages in the craft, from the primitive craftsman who works in the beech glades to the highly mechanised factory employing hundreds of specialists, could be seen until recently. In making a Windsor chair the services of at least three craftsmen are required. The first of these is the bodger, who in the past always worked in the woods and was responsible for making all the turned parts of the chair. In the early fifties there were at least four of these craftsmen practising their trade in the woodlands, but today with the death of the last bodger, Owen Dean of Great Hampden, the tradition of at least five hundred years has completely disappeared. The second specialist engaged in chair making is the benchman, who works in a small town or village workshop and is responsible for cutting the seats, back splats and other sawn parts of the chair. Lastly the framer assembles and finishes the chair.

The last of the Chiltern chair bodgers was a short, slim middle-aged man who spoke with the musical 'burr' of Buckinghamshire country folk. His father, grandfather and countless generations before him had obtained a living from chair bodging in the solitude of the beech glades. To reach his workshop in Hampden Wood, some six miles from High Wycombe, one passed through a rolling countryside of gentle grassy downland and smooth rounded curves that Huxley thought so suggestive of 'mutton and pleasantness'. Here and there were trim villages of timber and thatch, flint and brick, while above were the chalk pastures with grazing flocks of sheep. Crowning the hills were the glades of beech, shimmering green in the sunlight. Soon, one left the road for the thick glades of Buckinghamshire weed, so thick that the rays of the sun failed to penetrate it completely. Here and there young saplings sprouted while everywhere tree stumps marked the progress of some bygone bodger or woodman. Quite suddenly there was a gap in the trees and there in a clearing was the bodger's simple hut, surrounded by felled logs and hedgehog-like groups of drying chair legs and stretchers.

Although fine Windsor chairs have been made of yew and cherry, the common Windsor was usually of beech with an ash bow and elm seat. Since prehistoric times the upper reaches of the Chilterns with their cover of flinty clay overlying the chalk have borne thick glades of beech. Here countless generations of chair bodgers have worked, drawing on the forests for their raw material. Beech is particularly well suited to the needs of the chair leg turner, for it cuts very smoothly while still green and it can also be cleft and left to dry for a considerable period without danger of warping or cracking. So profuse is the beech growth in the Chilterns that the tree is often called the 'Buckinghamshire weed' and it seems surprising that after hundreds, if not thousands, of bodgers have drawn on the wood over the years, that the tree growth has remained as profuse as ever. This is in no small measure due to the techniques of felling adopted, a system that is known as 'the selection system'. When a bodger buys a stand of timber he does not proceed to cut it down indiscriminately, but he selects those trees that will suit his purposes. The beech trunks that he uses must not be too old, they must be straight grained and have grown rather quickly. By the selection system the trees that are too small are left to grow, while any gaps in the forest will soon be filled by seedlings falling from the surrounding trees.

The tools and equipment required by the chair bodger are few and simple, and this together with the fact that there is a great deal of wastage of raw material, explains why chair leg making throughout the centuries always remained a woodland craft. In a trade where more elaborate tools are required, and where there is little wastage of timber, underwood industries have tended to become localised in village workshops. It is so very much easier for the craftsman to take his simple equipment to the woodlands than it is to have timber, often from inaccessible places, taken to a permanent workshop.

After buying a 'stand' of timber from one of the Chiltern landowners, the bodger moves into the beech glade and sets up his portable shelter. Although in recent times bodgers used prefabricated wooden or corrugated iron sheds, the traditional hut was built up of wood shavings. An elderly bodger interviewed in 1955 said, 'The straight saplings were chosen, cut in twelve foot lengths and split down the middle. The top was joined by boring a hole through each some ten inches from the tip through which a tapered peg was inserted and tapped tight. These formed the two ends and were braced three feet from the ground. These frames were erected at suitable distances to

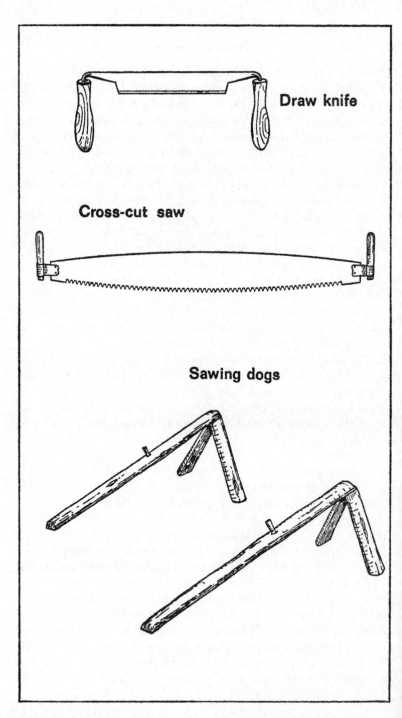

Draw knife

Cross-cut saw

Sawing dogs

Fig. 1. The Chair Bodger's Tools and Equipment: I.

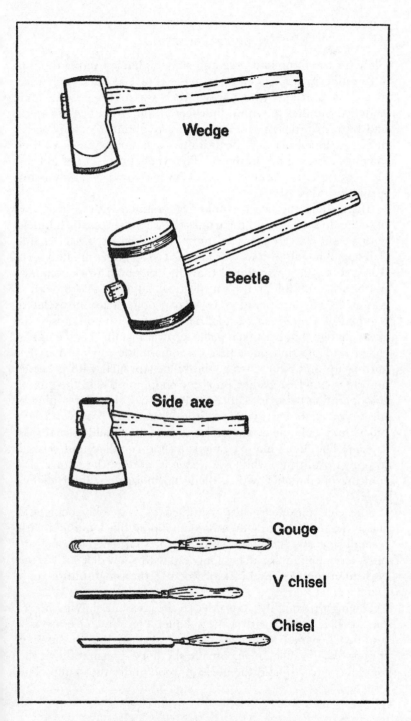

Fig. 2. The Chair Bodger's Tools and Equipment: II.

allow for the lathe and pole and shaving horse. Across the top and resting in the forks a cross-bar was placed. Side rails were nailed on and the whole framework was covered with four thatched bundles to within four feet of the ground. After work had been in progress and enough waste about, the walls were built . . . these huts were beautifully warm for the thick wall of shavings kept out all draughts.' The whole process of establishing a workshop in a new stand of timber could be easily completed in a day.

After felling the beech trunks are trimmed with an axe, the branches lopped off and the trunks cut into eighteen-inch billets with a cross-cut saw. This has unraked and widely set teeth and is designed to cut both ways. On a visit to a bodger in Hampden woods in 1958, it was found that the craftsman worked alone, but he was still able to use this particular type of saw though it was designed for operation by two people. The one isolated incident of a man using a tool designed for two epitomises the great change that has taken place in rural Britain. Each trunk is rolled into position on a pair of home-made sawing dogs for cutting up and after sawing, the billets are cleft with a beetle and short-handled wedge, on a low chopping block, the aim of this operation being to reduce the log to such sizes that will give pieces for chair legs, with as little wastage as possible. Some billets may only yield four pieces, others may yield as many as sixteen. The home-made beetle is a short-handled tool, ringed to prevent splitting, while the wedge is more in the nature of a splitting out hatchet with a blade no more than three inches wide.

The cleft pieces are next trimmed to a roughly octagonal shape the billets resting on a high chopping block and cut with a small side axe. This tool, with a blade sharpened on one side only, has a handle six inches long and with a few deft strokes the craftsman reduces the block of wood to the rough outline of a chair leg.

Placing the roughly shaped leg in the jaws of a shaving horse, the wood is shaved with a draw knife. The shaving horse is a low bench which many woodland craftsmen use for shaping timber. The craftsman sits astride the horse pressing down the foot lever so as to hold the piece of wood under the clamp. The bodger's horse differs from that used by other wood workers in that pieces of serrated steel are inserted in the clamping blocks. These are necessary to prevent the green beech from suddenly slipping into the workman's chest. The draw knife, which in the past was widely used by most woodland craftsmen, consists of a narrow blade basilled on its upper side with two handles fitted to it at right angles. It is pulled with both hands to shave chair legs to very nearly the correct shape and proportion of the finished product.

The final and perhaps the most complicated stage in chair bodging is the turning of the leg on the lathe. The bodger was the last of the woodland craftsmen to use a type of lathe that has been in use since the Iron Age – the pole lathe. Two beams of wood are fixed horizontally upon legs to form the bed of the lathe. They are parallel to each other, but a few inches apart, so that there is a groove between them. This groove receives the tenons of the puppets which are wedged to it. The puppets can be moved according to the size of material to be worked by removing the wedges. A fixed five eighths-inch screw is fitted to one puppet as a centre while the other centre is adjustable. The chair bodger's pole lathe differs from that of other woodworkers, such as that used by Bucklebury bowl turners, in that the driving string is wrapped directly around the material to be turned, and the lathe is not equipped with a chuck. The driving power is a twelve-foot ash or larch pole, firmly fixed to the ground and supported by the sides of the hut in the centre. A piece of string joins the end of the pole to the foot treadle, being wrapped once or twice around the material first. By pressing the foot treadle, which is hinged to the back of the hut, the pole bends and the material turns the spring back again when the foot is removed. The great disadvantage of the pole lathe is the fact that the chisel can only be applied on the forward movement of the material and the down stroke of the foot.

In turning a chair leg, one end is tapped on to the fixed centre and the cord passed around it twice. The other end is centred by turning the screwed shank of the adjustable centre. The wood is adjusted for true running and a small half-inch gouge is used to rough the surface. Traditional Windsor chairs have bobbin decorations on the legs, and are cut with V-shaped chisels. The turning process from start to finish takes no more than two minutes.

All this work is carried out while the wood is still green and the finished chair legs are stacked to dry for weeks before being transported to the Wycombe factories. The bodger is primarily a maker of the turned parts of the chair; other craftsmen, benchmen and framers, are responsible for the remainder. They, however, are not itinerant woodland craftsmen, but work in the factories and workshops of High Wycombe and the surrounding villages.

2. The Clogger

A craft that has almost completely disappeared from the rural districts within the last few years is that of clogmaking. The origins of this simply constructed piece of footwear are lost in the mists of antiquity, but clogs were certainly worn by rich and poor alike in the Middle Ages. In later times they were widely worn both on factory floors, in mines and on the land, particularly in Wales and the north of England. Although they may still be found in the textile mills of Lancashire and Yorkshire, the clogging factory still being fairly common in such towns as Huddersfield and Halifax, the old rural clogmaker is now a rarity. In Wales in 1918, for example, there were 65 specialised clogmakers, excluding those who were also bootmakers and repairers; in 1963 there were less than half a dozen working clogmakers. With the changes in fashion of the last few years the clogmaker has become a rarity and only a few representatives of the craft may be seen at work in Britain at a trade that demands considerable knowledge, not only of leatherwork, but of woodwork as well.

Despite the gradual disappearance of the clog and its replacement by rubber boots, it is still a very practical piece of footwear, particularly for agricultural workers. With thick wooden soles and iron rims, the wearer's feet are kept well above the level of a wet floor and, since each pair is made to fit the feet of each individual customer, they can be extremely comfortable and warm.

In the heyday of clogmakers there were two distinct types of craftsmen engaged in the trade. They were

(i) The village clogmaker who made footwear for a local market. He made clogs for each individual customer, taking accurate measurements of each foot, and cutting the clog soles to the shape of a paper pattern, made according to those measurements. His work will be considered later (pp. 235–6).

(ii) The itinerant clogger or clog sole maker was concerned only with the rough shaping of wooden soles which were sold to the clogging factories of Lancashire and Yorkshire. It was one of the most picturesque of all the rural crafts, but it has almost certainly disappeared completely from all parts of Britain. Before 1939, clogging gangs were a very common sight in all parts of Britain, but the alder groves of south Wales and the Border counties were particularly well known as their haunt. Like the Buckinghamshire chair bodger and the Dorset hurdle maker, the clogger represented an age-old tradition of craftsmanship; craftsmen who found it easier to take their few simple tools to the forests rather than take timber, often from inaccessible coppices, to a permanent village workshop.

For clog sole making the craftsman requires a timber that does not split easily, but on the other hand, it must be relatively easy to shape. As clogs are used on wet factory floors, mines and muddy fields, the sole must be durable in water and completely waterproof. Tough, resilient willow which lasts indefinitely in moist conditions is occasionally used by north country craftsmen, as is birch and beech, but in that area as well as in Wales nearly all the clogs are equipped with alder or sycamore soles. While many village clogmakers utilise sycamore, the itinerant cloggers by tradition are craftsmen in alder. Alder, a riverside tree, grows best in good fertile soil, with running water near the roots. It grows profusely in favoured conditions, its seed being carried from one place to the other by the streams. The timber it produces is soft and perishable under ordinary conditions, for it contains a great deal of moisture. In wet places, however, it is extremely durable and for this reason alder is widely used for such specialised tasks as revetting river banks. It can only be harvested in the spring and summer months and must be left to season for at least nine months before it can be used. Clogging was therefore a seasonal occupation and gangs of a dozen or more craftsmen wandered from grove to grove, living a hard, tough life in roughly built temporary shelters. In Wales the clogger reckoned that the amount of money made from selling waste material as pea-sticks and firewood should be enough to buy all the food that the gang needed while they worked in the woods.

After felling alder trees no more than twenty-four inches in girth, the clogger sawed the tree trunks into logs of fixed lengths of four sizes – 'men's', 'women's', 'middles' and 'children's'. Each log was then split with a beetle and wedge or with axe and mallet into blocks, which were cut with the clogger's knife into the rough shape and sizes of the clog soles. This process was known as 'breaking up'. If the alder trees used were small, nine-year coppice trees, their girth would be considerably smaller, and the splitting process with beetle and wedge was unnecessary.

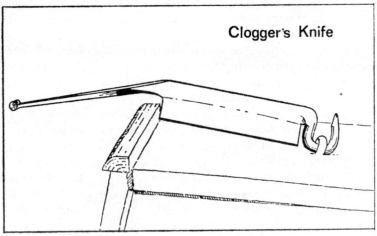

Fig. 3. The Clogger's Knife.

The work with the clogger's stock knife was highly skilled and intricate. The knife itself is made of one piece of steel, some thirty inches in length, bent to an obtuse angle in the middle. The blade is some four inches deep and thirteen inches long and the whole knife terminates in a hook. This hook was fastened to a ring on a wooden post driven firmly into the ground and forming one of the supports of a low bench. The clogger grasped the wooden handle, which is at right angles to the shank, while with his left hand he held an alder billet, resting on the bench and moving it as required. The large clogger's knife known as a 'bench', or 'paring knife', is still produced by some large-scale manufacturers, and with its stout hook and long handle it gives play to the craftsman who wishes to make rapid cuts at different angles. As such it is still used for some purposes in factories along with a variety of modern machinery. The clogger, stooping over the knife, cut an alder billet into the rough shape of a sole with great certainty and speed. A deep notch was cut in the block at a point where heel and sole were designed to meet, and the clog blocks were built into small conical stacks. These stacks, which had to remain in the open air for some weeks if not months were built in such a way that air could circulate freely between the blocks to hasten the drying process, for 'breaking up' was undertaken while the timber was still green and moist. The rough blocks were then sent to north country clog factories where they were finally shaped in workshops.

3. The Wattle Hurdle Maker

Near the well known village of Aldermaston one may still find a woodland craftsman practising an art that has remained almost unchanged since prehistoric times. He is one of the last representatives of a long line of woodland craftsmen in the district, who were dependent on the sheep farmers of the adjacent chalk downs for their livelihood. For nigh on sixty years, this strong, elderly man has worked in the solitude of the hazel coppices following his trade of wattle hurdle weaving. Year in, year out, he has worked in the woods, cutting, sorting and stacking hazel rods in the winter, and making hurdles, clothes pegs and thatching spars in the summer months.

Although at the present time few wattle hurdles are required by the sheep farmers, due to the widespread adoption of wire and electric fences, the craft is still a fairly flourishing one as there is a considerable demand for wattle as screening for town and market gardens. Nevertheless, despite the apparent prosperity of the craft, it is rapidly disappearing as few young people are entering a trade that demands exactitude, strength and long hours spent in the solitude of inaccessible coppices.

In the past, the craft of weaving wattle hurdles was widely distributed throughout the south of England. Even in the far off Iron Age, wattle was in great demand for building purposes, while in later times it was widely used for such things as the laths of buildings and the bodies of carts and wagons. But it was in the Middle Ages, when England was a great sheep-producing country, that the craft really came into its own. Thousands of sheep grazed unhindered on the vast stretches of unenclosed downland. In such areas as Wales and the Pennines there was a plentiful supply of stones which could be used for building folds and fences, but on the chalk downs of southern England there was very little stone or timber growth which could be used. The prosperous sheep farmers of the downs had to look for another source of raw material and, from the twelfth century onwards, it became the custom to reserve the lower, more productive parts of each downland parish for the planting of coppice wood. The hazel and ash grown in these coppices could then be used to supply the needs of such craftsmen as hurdle and gate makers, sheep crib makers and many others. To this day, coppices have persisted in the chalkland counties of England and, though most of them are now overgrown, many still bear the name of their original planters. Coppice hazel, that is the straight sticks growing around the stool or trunk of an already felled tree, is eminently suited to the needs of a wattle hurdle maker. The craftsman, who is a 'free-lance' worker, buys up a few acres of woodland or he leases a coppice for a fixed annual rent. A hazel coppice has to be harvested at regular intervals of seven or eight years, and the cutting has to be carried out in the winter months.

The tools and equipment of the wattle hurdle maker are few and simple for he relies much more on strength and ingenuity in weaving rather than on experience and dexterity in the use of tools. For cutting a few acres of hazel he requires little more than a heavy felling axe for cutting the stouter poles, a long-handled slasher for clearing brambles and a billhook. Cutting is carried out in orderly lanes and the material is laid in swaths with all the hazel butts pointing the same way. When a section of coppice has been cut, the hazel is sorted according to quality and size. The shorter sticks are tied into bundles to be sold as pea sticks, others are made into bundles of firewood, others for thatching spars while the longer rods are reserved for wattle hurdles. The last group is again sorted according to length and thickness and the selected rods are piled into orderly heaps.

When all this has been done, the craftsman is ready to start his summer task of wattle hurdle making. With a number of home-made pieces of equipment and a few simple tools he sets up his workshop in a corner of the coppice. The only work bench that he possesses is a heavy log six feet long with ten holes bored on its top surface which is firmly embedded in the ground. This is known as *the mould* and on it the hurdle is woven. Behind the craftsman is a rough stand or *gallows* which consists of a roughly shaped cross-piece nailed to a pair of uprights and on this the sorted rods rest. In front of the mould is a vertical, roughly marked graduated stick which is used for measuring the rods.

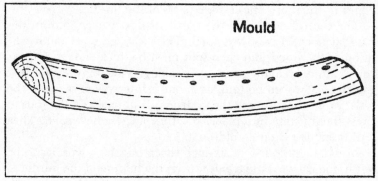

Mould

Fig. 4. The Wattle Hurdle Maker's Mould.

The process of weaving hurdles begins with the shaping of the upright *sails*. Taking the narrow-bladed spar billhook, the craftsman selects a number of the stouter poles from the

27

gallows. Holding each one against the graduated stick, he cuts it to the right length. The butt ends are flattened with the bill-hook and in most cases each rod is cleaved through the centre and placed in one of the holes in the mould. Cleaving is a task that requires great dexterity for a rod with a diameter of little more than two inches has to be cleft into two equal sections with nothing more than the point of a billhook.

When all the sails are in place (in a sheep hurdle there are ten of them) the craftsman selects two long thin rods and inserts them at right angles to one another in the gap between the first and second sails. Another pair is inserted in the next gap. These are known as *spur rods* and, taking each one in turn, the crafts-man twists and weaves them in between the sails to produce the bottom ten inches of the hurdle. The spur rods are always used in the round and never cleaved and each one has to be twisted twice around each end sail. For this reason, the end sails have to be much stronger than the other sails and in many cases they are not cleaved at all.

When the bottom has been firmly laid, the rods are trimmed with a special type of knife. In shape, this knife is similar to a billhook, but instead of having a blade ending in a point, it ends in a knife edge some three inches long. This is a very useful tool, for the projecting blade can be used for trimming loose edges in the more inaccessible parts of the hurdle.

The central portion of the hurdle is next woven and, in this case, cleft hazel is always used. The cleavage must follow the grain of the wood, but each split must be thick enough to bear the strain of weaving without breaking. Tucking the split into the already woven bottom, each one is interwoven between the sails. From time to time the craftsman will kneel on the rods to press them firmly into place. For this purpose he wears a knee pad fashioned from an old boot.

In making a four-foot six-inch sheep hurdle, a gap has to be left in the weave some two feet from the bottom of the hurdle so that the downland shepherd can thrust a stake or shore through the hurdles for carrying. The gap is made by inserting two uncleft rods, similar to the spur rods, in the weave. These rods are known as *twillies* and each one is twisted around the end sails. Most of the wattle hurdles made today are not used for

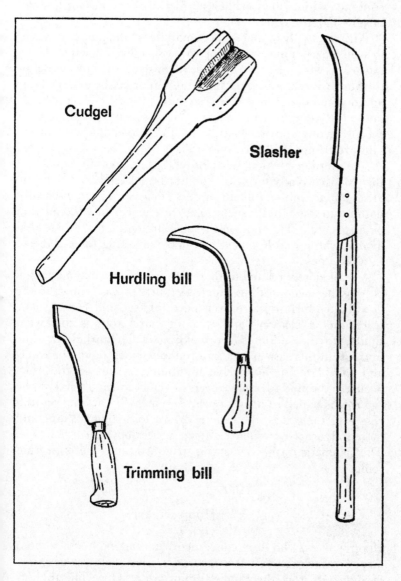

Cudgel

Slasher

Hurdling bill

Trimming bill

Fig. 5. The Wattle Hurdle Maker's Tools.

folding sheep and, unlike the true sheep hurdle, they are not equipped with twillies, while their sizes may vary according to a buyer's requirements.

With the twilly in place, the remainder of the hurdle is woven in cleft hazel. Finally, two or three springy, uncleft rods are taken and woven around the sails to finish off the hurdle. Before the hurdle is removed from the mould, it has to be trimmed and all unevenness and loose ends removed. A short cudgel is thrust under the end to be trimmed and with a sharp blow of the knife the projecting rod is cleanly cut. The projecting ends of the sails are trimmed in the same way.

The hurdles (which sold for 3s. 4d. a foot in 1965) are then stacked ready for sale. The hurdle maker's craftsmanship arises mainly in the difficult process of cleaving hazel rods with nothing to guide him except long experience. It is a craft that demands great skill and considerable strength and it is said that a good wattle hurdle maker can make anything up to a dozen hurdles a day.

A craft closely related to that of wattle hurdle making is that of weaving sheep feeding cages, a craft that was limited to the downland of Hampshire, Wiltshire, Dorset and Sussex. The technique of cleaving and weaving hazel rods is somewhat similar to that adopted for making wattle hurdles, but the uprights in this case are set in a round wooden mould or wheel and they are usually twelve in number. After several rows of cleft and round rows have been woven between the stakes, the top row is nailed so as to prevent slipping. By pushing an iron ring over the stakes, the cage is drawn to a conical shape and more rods are woven some eighteen inches above the first weave. This is made firm, the stakes trimmed and the iron ring removed.

4. The Hoop Maker

Hoop makers, who were concerned with making hoops to bind 'dry' or 'slack' barrels (see pp. 90–1), have almost certainly disappeared from the English countryside. They, like the dry coopers that they supplied, have become unnecessary in an age when more efficient containers than the slack cask have become available. The heyday of the dry barrel trade was the nineteenth and early twentieth centuries when many products ranging from gunpowder to apples and from salt to nails were packed and conveyed in barrels. At the present time dry casks are still used for fruit, vegetables and crockery, but the country craftsmen have been ousted either by foreign competitors or by large-scale industrial manufacturers. The last strongholds of the hoop shaving trade were Furness, the Weald of Sussex, Warwickshire and south Berkshire and, until 1939, most of these regions possessed a few elderly hoop shavers. The technique and equipment of the craft varied considerably from district to district.

The most popular raw material used for making hoops was coppice-grown hazel, eight or more years old. Occasionally chestnut, willow and even oak were used, while woodland hoop shavers were also responsible for making ash truss hoops for wet coopers (pp. 229–35). The seare still used for setting up casks, and they have to be strong enough to constrict the oak staves of a cask, over an inch thick. In addition the truss hoops have to be made with a splayed inner face to correspond with the taper of the cask. In the past, too, carefully shaped and spliced ash hoops made by woodland craftsmen were used by white coopers to bind the staves of plunger churns, cheese vats and washing tubs.

The first process in hoop shaving was cleaving hazel poles, and a variety of tools could be used for this purpose. Some craftsmen used an adze for this purpose, the adze being worked along the pole until it was split in two. A post stuck firmly in the ground kept the two sections apart as the hoop shaver worked along the grain. Other craftsmen used an L-shaped froe or dill-axe, with the cutting edge at right angles to the handle. The handle of this was pressed backwards and forwards until the pole had been split. Occasionally, in cleaving finer rods, some craftsmen used a hornbeam or box-wood cleaver similar in shape to the basket maker's cleaver, but much larger (Fig. 10). But whatever tool a hoop shaver used, his skill was shown in the number of hoops he could get from a single hazel pole. 'One old hoop maker considered that a good man could make as many as eight hundred more hoops per week than one less skilled, out of the same quantity of material.'[1] The piece of hazel to be cleaved could vary in length from thirty inches to as much as fourteen feet, depending on the girth of the cask that was to be made.

In cleaving, some form of brake for holding the material at different angles was essential, and these home-made pieces of equipment varied considerably according to region and the craftsman's inventive ability. The simplest described by Edlin[2] consisted of nothing more than 'two posts, one upright, the other nearly so, driven into the ground about nine inches apart at the base and bound together with a withe of twisted hazel'. Some, too, were in the form of a tripod standing some seven feet high with the posts firmly embedded in the ground. A pair of cross-struts ensured a firm horizontal hold. Other craftsmen used brakes similar to a rake maker's or the complex gate maker's 'monkey', but by far the most common consisted of a stout formed branch firmly nailed to two uprights and the diagonal post. The whole purpose of the cleaving brake was to hold the hazel in place at every conceivable angle while it was split.

After cleaving came the complex process of shaving the inner side of hazel. The bark was preserved on one side, but the inner core had to be shaved off to allow the hoops to bend freely. The exact method of doing this varied considerably from district to district[3], but again some form of brake was essential to hold the hazel in place while the inner side was shaved with the two-handled draw knife. The most common type of brake used resembled the chair bodger's shaving horse, others were in the form of a tripod described by Edlin[4] as 'a most ingenious contraption. It consists of a tripod of two slender legs and one stout one firmly fixed in the ground. The stout one of oak projects above the others and is cut out at the top to form a wide groove within which rests an oak beam free to pivot over the top of the tripod. The beam is set slanting down towards the ground; the hoop length is laid on it and the hoop shaver leans over it to draw his knife towards him. At its upper end a weight is suspended to act as a counter-balance, so that the beam can swing up and down like a seesaw. An iron pin fixed at the

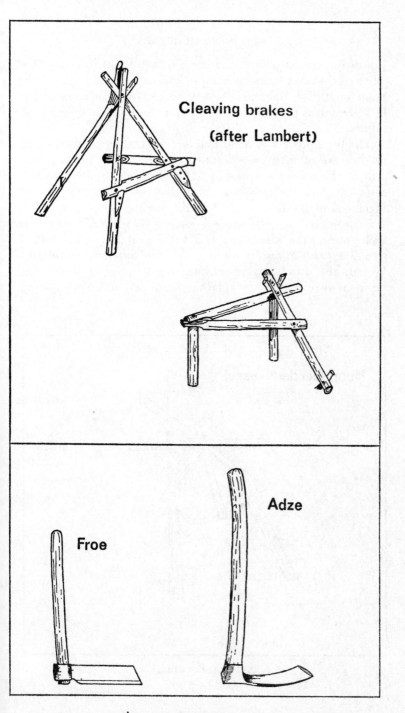

Cleaving brakes

(after Lambert)

Adze

Froe

Fig. 6. The Hoop Bender's Tools and Equipment.

top of the tripod secures the hoop length in such a way that when the shaver presses his left knee against the beam the hoop length is nipped in a vice-like grip; when he eases up the hoop length is immediately freed and can be shifted to a fresh position.'

The final process in hoop making was coiling, and although in the case of many woodland craftsmen, hoop lengths were sent to the cooper's workshop for coiling in bundles of sixty, some shavers undertook coiling themselves. A number of ingenious methods were used in this highly skilled process. It was considered essential to coil hoop lengths while the wood was still green, otherwise they would have to be steamed in a steaming chest to restore pliancy. In some districts, notably the Weald, the usual way of coiling was to pass the hazel rod between two arched iron plates, the upper and lower 'jaws',

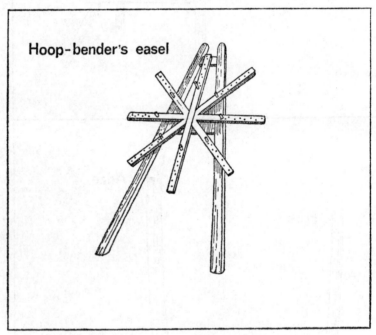

Hoop-bender's easel

Fig. 7. Hoop-Bending Easel.

so that the rod came out bent into a semicircle. The final bending was done inside a heavy truss hoop and the two ends scarfed together. In some areas, too, pieces of machinery somewhat similar to the tire benders used by country wheelwrights were used for hoop bending (pp. 119–20), while the final coiling was done on an easel, with six or more crossbars attached to the uprights. The arms of the easel were bored with holes into which wooden pegs were fitted. The pegs were placed in such a position that the rod coiled between them formed a circle of the required size.[5] A simple way of coiling was to soak the rods and bend them within a cylindrical tank, allowing them to dry there.[6] Some craftsmen used a peculiar type of bending horse for coiling. This consisted of a sloping beam fixed to a pair of vertical posts some eighteen inches high. The clefts were passed through the iron jaws of the horse and bent into a circle. The cleft was then placed in stout ash truss or shive hoops and the two ends nailed together.

Finally the completed hoops were packed in bundles of six, enough for a single cask, and sent to the cooperage.

A craft that is closely related to that of barrel hoop making is that of preparing crate rods for packing crockery, glass and hardware. Just as the country hoop maker supplied urban cooperages with a part of their raw material, so, too, did the rural rod maker supply industrial crate workshops with theirs. While the craft of crate making is concentrated in the Birmingham and Stoke-on-Trent regions, the crate rod makers are itinerant craftsmen drawing on the hazel coppices of Hampshire, Dorset and south-east England. Until recently it was common for lorries taking crates of crockery to the docks at Southampton to pick up loads of cleft hazel from north Hampshire on the return journey to the Potteries.

The raw material for crate rods as for barrel hoops is coppice-grown hazel, although oak, chestnut and birch are occasionally used. Due to the danger of introducing beetles and other timber diseases to foreign countries, neither elm nor ash are used for crates, although in the past both timbers were utilised. The process of preparing crate rods is somewhat similar to that used in preparing rods for wattle hurdles. The stouter poles, known as 'headings' are either roughly shaped or left in the round. The craftsman always uses winter-cut coppice hazel, and each rod must be straight enough to cut clear lengths of three or four feet. They are graded according to diameter and length, from seven feet to fourteen feet long, and from half an inch to two inches in diameter. They are packed in bundles and sent to urban crate makers, who again use the same technique of weaving as the wattle maker and the sheep crib maker.

5. The Charcoal Burner

From remote antiquity to the present day, charcoal has been made in much the same manner by itinerant craftsmen, in many of the well-wooded parts of Britain. Due to the fact that the timber used by the burners is heavy and difficult to transport from remote coppices, and due to the fact that charcoal is less bulky and is easy to carry, the craft of charcoal burning has always remained a true woodland craft. It was practised until recently in such well-wooded districts as the Forest of Dean, Furness, the New Forest and Berkshire, while it has persisted to this day in the Weald of Kent and Sussex, where the villages of Charlton and Bedgebury are centres of the trade. Although very few craftsmen in the region still practise the craft, charcoal is very widely used in the chemical and metal industries as well as in medicine and horticulture. In the chemical industry alone, charcoal is used in the making of a great range of products varying from penicillin to artificial silk, from sugar refining to making plastics and paints. In the metal industries it is used for such tasks as refining non-ferrous metals, insulating electric batteries, refrigerators and vacuum flasks, while the best shear steel is still made in charcoal-fired furnaces. [7]

Although today charcoal is not used as a fuel, in the past it was its qualities as a heating agent that made it such a vital element in the industrial development of Britain. It is almost the perfect fuel, yielding high, steady temperatures with no smoke and little ash. Before the invention of coke ovens in the eighteenth century, the iron and steel industry was entirely dependent on charcoal, and it became located in those regions such as the Weald, Furness and north Glamorgan where there was an adequate supply of timber that could be converted into this vital fuel. The itinerant charcoal burners were numerous and they were essential members of early industrial society. By using vast quantities of coppice oak, they, more than any other woodland worker, changed the natural landscape of Britain dramatically. Their product was also required in the non-ferrous metal industries, in the glass industry and for making gunpowder; indeed until the beginning of the present century the charcoal burner remained an extremely important person. Living in a primitive hut of logs and turves beside a slow-burning kiln in the heart of the woods, he was one of the most picturesque of figures. The modern charcoal burner is still a woodland craftsman, but he is no longer tied for long hours to watching his slow-burning kiln. The large, round metal retorts, which resemble large boilers with removable lids and chimneys, take some twenty hours to burn through but unlike the old open clamps they can be left unattended.

Charcoal burning is always carried out in the summer months, and although beech, alder, willow and many other timbers may be used, the best charcoal is obtained from coppice oak. In using oak, however, the craftsman must be very careful not to include too much bark as this leaves too much sulphur in the charcoal. The principle of burning is to heat wood in such a way that all the air is excluded, thus preventing complete combustion. Only a very small proportion of the wood in a clamp is actually burnt to ashes, the remainder is just charred. Water and volatile substances such as creosote and tar are driven out leaving a mass of solid carbon together with a small quantity of mineral ash.

The craft of charcoal burning demands no special tools or equipment, and after cutting rough wood into lengths of two or three feet, the timber is stacked for drying for several months before it is ready for burning. It is then carried by means of a wheelbarrow to the burning pit. This pit, which has a level floor of earth or ashes, is some fifteen feet in diameter, and a pole some six feet high is fixed at its centre. Around this, small pieces of wood which will catch fire quickly are arranged. The sticks are then piled up, sloping towards the centre pole. Split logs and round sticks are arranged in such a way that the clamp is a dome-shaped erection six feet high and fifteen feet in diameter. The wood is covered with grass, bracken leaves, turves and rushes and the whole clamp cemented down with damp earth and ashes. The central stake is then removed, leaving a chimney-like hole from the top to the bottom of the pile. A little cold charcoal is dropped into the flue followed by a shovelful of red hot charcoal and a few billets of kindling wood. More cold charcoal is used to top up the hole, and as soon as flames begin to appear, a turf is placed over the central hole to check the draught. Great care has to be taken in burning, for the clamp has to be checked at frequent intervals. If flames appear they are damped with water and more sods are placed on any gaps that occur. The craftsman always attempts to light his fire in a sheltered position, avoiding gusts of wind. Vital pieces of equipment are the portable canvas or corrugated iron shelters known as 'loos' which are erected on the windward side of the clamps. These consist of nothing more than rectangular pieces of canvas some ten feet high attached to a wooden framework. In the past these wind screens consisted of wooden frames wattled with bracken and supported by firmer sticks. As the craftsman has to make rounds of the burning clamps every two hours, he and his fellow workers live in the open air during the summer months. In the past huts of turf, wood and bracken were built. Nowadays caravans or corrugated iron sheds are used. The whole art of charcoal burning lies in the regulation of draughts so that the maximum quantity of wood is charred but the minimum burned.

The length of time required to burn a clamp varies according to the type of wood used. Dry timber may be completely charred within twenty-four hours, green wood requires a considerably longer period, but as soon as white smoke emanating from the clamp is replaced by a blue haze, the burning is nearly complete. When the fire is out, the charcoal is uncovered with a rake and the charcoal shovelled into sacks. Charcoal burning in the summer months is a continuous process, for as one clamp burns another is built up for further firing.

Although in some parts of the country, mostly Furness, charcoal burning is traditionally regarded as a separate and complete craft with its customs and lore, in other districts such as Sussex few men were recognised as charcoal burners, for the burning has always been done as a part of other forestry work. In Furness, too, the secrets of the craft have been passed down from father to son over many generations and the workers invariably practised their trade in groups of three.

A rival industry closely related to that of charcoal burning was that of producing oils and acids from waste wood. In the well-wooded Cothi Valley in Dyfed, for example, a wood distillation establishment was set up in the late nineteenth century. This flourished until the 1920's but, with bad roads and a haul of six miles to the nearest railway station, the cost of coal, essential for the distillation process, became excessive and the plant closed down. Naphtha oil as well as charcoal was produced in large retorts, rather than in clamps, and the by-products that would be lost under the old system of burning were regarded as being much more valuable than charcoal itself.

6. The Thatching Spar Maker

The making of thatching spars is not a specialised craft but is carried on in conjunction with some other woodland trade, such as wattle hurdle making. In some districts, such as the Vale of Glamorgan, the thatchers themselves are responsible for cutting and making spars from the hazel or willow growing locally. It is a seasonal occupation, for the spar maker is busiest in the spring and summer months, preparing for the thatching demands of the hay and corn harvests.

The term spar making includes making the spars themselves, that is making the spicks or broaches used for pegging thatch; it includes the making of liggers, the runners fixed to the exterior of the thatch, and the making of sways, the large rods traditionally used for binding each course of thatch. In many districts within recent years tarred twine, galvanised wire and metal spars have replaced the traditional hazel spars, liggers and sways, but the demand for wooden spars continues to be considerable.

39

Although coppice-grown willow is occasionally used for spar making, the traditional raw material is coppice hazel. This is harvested at regular intervals of from six to ten years and each rod has to be two or three inches in diameter. After the coppice has been cut in the same way as for wattle hurdles, each rod is cut into lengths of some twenty-eight to thirty inches. These lengths are known as 'spar gadds'. Each gadd is trimmed with a specially designed billhook known as a spar hook. This is a small tool with a curved blade varying between six inches and nine-and-a-half inches in length; it is very light and narrow and it can be used for all the necessary processes by the spar maker.

The most difficult task in the craft is the splitting of each spar gadd along its grain. Resting each rod vertically on a stone or block of wood, the spar hook is inserted at the thinner end of the gadd. Pressure is applied and the gadd is split cleanly down the centre by moving the hook gently to and fro. The craftsman's thumbs act as a guide during splitting for it is essential that each gadd is split into two equal halves. Each half-gadd is then split into three.

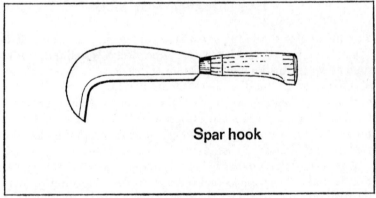

Spar hook

Fig. 8. A Spar Hook.

The next task is to remove all irregularities and rough edges from each split rod, and, with a leather pad over the right knee, the craftsman again takes his spar hook and shaves away the rough edges. If the spars are to be used fairly quickly, the ends are pointed with two or three sharp strokes of the hook. If they are not to be used immediately the pointing will be done by the thatcher himself. Finally the spars are bound with withy or wire into bundles of a hundred or more, ready for sale to the thatchers (at an average price of 1s. 6d. a score in 1965).

Before the spars can be used for pegging thatch, they have to be twisted to form staples. This is done by the thatcher by placing two thumbs in the centre of the spar and revolving the hands in opposite directions.

The method of making liggers is somewhat similar to that of spar making but the ends are bevelled for neat jointing rather than pointed. The sways, on the other hand, can be made from the smaller rods, one inch or less in diameter, left in the round and pointed as they can be split from thinner hazel, carefully trimmed.

III

Village Woodcrafts

1. The Osier Basket Maker

ONE OF THE OLDEST and certainly the most widespread craft is that of basket making. In its essential characteristics it is one of the simplest arts, involving only the manipulation of rods. As there is such a vast variety of baskets, the craft has completely escaped the application of machinery; at all levels of culture it has remained a true handicraft and the process of weaving has changed in no important particular since prehistoric times.

For many centuries one of the main centres of the willow growing and basket making industry in Britain has been the Sedgemoor district of Somerset. Small ribbon-like villages such as Stathe, Burrowbridge and Athelney provide the place of work for dozens of traditional craftsmen, while the flat marshy moors around the villages are extensively planted with willow, the basket maker's raw material.

For the last fifteen miles or more of its course, the slow meandering River Parret is tidal, and during the winter months, it often bursts its banks, flooding hundreds of acres of farmland. Fortunately the basket willow, varieties of the species *salix*, grows best on thick loamy soil, on land that is sometimes flooded, but at other times well drained. For this reason central Somerset has the ideal conditions for osier growing and willow cultivation which, combined with a certain amount of livestock-rearing and dairying, provides the basis of the agricultural economy of this part of the county.

Much of the area between the Mendips and the Quantock Hills is divided into a large number of square plots or *holts*, each plot bounded on all sides not by fences or hedges but by wide ditches known as *rhines*. These ditches are primarily irrigation and drainage canals but they are also widely used for carrying harvested willow, particularly in the winter months when the Parret is in flood.

There are countless varieties of basket willow, but the most common ones grown in Somerset are *Black Mawl* and the heavy cropping *Champion Rod*. Willow beds are replanted at infrequent intervals; indeed there are beds in Athelney that still bear annual crops of withy ninety years after planting. When a bed is planted, the ground has to be very thoroughly prepared and deep ploughing or digging is essential. In the past steam ploughing tackle was very widely used, indeed some growers believed that the plough had to be followed by a steam cultivator taken over the land at least eight times. If no steam tackle was available, then the ground had to be dug by hand with a spade to the depth of two spits. In present-day Sedgemoor, the ground is ploughed with tractor ploughs in the autumn and winter months, but before planting begins the plot has to be harrowed a number of times, all the weeds are cleared by hand and the ground thoroughly manured.

The willow grower purchases the best quality withy for cutting into sets at one of the many auction sales held annually in a number of Somerset villages. Regular auctions are held, for example, in the village halls at Langport and North Curry in the autumn, and it is at these auctions that local basket makers, as well as blind schools and prisons, obtain their raw material. The best quality rods are reserved for planting and the growers' first task is to cut each rod into twelve- or fifteen-inch sets. These are then placed in damp grass until the late winter planting season begins.

With the bed fully prepared, the planter, armed with the sets, begins the task of planting at the rate of between 18,000 and 24,000 sets to the acre. The planter pushes in each set with the palm of the right hand until only some seven inches of the set appears above the ground. They are planted in rows, each set being some fifteen from the next and with twenty-two inches between each row. Willow sets grow very easily for, as the sap rises in the spring, the buds in the soil will form roots, while those above ground grow very rapidly into the straight sticks that will form the basket maker's raw material.

During the early months of growth, the withy beds have to be hoed at frequent intervals and the crop sprayed with insecticides. In the autumn the maiden crop of willow is harvested and, although this is rarely used, harvesting is nevertheless essential to ensure the strengthening of the roots. It is only after three years that the willow stool will bear a full crop of usable willow, usually at the rate of some two or three tons of withy to the acre.

Harvesting is still carried out by hand and throughout the autumn and winter months, workers armed with simple harvesting hooks cut the rods as near the stool or stump as possible. A sharp upward movement of the hook is needed so that the cut ends are left as near vertical as possible so that the rain does not penetrate them. Good cutting is vital in willow harvesting for the stool has to bear a heavy crop of rods which have to be cut annually for many decades. After cutting, the rods have to be tied with willow bands into bundles known as *willow bed bundles* or *bolts*, each one measuring three feet one inch around the base. The average annual yield from an acre of willow is in the region of 100 bolts. These are transported, more often than not on flat-bottomed boats along the rhines, to the basket maker's workshops to be used there or to be sold at the auction sales.

The length of life of a willow holt varies according to the suitability of the soil, the variety grown and the care given to the crop. When the yield diminishes the beds are let down to grass and the land grazed for four or five years before replanting with willow.

Although only two or three species of willow are grown in Somerset, the basket maker uses three principal grades of raw material, each grade being known by its colour. These grades are obtained by the different treatment of the raw material after harvesting. All the willow in willow bed bundles is known as *green*. This is very rarely used nowadays although, in the past, it was used for making wattle hurdles and a cheap variety of basket. The three main types used by basket makers are:

   (i) Brown willow
   (ii) Buff willow
   (iii) White willow.

Brown willow: This is obtained by steaming sorted green rods in a steaming chest and then stacking them in the open to dry for many weeks. Brown willow is not stripped of its bark and green rods for browning may be cut at any time during the winter. Brown rods are widely used in Somerset for making wickerwork garden furniture as well as for making baskets for work exposed to damp, such as watercress baskets or those used in woollen factories.

Buff willow: To make buff rods green willow, after being sorted into foot sizes and again tied into bundles or *wads*, is boiled vigorously for five hours and kept in the water for at least another twenty-four hours. The tannin in the bark stains the rods to a rich golden colour. The green rods, up to a hundred wads in number, are almost invariably placed in boiling water, but, occasionally, when the withy is very dry, green wads are placed in cold water which is brought to the boil. After being removed from the large rectangular boiler, which usually measures six feet long, five feet wide and four feet deep, the boiled wads are stacked in heaps covered with willow bark, which, in dry weather, will be watered daily before the rods are ready for stripping.

White willow: Brown and buff willow may be obtained at any period of the year, preferably after green rods have been in store for at least six months, but white rods can be obtained only in the spring. Willow bed bundles that have been harvested in the autumn and winter are placed immediately in a few inches of running water in pits that have been especially designed for the purpose. They remain there until the spring. As the sap rises the bundles of willow are removed and the bark stripped. In Somerset a large proportion of the baskets made are from the white rods and, as pitted willow can only be peeled between the beginning of April and the middle of June, whilst the sap is rising and the willows bursting into leaf, that period is usually one of feverish activity in the withy beds. A great deal of female labour is employed during these three months.

Hundreds of different types of basket are made by rural basket makers at the present time. Most of them are common throughout the country, others are only known in a limited region. The *cran* and *swill*, for example, are peculiar to the fish quays of Yarmouth and Lowestoft, while the *peck cob* is known only to Suffolk farmers.[1] The products of rural basket makers may, however, be divided into five distinct categories.

Agricultural baskets for use on farms. With the mechanisation of agriculture, these baskets are less common than they were twenty years ago. Examples of agricultural baskets are: *Potato pickers* and the larger *potato hampers* formerly used for harvesting potatoes. *Cattle feeding baskets* and *fruit picking baskets*. Specialised local types are the *broccoli crates* of Cornwall, bushel baskets known as *rips* used on Sussex farms, and the *stable skeps* of the Newmarket district. Many Somerset craftsmen do produce these baskets, not only for the national, but also for the regional markets.

Market baskets for transporting fruit, vegetables or other material to markets. Examples of this type are the *bushel sieves* of the Vale of Evesham, *strikes* for carrying twelve pounds of tomatoes, *Flats* for cucumbers, *rim pecks* for strawberries, and *chicken crates* for carrying live birds.

Industrial baskets for use in factories. Examples of this type are the *Yorkshire skeps*, square open baskets some three feet high, often mounted on rollers and used in the textile mills, and *hampers* used in the Northamptonshire boot industry and the hosiery factories of Leicestershire.

Trade baskets for tradesmen's delivery, such as *laundry baskets* and *bakers' baskets*. The great variety of fish baskets, many of them with distinct local names, come into this category as well. Examples of fish baskets are the *prickle* of Sussex, the *cran* and *swill* of Yarmouth and Lowestoft, the *cockle Flats* of Ipswich and the *salmon baskets* made for Bristol fishmongers.

Domestic and fancy baskets. There are many varieties within this category ranging from barrel-shaped, buff shopping baskets to highly decorated needlework baskets and from picnic baskets to kitten baskets.

In addition to actual osier receptacles made by rural crafts-men at the present time, most of them extend their activities to making wickerwork furniture and wattle hurdles. The rural craftsman is facing intense competition at the present time, not only from such places as Hong Kong, Japan and Portugal, but also from institutions for the blind. This competition, more than any other factor, has caused the rural basket maker to extend his activities into other related fields.

Despite the fact that there are hundreds of local and trade variations in basket design, the process of weaving is basically the same throughout the world. Before he begins the day's work, enough willow rods have been soaked overnight to make them pliable and easy to handle, and the basket maker, seated on the floor with a lapboard in front of him, commences his task of weaving.

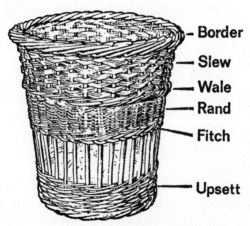

Fig. 9. 'Strokes' in Basket Making.

Whether a basket be round, square or oval, the base is almost invariably made first. If a rectangular or square basket is being made, the rods are first of all fixed in a small clamp made of two wooden blocks bolted together and the finer rods woven between the upright sticks. If it is a round or oval basket, however, a start is made with the slath which consists of

47

a number of rods overlapping crosswise. They are bound together and spread out to radiate from the centre like the spokes of a wheel. Finer rods are interwoven between the radiating stakes, and if the basket is large, more stakes are inserted as the work proceeds to make the base perfectly strong. When the base is complete, the edge being reinforced with a stouter weave, extra rods are inserted and bent up to form the side frame. A willow hoop is made and passed around the upright stakes to keep them in place as the work proceeds. Finer rods are woven round and round between the upright stakes from left to right, each rod being cut at the butt and inserted in the weave to overlap the end of the previous rod. The long ends of the stakes are finally woven along the rim to form a firm edge.

There are a number of strokes, or complete movements analogous to a stitch in needlework that the basket makers adopt. The principal ones are:

Randing. A simple rod is worked alternately in front of and behind the upright stakes.

Slewing. Two or more rods are worked together alternately in front of and behind the upright stakes.

Fitching. The rods are worked alternately under and over each other, gripping a stake at each stroke. This process is mainly used in making skeleton baskets, such as poultry baskets. The distance between the stakes has to be judged very accurately.

Pairing. Two rods are worked alternately over and under each other – the reverse of a fitch.

Waling. Three or more rods are worked alternately one by one in front of two, three or more stakes and behind one. This is a stout weave often used to edge the bottom of the basket.

Upset. Two, three or more rods of willow are worked alternately on the stakes immediately they are picked up from the base.

Although in most cases a basket is made from the bottom upwards there are exceptions to this rule. The well-known Yarmouth swill, for example, is built from the rim downwards, as is the Southport boat – a market basket used by Lancashire countrywomen and the Welsh *gwyntell*.

The main tools and equipment used by the osier basket maker are the following:

Brakes. These are used for stripping willow. Each one consists of two pieces of springy iron some twenty inches long set in an upright wooden frame, the iron blades being to pinch the willow rod as it is drawn between them. Women are often employed, particularly when peeling white withy in Somerset. The bark at the butt end of a withy rod is first loosened and the rod is then reversed and drawn right through the jaws leaving the bark behind.

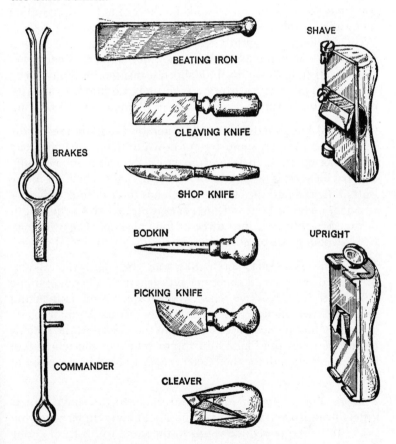

Fig. 10. The Osier Basket Maker's Tools.

Strippler. In some of the larger workshops, electrically driven peeling machines or stripplers have been introduced in recent years. The strippler stands some five feet high and two feet six inches wide and has the appearance of a winnowing machine. A rapidly revolving drum carries a series of scrapers, and as the craftsman places a bundle of willow against this drum, drawing it backwards and forwards, the bark is completely removed.

Sorting equipment. The rods in a willow bed bundle are only roughly sorted to size before they are put into store. Before they can be used by the basket maker they must be classified into foot sizes. A barrel is sunk in the ground and, standing alongside it, the sorter places a bundle of rods in the barrel. With the help of a graduated stick he draws out the longest rods, each one being around nine feet in length, and continues the process right down until the shortest two-foot rods have been removed. The sorted heaps are then tied into bundles or wads, each wad being thirty-seven inches in diameter at the bottom.

Cleaver. Although most of the white and buff rods are used in the natural round state, some are cut down to make finer material known as *skeins*. A little tool no more than four inches long, called a cleaver, is passed down each rod. A slit is first cut in the butt of the rod and the cleaver which has three or four radiating wooden, metal or bone cutting edges is pushed down the length of the rod, cutting it into three or four portions. Cleavers may be all-wooden, all-bone or wooden handled with metal blades.

Shave. This is a small plane-like tool through which skeins are passed to shave off the inner pith leaving a narrow, pliable band of timber. A shave has a wooden stock some four inches long and two inches wide, shod with metal. A small blade one and a half inches wide is bolted to the stock and the skein is passed between the blade and the metal shoe; the whole tool being small enough for the basket maker to hold in the palm of his hand.

Upright. This is similar in size and shape to the shave, but it differs from it in that it has two parallel blades underneath the stock. It is used to reduce skeins to the same width throughout their length, by drawing each one between the blades. The

width of skein can be adjusted by turning a small brass screw
on top of the stock.

Lap board. The basket maker sits on the floor with his back
against the wall. His work bench is a wooden plank some
seventy-two inches long and thirty inches wide placed between
his outstretched legs. If he wishes to raise the height of his
basket, then a sloping table, known as a lap board, can be
placed on the plank. This is some thirty-five inches long,
thirty inches wide and stands six or seven inches high at the
back.

Bodkin. To make openings in the weave for the insertion of rods
the craftsman uses a wooden, iron or bone bodkin, which
varies in length from as little as three inches to ten inches.

Picking knife. This is a very short knife with a blade not more
than three inches long for trimming finished baskets. It has
hardly altered in shape over the centuries, for with the beating
iron it appears on the Arms of the Company of Basketmakers
established in 1569.

Shop knife. This is a narrow-bladed knife, usually some seven
inches long for pointing willow rods before insertion. Some
craftsmen use an ordinary penknife for this purpose.

Beating iron or shop iron. This is a piece of iron approximately
nine inches long and three inches wide used by the basket maker
for beating the weave into place as the work progresses.

Commander. This consists of an iron rod, ringed at its tip for
straightening the heavier stakes and also for beating the weave.
The most common type measures some nine inches in length.

In addition to these essential pieces of equipment the basket
maker also needs a tank for soaking willow, a heavy weight for
placing in the base of the basket while he weaves the sides, and a
small pair of clippers or shears for cutting the thicker pieces of
willow. In addition some craftsmen have small horns containing
grease in their workshops. A bodkin is dipped in this as it is far
easier to use after greasing.

Willow basket making is a craft that requires, not only
great dexterity, but considerable strength, for willow, even

after soaking in water, is difficult to bend or weave. But despite foreign competition the craft in Somerset is still flourishing and the demand for traditional baskets is still high.

In Wales, the traditional basket is a round, bowl-shaped receptacle known as a *gwyntell*. In the past the *gwyntell* was widely used for potato picking and for carrying fodder to animals. In the Principality, however, there is no tradition of professional basket making as in Somerset, but it was carried on by farmers and labourers in their leisure hours. Indeed, to this day in most local *Eisteddfodau*, basket making is invariably included in the competitions and many amateurs, particularly in west Wales, have attained considerable fame as makers of *gwyntelli*.

The process of making a *gwyntell* begins with the selection of a suitable piece of hazel or blackthorn to make the rim or bool of the basket (*y wragen*). This is steamed and bent to a circle, the two loose ends being nailed together. In the past the rim was hung in the chimney to season for some months before it could be used, but in more recent times the hazel was tied around an old bicycle wheel and allowed to set and dry out.

After the rim has been prepared, the ribs of the basket have to be put in place. Cleft hazel or willow laths, each one-inch wide, are tied to the bool with strips of green willow. The four centre laths are attached first and before the others are inserted the centre laths are attached firmly to the rim by weaving some three rows of osier at right angles to the laths and parallel to the rim. Four or six other curving laths are then attached to the rim and weaving continues until the whole basket is completed. Each row of osier is firmly attached to the rim by being twisted around it. A pair of carrying handles are provided by leaving a gap in the weave and the basket is ready for use.

Not only is the Welsh *gwyntell* different from many others in that it is one of the few osier baskets started at the rim and finished at the base, but in many features it resembles the English spelk basket. Like the spelk basket it is round or oval in shape, it has a bool of seasoned hazel and a number of cleft laths. Its uses for potato picking and fodder carrying were also somewhat similar.

2. The Spale Basket Maker

It is rarely that one associates hard and durable oak with the art of basket-making, but nevertheless in the Furness district of Lancashire and in the Wyre Forest of Worcestershire coppice-grown oak provides the raw material for a once important industry, that of spale or spelk basket making. These tough, durable baskets, known in some parts of the country as *whiskets, slops* or *swills* are made of interwoven oak laths or spelks, and they are still widely used in the north and Midlands for carrying a great variety of products, ranging from shellfish to coke and from animal fodder to cotton waste. In addition to its durability and toughness, the advantage of the spale over an osier basket is the closeness of its weave, indeed, so close is the weave that it is possible to carry powdery material in it. In the past side slops or kidney lips made in the same manner as spale baskets were widely used in northern districts for broadcasting seed.

The spale basket is almost bowl-shaped and measures some two feet to three feet across the rim. The rim, known as a bool is made of hazel, although birch, ash or even oak may be used as an alternative.

The process of making a spale basket begins with the shaping of the bool. Coppice-grown hazel rods are cut in the winter and softened by boiling or steaming until they are quite pliable. Each rod, an inch or so in diameter, is bent to a round or oval shape and the loose ends fastened with a nail.

The spale basket maker obtains oak from neighbouring coppices, but great care must be taken in the selection of raw material. The oak, usually twenty-five or thirty years old, must be straight grained and free of knots, and each pole must be approximately six inches in diameter. After cutting, the poles are transported to the craftsman's yard for lengthy seasoning, and when required for use, they are cut into lengths of four or five feet. The bark, which in the past was in great demand in the oak bark tanneries, is removed and the poles are immersed in boiling water for several hours. For this purpose, the craftsman has a metal tank measuring some five feet long, three feet wide and two feet deep resting on parallel brick walls two feet high. A fire of shavings is lit underneath the tank, the smoke being carried away through a chimney at the back.

After some hours of boiling, each pole is quartered by means of a beetle and wedge while it is still hot. The wooden beetle used by spelk makers is usually a home-made affair with a head of apple wood, pear or elm with an ash handle. The wedge is usually an L-shaped froe with a blade up to ten inches wide and a handle some twenty inches long. The cleft must pass through the heart of the oak pole, following the grain to produce symmetrical sections. The froe, after being started with sharp blows of the beetle is levered up and down until the pole is completely split.

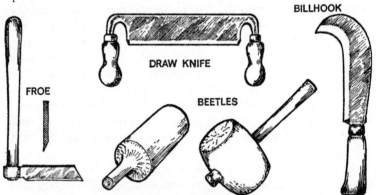

Fig. 11. The Spale Basket Maker's Tools.

The next process calls for considerable skill, for each quarter has to be split into thin strips, each one no more than a sixteenth of an inch thick. Great care has to be taken in splitting, for the spelks have to be of the same width and thickness throughout their length. For spelk making a small L-shaped froe is used by most craftsmen. This has a blade of mild steel, six inches long, sharpened on one side only, attached to a handle some sixteen inches long. Other craftsmen, however, prefer a small billhook, similar to the thatcher's spar hook. Both billhook and froe are inserted in the quartered pole, worked from side to side, so that a thin strip of oak can be ripped off by hand.

Before weaving, the spelks have to be trimmed and smoothed with a fine spokeshave, for the nature of the finished basket

54

will be such that this cannot be done after the completion of the whole process. The spelks are placed on the shaving horse for shaving. This is a low bench on which the craftsman sits astride, pressing with his foot so as to hold fast the spelk under the projecting clamp bench. The spelk, being thin and springy, is placed on the curved platform on top of the horse. In the past some craftsmen used upright shaving vices, somewhat similar to those used by hoop shavers (p. 30).

The spelks are next immersed in water and the stouter ribbons are fixed to the bool to form the warp of the basket. The largest of the wide spelks is fitted across the centre and successively shorter ones are added until the warp is complete. The thinner, shorter ribbons, known as 'chissies' are then inter-woven through the warp until the whole basket is completed.

The strength and resilience of the spale basket is due to the fact that moistened pliable oak can be moulded to a new shape. As the water in the spelks evaporates, they are set to that new shape. Spale basket making is a disappearing craft, for today there are no craftsmen at work in the Wyre Forest, and few remain in Furness. Like the osier basket maker, the spelk maker depends almost entirely on skill and dexterity rather than on any elaborate equipment. By tradition it is a hereditary trade, which not long ago demanded an apprenticeship of seven years.

3. The Trugger

While in the Midlands and north the closely woven spale basket is popular, its southern equivalent is the trug. The word 'trug' is derived from 'the Old English "trog", a tub or boat, a name suggested by the appearance of the basket which is oblong and shallow with a curving bottom. It has a tall handle and stands on two wooden feet that run across each end of the basket.'[2] The craft is concentrated in Sussex, particularly in the village of Hurstmonceaux, where Thomas Smith began to make trugs in the late eighteenth century. But the tradition of trug making in Sussex is even older, for truggers are mentioned as far back as the sixteenth century. Trugger's tools left by John

Edwards, a Slaugham trug maker, to his son James and described in his will are almost exactly the same as those used at
the present day by the truggers of Hurstmonceaux.[3]

Like spale basket making, trug making is a craft that demands
skill and exactitude of a high order, but unlike the craftsmen of
the Wyre Forest and Furness, those of Sussex have adopted
some mechanical techniques. In the trug making industry there
is no division of labour, for one man makes a trug from first to
last. The result is that each trug bears the unmistakable stamp
of a particular craftsman, and it is said that the expert will
recognise the maker of a trug by the workmanship and finish of
a basket.

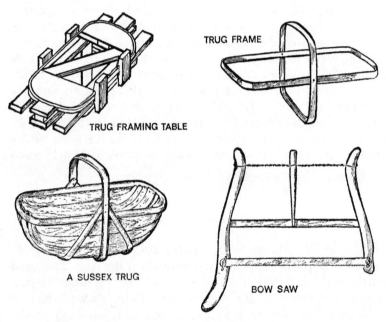

TRUG FRAME

TRUG FRAMING TABLE

A SUSSEX TRUG

BOW SAW

Fig. 12. Method of Trug Making.

Trug making begins with the shaping of the frame. The ash
or chestnut rods which form it are cut into convenient lengths
and cleft in two with the froe. The bark is left on the outer
surface, while the inner surface is shaved with a draw knife and

spokeshave, each rod being clamped in the jaws of a four-legged shaving horse for this purpose. Each rod is reduced to a width of two inches and a thickness of three-quarters of an inch. The rods are then steamed in an elm steaming chest, which is some six feet long, two feet wide and two feet deep. A pipe from a boiler nearby leads to it, carrying the steam which will make the rods pliable. The most important pieces of equipment in the trugger's shop are the simply made setting frames. The trugger possesses

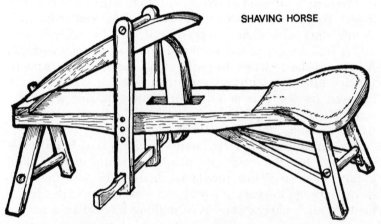

SHAVING HORSE

Fig. 13. A Trug Maker's Shaving Horse.

a large number of these varying from as little as eight inches in length to as much as four feet. The setting brake consists of a wooden frame, oval in shape with blocks of wood at each extremity. The frame of the trug is shaped on this, for as the pliable, steamed rods dry out, the timber is set to the shape of the frame. The overlapping ends of the frame rod are next nailed together. A smaller oval, which will form the handle of the basket is next nailed at right angles to the frame.

For the body of the trug, white pollard willow some seven years old is used. The logs are first cross-cut into convenient lengths and cleft repeatedly into strips no more than one-eighth of an inch thick. In some workshops a finely toothed band-saw is used for cleaving, but in others the traditional method of cleaving with a beetle and wedge along the grain of the willow still persists. The boards are next clamped in the shaving horse and smoothed with draw knife and spokeshave. This thinning, shaping and smoothing is the most skilled part of the trugger's work, but in some workshops the strips of willow are sent through a machine, which saws and shaves it to the required thickness. However, this cuts the grain and weakens the fabric of the basket, but as shaping by hand is such a slow and arduous process, the machine-made trug is considerably cheaper, even though it may be weaker and less attractive.

The boards are next sorted according to size and curve. The longer, thinner ones with straight ends will be 'centre boards'; shorter ones with slightly tapered ends will be 'seconds' and others with a more pronounced end-taper will be 'side-boards'. A medium-sized garden trug will usually have one centre board which is fitted first with two seconds on each side of it. These are followed by one pair of side-boards, thus making a total of seven boards for a medium-sized trug. The largest-sized trug has six seconds, making a total of nine boards.

After soaking in water, the boards are finished with the spokeshave and like the frame and handles they are steamed until pliant. Their boat-like profile is obtained by levering each board between the bars of a setting brake. This, like the device used by rake makers, consists of nothing more than a pair of pegs, some two inches apart, firmly fixed to an upright post.

Finally the various parts of the trug are assembled. The dried boards are taken and dipped in rain water to make them supple and pliable enough for bending into the trug frame. The centre board goes in first and this is nailed to the frame, the craftsmen knocking the nails in with a flat-headed hammer. Each nail is clinched as it emerges from the frame. The centre board is then followed by the seconds and side-boards, each board being nailed to the frame and handle. All the boards overlap so that in construction the trug is not dissimilar to a clinker-built boat. Cross-pieces of willow are added to give the basket stability and a pair of feet on stands are carefully shaped and nailed to the bottom of the basket.

The trug basket is exceptionally strong and durable and it is ideal for the farm and garden. Not only will it withstand many years of hard and constant use, but it is also light in weight and easily repaired.

4. The Bowl Turner

In rural west Wales, the sycamore tree is a very conspicuous element in the landscape, for although it rarely grows in plantations, coppices and natural forests, it occurs everywhere in farm hedgerows, as animal shelterbelts and on the banks of the numerous rushing streams. Indeed, sycamore is one of the few trees that can withstand the great force of the salt-laden winds that blow in from the Irish Sea. For many centuries the sycamore tree has provided the raw material for a number of important village woodcrafts whose fame has spread far beyond the boundaries of Wales. The most important of these crafts were those of bowl turning, the carving of wooden spoons and the manufacture of all kinds of dairy equipment, ranging from carved butter prints to coopered cheese vats. It is said that sycamore is eminently suited for many dairy and cooking utensils, as it is one of the few timbers that does not taint foodstuffs. In addition, like beech, it can be turned and carved while still green and it can be immersed in water at frequent intervals without cracking or warping. Its beauty lies largely in its pale, lustrous colour, for unlike yew or oak it has no strongly marked figure or pattern. On the other hand, it may be steamed to darken its colour to a pale yellow and should a craftsman wish to produce a coloured article, then sycamore will absorb chemical dyes of any colour without the natural grain being obscured. Above all it is the timber's quality as a carving medium that made bowl turning and spoon carving such an important industry in the counties of Cardigan, Pembroke and Carmarthen in the past.

In the past, when wooden utensils were far more widely used in the farm and home than at present, the craft of the bowl turner was widespread in all parts of the British Isles. Like the carpenter, the blacksmith and the wheelwright, the turner was an essential member of the rural community, for not only did he supply essential table and dairy ware, but his products were needed on the farm. Pulley blocks, milking stools as well as many other necessities were made by him, while in many cases some turners were competent to carry out the work of the white cooper, the craftsman who made pails, wash tubs, butter churns and other utensils for use in the dairy.[4] A rhyming signboard of early fifteenth-century-date from Hailsham in Sussex gives some idea of the range of products made by such a country craftsman.

> As other people have a sign
> I say just stop and look at mine,
> Here Wratten, cooper, lives and makes
> Ox bows, trug baskets and hay rakes.
> Sells shovels both for flour and corn
> And shauls and makes a good box churn
> Ladles, dishes, spoons and skimmers,
> Trenchers too, for use at dinners.
> I make and mend both tub and cask
> And hoop 'em strong to make them last.
> Here's butter prints and butter scales.
> And butter boards and milking pails.
> N'on this my friends may safely test
> In serving them I'll do my best.
> Then all that buy, I'll use them well
> Because I make my goods to sell.[5]

The turner was concerned entirely with producing something essentially functional and utilitarian. And if at times his products displayed some beauty of form, then that beauty was purely coincidental.

With the advent of cheap china, plastics and tinware, and with the virtual disappearance of domestic butter and cheese making, the turner is no longer the essential member of the rural community that he once was. Consequently the craft has almost completely died out within the last twenty years and the few elderly representatives of a long tradition have tended to limit their activity to producing decorative ware rather than utilitarian objects. The market for domestic woodware has almost completely disappeared in this age of mass production. The craft itself is of great antiquity, for bowls and trenchers excavated from prehistoric lake dwellings differ but little in shape and workmanship from those made by twentieth-century craftsmen in rural Britain. Pole lathes similar to those used until recently by turners in Berkshire and Buckinghamshire have been excavated from ancient Glastonbury, while the tradition of craftsmanship in those villages which attained pre-eminence as centres of bowl turning goes back at least to the Middle Ages.

One such village is the small isolated north Pembrokeshire hamlet of Abercuch, which until recently was a great centre of woodland craftsmanship. No more than forty years ago there were at least seven families who were entirely dependent on the craft of bowl turning; there were others who worked on a part-time basis combining farming or some other occupation with a certain amount of bowl turning. The fame of Abercuch as a centre of remarkable craftsmanship had spread far beyond the boundaries of Wales, and even as recently as 1935 the prospects of the industry were regarded as excellent. A Guide issued in that year says 'a growing recognition of the aesthetic beauty of the well-turned bowl is creating a new demand for the products of the wood turner'; yet twenty-five years later all the craftsmen with the exception of an elderly workman had disappeared. They disappeared because of the availability of mass-produced goods and also because the Abercuch turners had been unable to find apprentices to learn a trade that demands great craftsmanship and long experience before full competence is achieved. The woods of Cwm Cuch, which not very long ago were alive with the sound of the woodman's axe, are silent; the doors of the once busy workshops are closed and the buzzing of a dozen pole lathes has ceased. For the first time in its long history Abercuch has become a quiet, isolated village which has little to show of its past glory as a centre of woodland artistry.

The last representative of this long tradition of craftsmanship is John Davies, who for well over sixty years has practised the craft of his forefathers in a small workshop in the heart of the woodlands of Glyn Cuch. In those very same woods the knights of the *Mabinogion* hunted the wild boar, but in later times the trees provided the raw material not only for dozens of bowl turners, but other craftsmen as well. Rake makers, broom makers, coracle builders and many others drew on the profuse timber growth of the valley to produce a great variety of goods for farm and household use.

With the virtual disappearance of domestic butter and cheese making, a great deal of the decorative ware made at Abercuch today is from timber other than sycamore. Cherry, chestnut, walnut, oak, mulberry, yew and many of the other timbers that occur locally are used to make the bowls, platters, candlesticks, egg cups and many other things for which there is still a great demand. All the timber used in bowl turning is winter cut as this ensures a good colour in the finished bowl.

After cutting, the tree butts are cut into logs which vary in diameter according to the girth of the tree, and vary in depth according to the type of bowl which is being made. If a bowl is to be of no more than three inches in diameter, then the trimmed logs will be no more than five inches in depth. The sapwood is removed from each log, and the blocks are then stacked under cover to dry out and season before they can be used by the craftsman. The length of seasoning may vary from six months to a year.

The process of bowl turning begins with the shaping of the outside of the bowl, and for this the craftsman uses a one-inch gouge which is used to reduce the roughly octagonal block into a rounded disc. The lathe used by the Abercuch craftsman at the present time is electrically driven, but until recent years he used the older type of treadle lathe. Here the driving power was provided by the craftsman's foot which caused the bowl to revolve continuously. An even older type of lathe, used by craftsmen until 1938, was the pole lathe. The driving power for this piece of equipment was supplied by a horizontal ash or larch pole anchored firmly to the ground at its butt. A piece of string joined the free end of the pole to the foot treadle, being passed around the lathe chuck first. When the treadle was pressed, the pole bent, the chuck turned, only to spring back again as the foot was removed. On each forward motion of the block of wood, the gouge or chisel was applied.

After shaping the outside of the bowl, the craftsman again takes a one-inch gouge and carefully shapes the inside, removing the core at a considerable speed. Smaller gouges and chisels are then applied until the inside of the bowl is quite smooth. At this stage only a thin pillar of wood connects the inside of the bowl to the lathe centre. Taking a little beeswax the craftsman applies it to the rapidly revolving bowl until it is fully polished. Excess wax is removed with wood shavings, the lathe is stopped and the bowl removed for final trimming. The pillar of wood which connected the bowl to the centre screw of the lathe is scraped and the chuck marks cleaned off with a knife.

In the past the Abercuch turners visited all the markets and fairs of west Wales, and the turner's stall was a feature of the Cardigan, Carmarthen, Aberystwyth and many other fairs. Although the last representative of the craft still set up his weekly stall in the Cardigan market place until 1962, most of his products are now sold to a number of large city stores. The days when the turners left the village by pony and trap well loaded with the products of the lathes has long passed, but the spirit of true craftsmanship still lives in the isolated workshop in Glyn Cuch. The bowl turner is in the full sense of the term a creative craftsman, who uses no written measurements or templates, for he has the shapes in his head and hands; shapes that have remained virtually unchanged from the dawn of civilisation.

At one time Bucklebury Common in Berkshire with its dells and dips and maze of minor roads was, like Abercuch, a great centre of woodland craftsmanship. There were rake makers and broom squires, wattle hurdle weavers and tool handle makers, together with many others who drew on the profuse timber growth of the common to produce a great variety of goods for farm and household use. Some of these craftsmen worked on a part-time basis; many of them grazed horses on the common land, but most were employed as full-time craftsmen. One of the best known of all the Bucklebury craftsmen was the bowl turner George William Lailey, who, for nearly eighty years, practised a craft that had been in his family for over two hundred years. Indeed so important was bowl turning in the life of Bucklebury Common that the small hamlet where Lailey lived and worked bears the name of Turner's Green. In December 1958 George Lailey died; his equipment was given to the University of Reading's Museum of English Rural Life and with his death a tradition of craftsmanship also died.

Although a great variety of woods may be used in bowl

turning, the Bucklebury turners used elm almost exclusively. Elm occurs widely on the common, and in turning it possesses one great advantage in that it does not crack or split very easily. Due to the tough nature of elm, Lailey could turn a number of

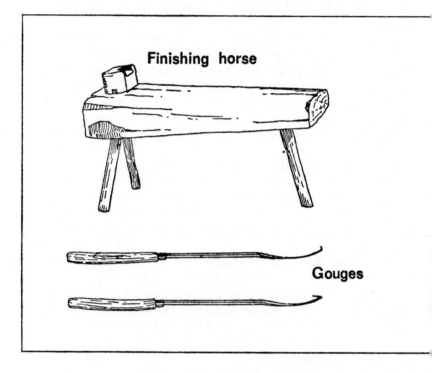

Fig. 14. The Bucklebury Bowl Turner's Equipment.

bowls from a single block of wood, one bowl inside the other with very little wastage. The Abercuch craftsmen using syca-more could never adopt this technique, but George Lailey using elm could cut perhaps four bowls, ranging from a large-sized fruit bowl to a small pin bowl from a single block. The Buckle-bury turners, unlike the Welsh craftsmen, were specialists in decorative woodware. The elm produced bowls of an attractive warm, rosy brown colour whose beauty of grain could be brought out very effectively with constant polishing. The main products of the workshop were bowls and platters, candlesticks and bellows, egg cups and trays that were sold locally or to some London stores.

Lailey's workshop was a lop-sided wooden hut with a red tiled roof built nearly a hundred years ago. It measured some twenty feet long and thirteen feet wide and was equipped with a wide doorway and three windows located near the lathe. In a corrugated iron lean-to behind the hut seasoning timber was stored and there the initial stages in the making of a bowl were carried out. The elm was cut into blocks in such a way that the grain ran across the opening of a bowl, but the blocks had to remain in store for at least five years before they could be turned. Inside, the actual workshop was very gloomy and a thick carpet of woodshavings covered the whole floor except behind the lathe where the craftsman's feet had stood and bored a deep hole in the carpet. The pole lathe dominated the workshop and although an electric power cable passed within a hundred yards of the workshop, Lailey clung to this piece of antiquated equipment. The driving power of the lathe was a springy alder sapling, twelve feet long anchored at its base with wedges and dozens of pieces of old iron. Running from the free end of the pole was a string which was wrapped around the chuck and attached to the foot treadle. As the craftsman pressed the treadle the chuck and the piece of elm that it carried revolved. At the same time the firmly anchored pole would bend and spring back again when the treadle was released.

Near the lathe a great variety of chisels rested; some were straight-shaped for shaping the outside of the bowl; others were sharply curving so as to reach the very core of the elm block. All were made by the craftsman himself from old files, and while the V-shaped chisels were used for the outside of the bowls, the L-shaped tools were used for the intricate process of shaping the inside of the bowls.

Unlike John Davies of Abercuch, George Lailey had to finish his bowls on the bench or on the specially designed shaping horse. This was a low bench, similar to a shaving horse, but with a round shaping device at the front. Each bowl was upturned on this and all irregularities removed with spokeshave, files and sandpaper. The bowls were then placed in the open air to dry out before being sold.

5. The Spoon Carver

In the past wooden spoons were widely used in country house-holds for a great variety of purposes. In Wales, for example, small ten-inch spoons were always required for eating *cawl*, that unique broth of bacon, leeks and other vegetables, the recipe for which seems to have been limited to the western counties of Wales. *Cawl* still remains extremely popular in Welsh farm-houses and many people will not eat it with anything but a wooden spoon. The spoon carvers, in addition to making broth spoons, also make a variety of large spoons and ladles ranging from butter scoops for use in the dairy, to kitchen spatulas and stirrers. All these are made by hand and with a few simple tools.

The process of making a spoon begins with the felling of suitable timber in the winter months. There is a tradition that sycamore for bowls and spoons should be winter felled as this ensures a pale lustrous wood, free of all blemishes and stains. After felling, the sycamore butts are cut by means of a cross-cut saw into logs, each one approximately twelve inches long. With the aid of a small cleaving iron and hammer, each log is cut in two and the process of shaping the spoon begins. Sitting on a three-legged stool, the craftsman rests the sycamore log on the chopping block in front of him and with a short-handled axe cuts the log to the approximate shape of the spoon. With a few deft strokes the handle and the shoulders of the spoon, as well as the rough outline of the bowl, are cut. For this process the craftsman depends entirely on eyesight and long experience for the shoulders have to slope at the same angle and the spoon has to be perfectly symmetrical. No written measurements or patterns of any kind are used by Welsh spoon carvers.

After roughing out with the axe, the half-finished spoon now needs hollowing and this is done with a peculiarly shaped knife known as a *twca cam*. This tool, which has a handle some eighteen inches in length, has a small curved blade, usually made by the craftsman himself from an old file or chisel. It is kept extremely sharp and to use it the handle is tucked under the user's right arm and tightly against his body, while the blade is grasped firmly in the right hand. With the tip of the handle acting as a fulcrum considerable power is applied to the blade and with a few short sweeping movements the core of the spoon is removed cleanly.

The convex side of the spoon and the handle has to be smoothed next and this is done with an ordinary, small-sized spokeshave. This held in the palm of the hand is used to smooth away all unevenness. Finally, the tip of the handle, the edges of the spoon and the shoulders are cleaned and finished with a short-bladed knife. The whole process of making a broth spoon takes little more than fifteen minutes from the moment when the sycamore log is cleft to the final stage when the spoon is cleaned with the knife.

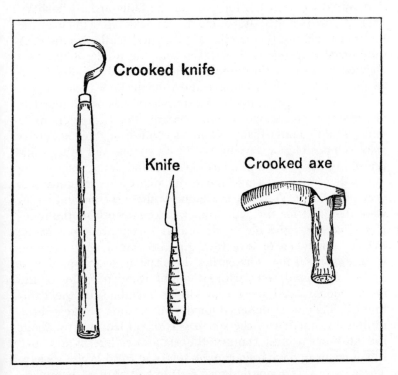

Fig. 15. Spoon-Carving Tools.

To make the large ladle which is used for a number of tasks in the home and dairy, the process is rather different. Since the ladle will be at least fifteen inches long, the logs have to be larger. Each one is roughed out in the same way as the broth spoon except for the fact that the tip of the handle has to be shaped into a hook. This hook is necessary for hanging the ladle on the edge of the milk bucket or shelf and it is shaped during the first stage of roughing out with the axe. Since the bowl of the ladle is considerably wider and deeper than that of the broth spoon, something stronger than the *twca* is required to shape it. The roughed out ladle is therefore clamped in a vice and a short-handled adze with a one- and-a-half inch gouge blade is taken. This adze, known as a *bwyall gam*, is a unique tool which, like the *twca*, has remained unchanged for many centuries. All that is required to clean the top part of the ladle are a few sharp knocks with the adze, but since it cannot be used to clean the lower end, nearest the handle, a gouge and mallet are used. A large-sized *twca cam* is then taken and the inside of the base cleaned exactly in the same manner as in the smaller broth spoon. Finally, with spokeshave and knife the ladle is completed.

The wooden spoon, despite its simplicity, has been an article of great importance in Welsh peasant life. Although many villages and country districts had their full-time craftsmen who were responsible for carving the broth spoons and other utilitarian objects of use in the farm kitchen and dairy, the carving of wooden spoons as a pastime in the long winter evenings was very popular on Welsh farms. Some of those spoons and ladles were designed for use, but from the seventeenth to the nineteenth century, the highly decorated spoon presented by its maker as a token of love to a girl, became a very common feature of rural life. The earliest love spoons were simple and undecorated and were without doubt wooden copies of the metal spoons used by the wealthier members of the community. They were designed for use but as time progressed the utilitarian function of the spoon was discarded and by about the mid-seventeenth century the elaborate, but useless love spoon seems to have been commonplace in rural Welsh society. These spoons were not designed for use and most of them were very intricate and elaborate in design, with slotted handles, chain links and carved patterns or initials. The aim, wherever possible, seems to have been to carve an intricate pattern out of a single piece of wood, and since the donor of the love spoon was also its maker, he tried to emphasise the feeling and care that had gone into its making by elaborating the design as much as possible, as a symbol of the fervour of the carver's passion.

While early spoons were, on the whole, simple, elaboration of design took place especially in the late eighteenth and nineteenth centuries. First, the handle of the spoon was en-larged either by making it rectangular or by giving it the flat form of a panel. The increased surface of the handle gave the carver an opportunity to express his skill by carving fretwork designs of various symbols of affection. Hearts, anchors, bells, locks, keys, as well as geometric designs were carved; reliefs of vine and bay leaves were carefully moulded with a penknife; and narrow channels for the insertion of black and red sealing wax were cut in the handle. Sometimes too the date of manu-facture and the initials of the girl that had taken the carver's heart were inscribed on the handle, while in later examples a circular or rectangular panel for the insertion of a picture or a glass-covered inscription was prepared. Fretwork designs were endless in their variety and shape, but perhaps the most striking of all spoons were those with rectangular or circular stems hollowed out with wooden balls running in the cavity. The aim wherever possible was to make both spoon and balls, as well as chain-link for hanging, out of a single piece of wood and it was this feature that revealed the ingenuity of many makers of love spoons. In some parts of the country, notably in west Wales, it has been said that the number of little balls running freely in the cavity of the spoon handle denoted the number of children that the young man wished for after marriage.

While the handle of a love spoon lent itself to considerable variation in carving, it was very rarely that the bowl of a spoon was carved. The development here was the introduction of twin or even triple bowls, normally with the accompaniment of a broad panelled handle. Examples exist too of love tokens equipped with a spoon in the centre flanked by a carved knife and carved fork attached to a piece of carved wood with a chain link.

Little is known about love spoons except that their presentation was a custom associated with courtship in Wales. Possibly the offer of a spoon by a suitor and its acceptance or refusal by a girl could have developed into a ritual of betrothal, but there is no evidence to suggest this. That the spoons were made by the thousand in rural Wales, can not be doubted, but their ritual significance and the customs associated with their presentation must remain a mystery.

In the same tradition as love spoons were the knitting sticks or needle sheaths that were also presented as love tokens. A sheath was used to support a needle to work from during knitting and it had a hole in the end to receive the needle. The sheath was inserted in the apron strings and although many are straight pieces of wood, many are most intricately carved with initials and symbols of love.

Stay busks were also presented as love tokens and these elongated pieces of wood designed for insertion into a girl's stays were most elaborately carved and decorated but, like the love spoons, they developed into articles of conspicuous waste, rather than objects that could be used.

6. The Rake Maker

In the past, hand rakes were an essential part of farm equipment, but within the last forty years, with the mechanisation of the hay harvest, rakes are not the indispensable tools that they once were. Indeed, so low and seasonal is the demand that the work available is very often not enough to keep one craftsman fully occupied throughout the year. For this reason a large number of rake makers have given up work, while others have developed some secondary occupation such as making clothes pegs, hurdles and tool handles. But in the past, rakes were indispensable for collecting hay into rows and ready for loading on to a cart or wagon. They were required for such tasks as combing and straightening the sides of ricks, while thatchers often required rake heads to comb the thatch.

The hand rake is a tool of great antiquity, for rakes not unlike those made by country craftsmen in Hampshire and Ceredigion at the present were frequently illustrated in medieval manuscripts and psalters. Within the last forty years the hay harvest, once a vast communal affair, has been greatly mechanised, and with mechanisation, hand rakes, though required in limited quantities, are less essential than in the past. Only a few representatives of the ancient craft of rake making still remain at work in Britain, and they are easily able to fulfil the small seasonal demand that still exists in some regions.

As recently as 1930, when the hay harvest was not mechanised to the same extent as at present, rakes were in considerable demand, and wherever suitable coppice wood existed, then a rake maker's yard was found nearby. In north Hampshire and west Berkshire, for example, the craft was widespread, for the Kennet Valley was particularly rich in willow, the Hampshire rake maker's raw material. Today, only one rake maker still remains at work in this region, and in a small thatched workshop he follows a tradition of craftsmanship that has been in his family for well over two hundred years. Working alone, on a part-time basis only, he is able to meet the demand for hand rakes from all parts of Southern England. In 1953 he worked on a full-time basis and his two sons were also employed in the trade, but after that date the demand fell off to such an extent that he no longer needed to employ any workers. In the same thatched workshop, using the same techniques of manufacture and even the same tools used by his forebear when he established his business in the eighteenth century, Ernest Sims, the last of the Tadley rake makers, still produces the light, long-handled Hampshire hay rakes.

Hand rakes vary tremendously from one part of the country to the other, and there are many variations in the methods of making them. Some, like those of Yorkshire, are short-handled, others like those of Hampshire are long-handled. Most have heads at right angles to the handle, but those of Glamorgan, designed for raking hay on sloping fields, have short heads at an angle of forty-five degrees to the handle. There is considerable variation in the type of wood used; those of Hampshire are of tough springy willow, while those of Wales are of ash. In other parts of the country pine, birch and alder are also used. In northern and western Britain, where the hay is often grown on sloping fields and is short and springy, the hay rakes are by tradition small and well constructed, with the heads supported by braces and bows. In those districts, the rakes are expected to last for many years. The rakes of Southern England, on the other hand, designed to cope with the lush grass growth of lowland meadows, are much larger and less strongly constructed. The butt end of the handle is sawn along the centre to provide a pair of split ends morticed into the head. This is the simplest and quickest type of rake to make and the southern farmer rarely expected his rakes to last for more than one season, and consequently the rakes made in great quantities by such craftsmen as Ernest Sims were sold at amazingly low prices.

In the past, rake makers were also engaged in making specialised types of rakes, in addition to the ordinary hand variety. For example, some craftsmen made the wide-headed drag rakes for gathering hay and corn, others made thatcher's rakes and offal rakes, but whatever type the craftsmen made, the process of making always appeared simple to the casual observer. It has been estimated that the wood from which a hand rake is made, passes through the craftsman's hands at least fifty times from cutting in the woods to the final touches. In order to make a tool that is durable, strong and light, considerable experience and skill are required. A good rake must be as light as possible to avoid fatigue during the long hours of harvesting. The teeth must not be set in the head at too sharp an angle, or the tool will not gather the hay efficiently. If the angle between the teeth and the head is not sharp enough, then the tines will tend to stick in the ground, and are quite likely to break off. With no pattern, templates or measurements, and no guide but that of long experience, the craftsman has to ensure that his rakes fulfil all these conditions.

In Hampshire, hay rakes are fitted with tines of tough, resistant willow and vary between eleven and fifteen in number. They are generally equipped with ash handles, split and divided at the bottom before entering the head. Although ash is preferred for the handles of rakes, as for other farm tools, other timber such as hazel, alder, birch or willow is also widely used. Rake handles must be very smooth, however, so as to slip easily through one hand as the hay is raked with the other.

After the craftsman has cut his willow and ash, the timber is stored in his yard for many months before it is ready for use. The rake maker's yard in the hamlet of Pamber End in Hampshire is large; there are huge stacks of seasoning timber, while everywhere peeled bark, broken tines and wood shavings provide a thick carpet underfoot. Although the craftsman possesses a low thatched building where a great variety of tools and finished as well as half-finished rakes are kept·he very rarely works there when the weather is dry. The yard is littered with a number of primitive-looking vices, shaving horses, sawing horses and tining horses. Here and there may be seen some of the peculiar tools used by the craftsman, some of them dating back to his great-grandfather's day.

The first task in making a hand rake is the shaping of the handle, and from the large pile of seasoning timber the craftsman selects a suitable ash stick and with a broad axe he carefully flattens the lower twenty inches of it. He continues with this work until he has a large number of sticks, some straight, others crooked. Each handle is then clamped in the jaws of the brake, a primitive home-made vice firmly embedded in the ground. This consists of a rectangular frame some seven feet high and the jaws are opened with a lever and closed by the heavy weight of pieces of old iron and clock weights. With the ash stick firmly held in the brake, the craftsman takes a draw knife or round shave and with a few dexterous strokes, removes the bark.

Ideally each ash stick should be perfectly straight, but this is very rarely·the case, so that each handle has to be straightened artificially by steaming. Standing in the corner of the workshop is a large coffin-like elm box, measuring some six feet long. This is connected by a series of pipes to a large copper boiler. The boiler is filled with water, a fire of wood shavings is lit underneath and the steam emanating from it passes through the elm box which is filled with a dozen or more rake stails.[6] After an hour or so in the chest the fibres of the stails are pliable and each one can be straightened on a setting brake or pin. This consists of nothing more than a stout upright post, perhaps a supporting pillar of a building to which are fixed a pair of wooden pegs, the one above and behind the other. By placing the steamed stail between the jaws of the pegs it is levered to the desired shape.

Once again the rake handles are clamped in turn in the upright brake and smoothed with a special type of plane known in Hampshire as a 'Stail Engine'. This consists of two blocks of wood fastened together, with a hole large enough to admit the stail in the centre. Some stail engines have two blades, one in either block, and the tool is worked right down the length of the pole with a circular movement that provides a smooth finish. The rake handle may be tapered if necessary by screwing the two halves of the engine and so moving the blades closer to one another. After the final smoothing with a small semi-circular-bladed draw shave, the butt end of the handle is sawn for some twenty inches of its length on the sawing horse, a low, four-legged stool with a long slit on its top surface. A piece of tin is nailed around the saw cut to prevent further splitting. The stails are then stored in a corner of the workshop until required.

The process of making a rake head is equally intricate and the craftsman requires a number of tools for this work. In Hampshire, rake heads are made of Dutch willow and the tines or teeth from locally grown pollard willow. The craftsman selects a log some thirty inches in length from the heap of seasoning timber, and with a large felling axe, the log is quartered. With the broad axe, each quartered piece is chopped to shape – a most skilful and intricate process, for a few strokes of the axe reduces the billet to very nearly the shape of the finished head. Indeed all that remains is to shave and smooth the rake head with the draw knife.

Clamping the head between a pair of wedges on a low table, the rake maker bores a series of tine holes. These vary between eleven and fifteen in number, but the craftsman knows from experience where to position those holes knowing that the tines should be no more than three inches apart. In the Hampshire workshops these are bored with an electric drill, the only feature of the mechanical age in this rural workshop.

The smallest pieces of willow are sawn into lengths of approximately six inches, they are quartered with the axe and rounded by the tube-shaped knife of the driving stool. The craftsman sits astride this stool and the roughly cleft pieces of

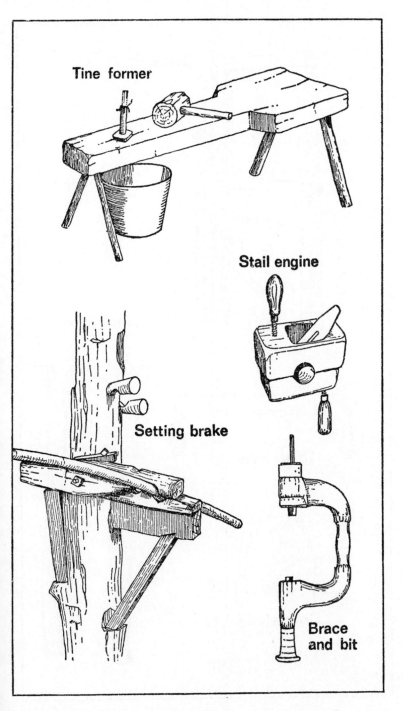

Tine former

Stail engine

Setting brake

Brace and bit

Fig. 16. The Rake Maker's Tools and Equipment: I.

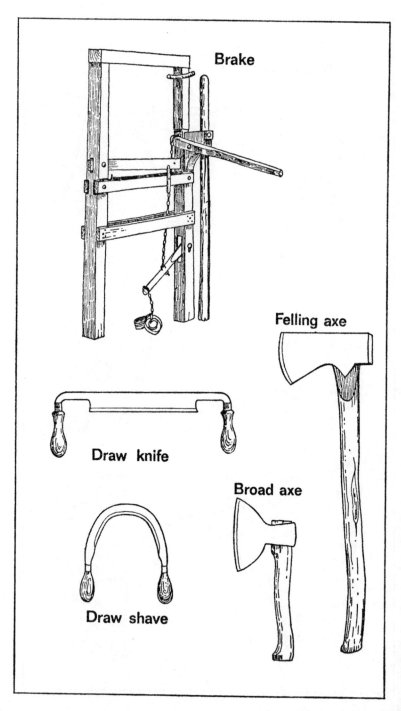

Fig. 17. The Rake Maker's Tools and Equipment: II.

willow are in turn passed through the cutting iron in front of
him. A peg is driven with a mallet through this and just as it is
flush with the cutting edge, the next is placed on top to follow
it. Each rounded tine falls into the waiting basket beneath and
when a large number have been made in this way, the process
of tining begins.

The tining horse consists merely of a flat table some three
feet high. The head is clamped in the jaws of a small vice at one
corner, as the craftsman armed with a small hammer knocks
in the tines. Taking a tine from the large heap on the table,
he dips it in water so that the fibres swell and are fixed tightly
in the head.

Once again the upright brake is required, for each tine must
be pointed with the half-round draw shave. The head is finally
trimmed with the axe and draw knife and the two holes into
which the split ends of the stail will fit are bored with a wooden
brace and bit. Long experience alone tells the craftsman where
these holes have to be bored, for he uses no written measurements or pattern, yet, not only is he able to gauge the position
of the holes, but he must also ensure that the angle of boring is
slightly acute. If this is not done, the finished rake will not be
able to gather hay without jumping.

With all the various parts of the rake completed, the final
stage consists of assembling and smoothing the tool. The split
butt end of the stail is opened and each section inserted in the
drilled holes. A small nail is passed through the head and forked
ends of the handle and with penknife, draw knife and sandpaper,
the finished tool is cleaned and shaved. The rakes are then
packed in bundles of six, ready for sale.

Deep in the heart of the Welsh hills in the hamlet of
Llanymawddwy, another rake maker was at work until 1966.
His methods of manufacture were entirely different from those
of the Hampshire craftsman, for his rakes were expected to last
for many a year; they had to be much stronger to cope with
tough springy grasses and the loose stones that may have found
their way to the hayfield.

In making rake handles William Thomas of Llanymawddwy
sawed an ash plank into long strips some three inches square.
With a small rounding plane he shaped the handle until it was

perfectly round and smooth. The rounding plane is quite different from the stail engine, for it resembles an ordinary carpenter's plane, but with a concave sole and blade some two inches wide. The handle was firmly held horizontally on the bench with the left hand during the shaving process.

While Ernest Sims saws the butt end of the stail, the Merioneth craftsman carefully flattened the butt end with a knife and split it for no more than ten inches of its length. A pair of holes at right angles to the split, into which the curved ash bows would be fixed later, were bored in the handle a few inches above the split. The technique of head making differed considerably from the rough and ready method adopted in Hampshire. The ash for the head was sawn out of a solid plank and the position of the fifteen or more tines carefully marked at a distance of no more than two inches from one another. The tine holes for the rake bow were carefully marked out and bored with brace and bit. The technique of tine cutting and fitting in both workshops was similar, but after assembling the rake, the Merioneth craftsman had to shape and fit the semicircular bows that gave added strength to the rake. These were shaped with a spokeshave and were gently fitted into place to make an extremely strong and durable tool.

These two craftsmen, the one practising in a small workshop, that was once in the heart of the English countryside, the other working in an isolated workshop in the solitude of the Welsh mountains belonged to a different tradition of workmanship. The one works in the age-old tradition of the woodland worker, producing a cheap rake very quickly, the other belonged to the tradition of highly skilled woodworkers, carpenters and joiners, to produce a much more expensive, durable tool. Both were reminders of the days when a village community looked no further than the bounds of its own locality for the means of life.

The tool handle maker uses the same basic methods for shaping his products as the rake maker employs for making rake handles. Usually his raw material is held in the jaws of a shaving horse, similar to that used by chair bodgers, and the shaping and smoothing is completed with a draw knife, stail engine and spokeshave. His trade, too, has almost ceased to be a rural one, for tool handles are usually made by town

workers who are often employed by the large-scale manufacturers of edge tools.

7. The Gate Hurdle Maker

Unlike the wattle hurdle maker, the craftsman who builds gate
or open hurdles is a village rather than a woodland worker.
Instead of spending the greater part of the year in the wood
coppices, the gate maker transports his raw material to a
village workshop where, in the spring and summer months, he
spends his time building hurdles.

The hurdle maker's raw material is winter-felled willow, a
timber eminently suited to the needs of his craft. Willow is
light, yet resistant to shocks and hard usage; it is soft and very
easy to cleave. Along the banks of slowly meandering streams in
southern England the willow grows profusely and in the moist
river valleys of Hampshire and Berkshire, in particular, the
craft of gate hurdle making was once very widespread, especially
as there was a ready market for the hurdles among the sheep
farmers of the adjoining downs. Along the banks of the Kennet,
for example, the willow grows well and this plentiful timber
supply provided the basis for a large number of crafts in such
villages as Aldermaston, Woolhampton and Thatcham. In the
past, these villages supported a large number of basket makers,
rake makers and many others, while today, willow grown in
the region is widely used for manufacturing cricket bats in
town workshops.

A group of important craftsmen in these villages in the
past, were those supplying the needs of sheep farmers on the
Hampshire and Berkshire Downs. Each village supported sheep
crib makers, makers of feeding baskets, wattle weavers and gate
hurdle makers. Though both gates and wattle hurdles may still
be required in limited quantities by downland shepherds, the
demand has diminished very greatly within the last few years.
The demand for gate hurdles in particular, is very low, for they
do not provide the weather screens that closely woven wattle
provides for lamb folds on the windswept downs. The folding
of sheep is less frequently practised than in the past and while

the popularity of wattle as garden screens has been the salvation of the wattle weaver as a craftsman, the gate hurdle is completely unsuitable for decorative or screening purposes. For these reasons, the number of workers engaged in the craft has declined remarkably within the last few years. The few that are still engaged in the trade tend to spread their activity over a much wider field and make a variety of products ranging from clothes pegs to hand rakes, in addition to hurdles.

The best-known centre of the gate hurdle trade in southern England was the village of Baughurst in northern Hampshire. In 1959 the last of the gate hurdle makers in this village was forced by economic circumstances to find alternative work in a neighbouring village, due to the low demand for his range of products. His hurdle making has remained a part-time occupation.

Hurdle making is a summer craft, for the winter months are spent on the river banks, cutting and sorting willow. The craftsman buys a quantity of standing willow in the early autumn and, with felling axe and billhooks, he cuts and trims the straighter, stronger poles that he requires. The raw material used for gate making is pollard willow, the crown of branches radiating from the trunk or stool of an already felled tree. The poles are harvested at regular intervals of seven years. They are lopped in the winter months, but in the following spring the willow stool again puts out a large number of green shoots. Lopping may be repeated indefinitely for, even though a willow trunk may be hollow and rotten, it will continue to bear its crop of poles for many a year.

When all the suitable poles have been transported to the craftsman's yard and sorted according to length and thickness, the task of hurdle making begins. The craftsman likes to begin this work as soon as possible, while the willow is still green, pliant and easy to cleave. It is only after the whole hurdle has been assembled that the seasoning of timber takes place.

In Hampshire a gate hurdle measures six feet long and three-and-a-half feet high; it has six or seven horizontal bars, with one upright and two diagonal braces to give it added strength. The distance between the rails may vary according to the requirements of the local sheep farmers. In some cases, when the hurdles are required for lamb folds, the distance between the two bottom rails may be large enough for a lamb to pass through in order to reach fodder placed on the other side of the fold, but the rails are too close for the ewe to follow its offspring. This type is known as a lamb-creep hurdle and is but one of a great variety of hurdles made.

The first stage in the construction of a gate hurdle consists of cutting and shaping two stout rods to form the vertical heads. Each pole is trimmed with a saw to a length of three feet six inches, and fitting this firmly in the jaws of a brake or 'monkey' the pole is cleft into two equal halves. The hurdle maker's monkey is a roughly made frame some five feet long and four feet high with rails and diagonals running at all possible angles so as to clamp a piece of wood for cleaving at any desired angle. Another variety of brake consists basically of two wooden cross-pieces nailed to two pairs of firmly embedded uprights. The two cross-pieces are some twenty inches apart and at a different level, so that when a pole is fitted into a U-shaped gap in it at a downward slant, it is held firmly in place. Some twenty-four inches in front of the brake is another upright, on which the pole rests when shaping. To cleave a pole, the hurdle maker uses an L-shaped froe, and after the blade has been tapped in with a mallet, the cleaving is completed by moving the tool backwards and forwards until it is cleanly cut into two sections.

After cleaving, the craftsman takes each cleft pole, clamps it in the brake and with a two-handled draw knife strips the bark from it. It is then removed from the monkey, rested on a chopping block and pointed with a billhook. A point is essential on hurdle heads, for when in use they are moved frequently, and the pointed ends mean that the shepherd need not dig preparatory holes whenever he wants to move his hurdles.

The hurdle heads must next be marked and the mortice holes for the horizontal rails cut. The head is placed on a roughly made, marked table, and the six or seven mortice holes are marked in pencil. The head is returned to the monkey and with brace and half-inch bit a pair of holes are bored at each end of the marked mortices. The wood in between these borings is removed with a peculiarly shaped knife known in various parts of the country as a 'tomyhawk', 'dader', 'twobill' or 'twivel'.

This knife is some fifteen inches long; at one end it has a sharp triangular blade for cutting in between the borings, while at the other it has a hook to pick out the wood. This tool is peculiar to the gate hurdle making trade, and were the timber to be harder than willow, it could not possibly be used. With the heads completed, the rails are now shaped. The longer, lighter poles are cleft with the froe and rinded with the draw knife in

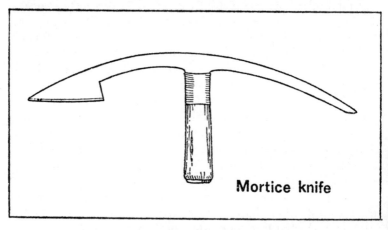

Mortice knife

Fig. 18. Hurdle Maker's Mortice Knife.

the same manner as the heads. In this case, however, the ends are not pointed but only flattened with the axe. The rails of the gate are roughly six-sided in cross-section and, although all the corners are shaved away, the centre of each rail is thick, so as to be strong where the nails connect it to the diagonal braces. The braces themselves are made in exactly the same way as the heads and rails.

When all the sections of the hurdle, the two pointed heads, the six or seven rails and three braces have been completed, the task of assembling begins. Once again the craftsman has a special device, standing in the open air for this purpose. This consists of a low, flat framework, standing some three feet high, which is exactly the same size as a hurdle. The various sections are placed in the right position on this table and the heads are tapped firmly on to the rails. The braces are placed in position and nails are knocked in at the junction of each one with the rails. Ideally, rose-headed cut nails should be used, but due to the difficulty and cost in obtaining them, the craftsman uses ordinary wire nails. Before use, the point of each nail is flattened, so that it is less likely to split the wood, while the nail tops coming through the rails are clinched to lie absolutely flat against the surface of the gate, so that they do not tear the sheep or shepherd.

Finally, the hurdles are stacked in batches of a dozen under the mellowing influences of the wind and the rain. Each pile has to be weighed down with stones so that the hurdles are perfectly flat when sold. A great deal of skill goes into the making of a gate hurdle, for they must be strong enough to withstand the thrust of hungry sheep and lambs, while they must also withstand a great deal of moving and handling. Nevertheless, hurdle making is a rapidly disappearing craft which has been unable to face the competition of the electric and wire fence.

8. The Broom Squire

For many centuries the small village of Tadley on the Hampshire–Berkshire borders has been well known as the home of a large number of woodland craftsmen. In the past it supported a large number of rake makers, besom makers, hurdle makers, turners and many others who drew on the profuse timber growth of the Kennet Valley and surrounding heathland, to produce a variety of products for farm and household use. Up to a few years ago Tadley was a typical English village with the majority of the inhabitants depending almost entirely on the soil and its products for their livelihood. Perhaps the best known of all these Tadley woodworkers was the broom squire who utilised local raw material to produce the famous Tadley besom or birch broom.

Today in an area famous for its woodland craftsmen only a few still remain at work. Basket makers, scythe snead makers and bowl turners have almost completely disappeared, while only two people are still engaged in broom making as a full-time occupation. In 1953 there were at least ten broom squires in the Tadley district. Some were itinerant woodland craftsmen, others worked in permanent village workshops. A few years ago however, the Atomic Weapons Research Establishment was set up in the neighbouring village of Aldermaston. This vast undertaking was established on the sandy, well-wooded heathland of south Berkshire, where countless generations of woodland craftsmen had obtained their raw materials. But a more serious threat to rural life that this new undertaking presented was the fact that its very existence provided alternate, more secure and remunerative employment to the inhabitants of the village of Tadley. Local society has been robbed of its craftsmen, who have left their traditional way of life for the greater security, shorter hours and high wages of the Establishment.

Hampshire besoms are invariably made of birch twigs, bound together by wire or withies, but in other districts such as north Wales and Yorkshire, heather is widely used. The besom itself is of considerable antiquity and has been known in Britain at least since Saxon times. Few records of the craft in Hampshire have survived, but it seems probable that the craft has been carried on in the villages of Tadley and Baughurst since the fourteenth century. It is known that one workshop in Tadley has been in existence since the mid-sixteenth century and is still very flourishing, the craft having been passed on from father to son over the centuries. Here in a low, long building, Alfred West, who is likely to be the last of a long line of broom squires, may still be seen at work. He uses exactly the same techniques of manufacture and the few simple tools that his ancestor used, when, four hundred years ago, he established his business on the brow of Mulford's Hill.

A living can still be made from making besoms, for not only are besoms required for such tasks as sweeping leaves and sports grounds, but they are still widely used in the modern steel industry for sweeping away impurities from newly made steel plates. In vinegar brewing, too, the bottoms of the vats are lined with handle-less besoms known as 'swales' to a depth of three feet. The birch used in besoms helps to create acetic acid and helps to filter malt liquor. Despite its antiquity and its simplicity, the birch besom still has its place in twentieth-century Britain.

The broom squire's yard is completely dominated by huge, orderly stacks of maturing birch, carefully built up and thatched, so that winter snow and rain does not damage the selected brushwood. In broom making, seasoning is of great importance, for should the birch be used too soon, the finished besom will be too brittle and of little use. Here and there in the yard are lower stacks where roughly hewn hazel, ash and lime handles are stored for use. Other handles, their barks removed and ends pointed lean in orderly piles against incredibly old apple trees. One walks through endless corridors, with vertical walls of reddish-black birch almost obscuring the daylight. The besom maker's yard seems uncannily quiet and peaceful, for he uses but a few simple tools. He requires nothing more than a pair of pliers, a billhook and short-handled axe, for he depends far more on long practice, and a strong pair of arms, to make besoms, which Alfred West can produce at the rate of twelve dozen a day.

The besom maker generally buys standing birch by the acre, and although countless generations of craftsmen have drawn on the timber of the sandy heathlands, the rapid-growing, hardy birch trees are as profuse as ever. The material for besom making is selected from the crown of the tree, a tree that must be at least seven years old and bearing a thick, rounded crown. After selecting and cutting, the birch is tied into large bundles and delivered to the besom maker's yard. Here it is carefully stacked or 'piled' and allowed to mature and season for several months. The piles must be built up in a special way, for they must be open enough to allow the winds to penetrate and thus assist the seasoning process, yet they must be built in such a way that rain and melting snow do not penetrate into the heart of the stack and cause rot. The bundles of brush wood, which the craftsman knows as 'brish' are very carefully built up into piles, that must be perfectly level and square so that they do not collapse with high wind. The bundles are built up in layers alternately laid lengthways and crossways, each bundle laid head to tail with the next. When the squared pile is some fourteen feet high, it is thatched with other bundles of brush, their heads pointing downwards at a sharp pitch so that rain is easily carried away and does not penetrate the stack. The brushwood

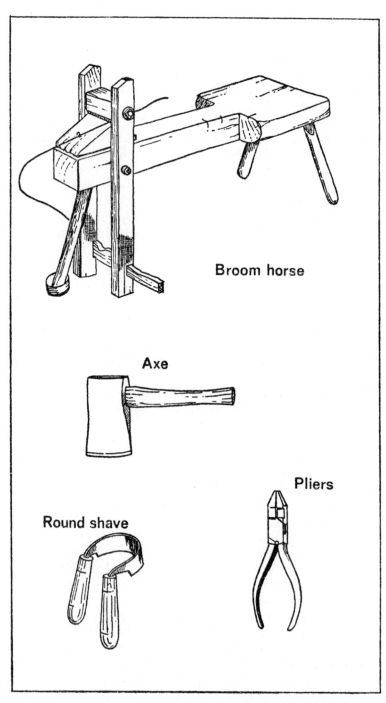

Broom horse

Axe

Pliers

Round shave

Fig. 19. The Broom Squire's Tools and Equipment.

is kept in these large stacks for many months, until each twig is hard yet pliant and tough, all ready to be used for making besoms.

In addition to birch, the craftsman also requires a large number of handles. A great variety of woods may be used for handle making, although custom has dictated that the best broom handles are made from hazel, ash or lime rods. After these have been selected, cut and stored in thatched piles for many months, they are placed in a shaving horse, and the bark removed with a straight, double-handled draw knife. They are then smoothed with a small two-handled semicircular bladed draw shave, their ends pointed with an axe and carefully piled in close proximity to the workshop, ready for use when required. Since broom handles need not, of necessity be perfectly straight, the craftsman is very often able to buy inferior quality wood, considered not good enough for other woodworkers.

The only other raw material that the broom squire requires is something to tie the besom head together. Once again the tying material is varied, although at the present time galvanised wire is in general use. In the past, however, a great variety of local timber was adapted for making bonds, the most popular in this area being willow twigs, willow being particularly abundant in the damp Kennet Valley. In addition to willow, strips of ash, thin pieces of oak cleft with a wooden bond splitter, lime bark, chestnut strips and bramble were all widely used. Later these were replaced by bonds of imported cane, but with the outbreak of war in 1939 and the consequent short supply of cane, craftsmen either reverted to traditional wooden bonds, or more often used galvanised wire to tie the besom heads.

The first stage in the manufacture of a besom consists of opening up one of the piles of seasoning timber. The bundles are trimmed with a short-bladed billhook and then sorted by hand; a task very often performed by the village women and children. Sitting on an old box in the open air, the sorter, sometimes armed with a narrow-bladed stripping billhook, cuts away all pieces that are too small and brittle for besoms. The rejected material will be later tied into bundles and sold as firewood. The brush is sorted into two distinct groups, the first containing the longer, rougher material for the core of the broom, the second containing the smoother, shorter strands of birch for the outside of the head. The sorted twigs are again tied into bundles and stacked outside the workshop door, all ready for the broom squire to carry in to the workshop as he requires them.

The craftsman himself very rarely does any sorting, for this is unskilled work which can be entrusted to women and children. He, clad in a leather apron, smooth and shiny after years of constant use, works in a low-ceilinged workshop, that seems to be full of finished besoms, heaps of besom heads, coils of wire and heaps of unused and rejected birch. In a very small space within these mountains of birch the craftsman, sitting astride his home-made broom horse works at a fantastically rapid pace. His tools are few and simple; he requires nothing more than a pair of pliers and an axe to make the heads, while his four-legged broom horse is a roughly made affair. The squire sits astride this horse, the galvanised wire from the coil on the floor beside him being guided towards the jaws of the horse by a small staple at the front. The wire passes through this, and then passes through the clamping jaws of the bench, the wire being locked or released at the craftsman's will by the pressure of both feet on the treadle. In many respects this work bench is similar to the shaving horses used by the majority of woodland craftsmen, but it is a horse specially adapted to the needs of the besom maker.

The craftsman picks up a small handful of the longer, rougher birch twigs from the bundle on his left-hand side. He arranges the twigs, rolling them up and down on his apron. He then picks up a bundle of shorter, smoother twigs and arranges them round his first handful. Besoms are known by their size in inches, each size being measured around the circumference of the head. No rulers or calipers are used for this, but the crafts-man knows that where his thumbs and fingers just touch as he places them around the base of the broom, then he has a twelve-inch broom. Where his fingers and thumbs overlap slightly, then he knows that he has made the smaller ten-inch broom. When he is satisfied with the size and shape of the besom, he inserts the end of the wire into the birch, some four inches below the base. By rolling the besom towards him, the wire is twisted around the base a number of times. Pressing forwards with both feet, he locks the wire in the jaws of the horse; he leans back pulling on the wire so that the birch twigs are rigidly held together. He then cuts the wire, twists it and taps it down with his pliers. The process is repeated with another length of wire twisted around the broom head, some three inches below the first bond. When the birch has been tied in this way, the besom maker gets up from his bench and leans over to the high chopping block beside him. This is nothing more than an old tree trunk some three feet high, where the butts of each broom head are chopped away with a short-handled axe. He then throws the finished head to the ever-growing pile at the other end of the workshop, and continues with the process of making heads until there is very little room left to work in.

The next step is to fit the handles to the besom head. He inserts a handle into the base and with sharp blows against the low chopping block he drives it home into the head, making quite sure as he does so that it goes in squarely. A nail is then knocked into the handle between the two bonds in order to keep the head in place. In some cases a hole is bored in the handle with a small spiral auger, and a wooden peg inserted in place of the nail.

After a large quantity of besoms have been made in this way, they are stacked ready for sale to all parts of the world in bundles of twelve.

9. The Cooper

One of the most intricate of all woodcrafts is that of cask making, for the cooper rarely uses any written measurements or patterns to make a cask of specified girth and capacity. One of the secrets of his trade is to know the number and dimensions of the staves that are required to make a vessel of a particular size and in the accurate shaping of those staves to fit tightly together. Not only must the craftsman make his casks so that they are perfectly watertight, but he must also ensure that each one holds the exact intended contents of liquid. Each cask must also be strong enough to withhold the great force of fermenting liquids; it must last for many years, despite rough and frequent handling.

The craft is one of great antiquity; there are references to it in the Bible, it was known in Ancient Egypt, while it is probable that the Roman invaders brought it to this country. Like so many other crafts, the art of cask making disappeared with the departure of the Romans from this country, but it was re-introduced by the Anglo-Saxons. By the close of the Middle Ages, the cask was the standard package in most European countries, and the craft of coopering was very widespread. On board ship, for example, almost everything was stored in casks, and the coopers, regarded as a hard-drinking, hard-swearing group, continued to be important members of ships' crews until the mid-nineteenth century. It was customary to load ships in British ports with a large number of roughly shaped staves. On the outward journey to some far corner of the globe, the coopers would be busily engaged in making casks in which the cargo of sugar, wine or spirits would be stored for the return voyage.

On land, too, master coopers were numerous, and they were engaged on a variety of tasks from making washtubs to brewing vats. In 1501, the Cooper's Company received its Charter of Incorporation, though the earliest reference to a Company was in 1298. In 1501, however, a beadle was employed by the Company to search for unauthorised practices, one of which was the making of casks in a brewery. It was not until the late eighteenth century that brewers were allowed to make casks on their premises, but by the end of the nineteenth century master coopers were rare, and the majority of workshops were to be found in the breweries. Today, the number employed in cask making is very small indeed, yet the craft remains a highly complex one. Machine technique has not replaced the age-old methods. The tools of the trade, too, are complex and numerous and differ considerably from those used by other woodworkers.

The least specialised category of coopering is that known as dry coopering. The dry cooper is concerned with making casks to hold non-liquid substances, such as flour, tobacco, fruit, vegetables and crockery. The work is far less exacting than that of wet coopering for the staves are less tightly held together and the barrels, which are bound with wooden hoops, are far less bulged. Douglas fir is mainly used for the staves but elm, spruce, poplar, beech and many others may also be used. At an early date machinery replaced hand-work in the manufacture of slack barrels, and both heads and staves are cut into shape with modern machinery. They are then steamed until pliable and, after the staves are arranged inside a truss hoop, a windlass is employed until the free ends are drawn together to the shape of a barrel. The cask is then fired, trussed and shaved with a variety of shaves and knives. If the barrel is required to hold a powdered substance, such as gunpowder, the staves are tongued and grooved by machinery to provide a tight joint. This category of the trade is known as dry-tight coopering.

The second main category of the craft is white coopering, a category that disappeared almost completely in the late nineteenth and early twentieth centuries. The white cooper made pails, butter churns, washtubs and other utensils for dairy and household use. He was often a bowl turner, a rake maker and trug maker and some idea of the range of products may be seen in the rhyming signboard from Hailsham, Sussex, quoted on page 60. The main materials used by the white cooper were oak and sycamore together with a certain amount of ash. The process of manufacturing a tub or bucket is substantially the same as that used in wet coopering except that in the manufacture of a tight barrel the shaves are used to cut along the grain of the wood when smoothing the inside of the cask, while in white coopering, the shave is used across the grain.

The third category and by far the most specialised and common is wet coopering, the manufacture of tight casks to hold liquid substances. The work is very careful and exact, for not only must the staves fit exactly together, but the cask must be strong enough to bear the strain of fermenting liquids and resist rough handling during transportation by sea and land.

The only timber used in wet coopering is oak. For spirits, American oak is preferred; for wine, oak grown south of latitude 50° is preferred, while for beer and ale, oak grown north of latitude 50° is used. In Britain, very little native oak is used today, and the main sources of supply are Germany, Russia and Iran. Different qualities of wood are required for different classes of work. For example porosity is essential in some wine casks to allow for the passage of air through the wood to assist fermentation. For spirits the wall of the cask must be so tight that neither water nor alcohol can escape, and for this reason staves cleft along the radius of a tree trunk are used; the natural concentric rings of the tree making the barrel perfectly tight.

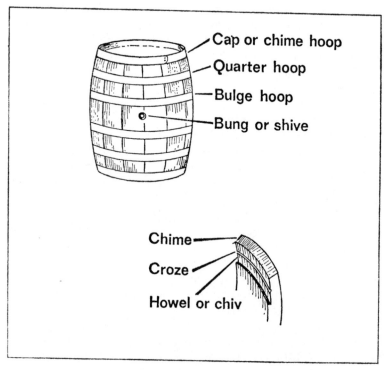

Fig. 20. A Cask and Its Parts.

The manufacture of a tight barrel starts in the woods where oak trees averaging two hundred years old are selected and felled. These are cut with cross-cut saws to roughly the lengths required for staves. The logs are then quartered with beetle and wedge and further broken down to the required shape with a long handled fromard. They are then shaped roughly with a draw knife, and cut to the exact length of the required stave.

The rough staves are then thoroughly dried by piling in the open for a length of time, which varies according to moisture and temperature conditions. So far, preparing the staves has been the province of the woodland worker, and it is not until the rough staves are dried down to an uniform moisture content, that they are taken to the cooper's workshop.

The processes involved in the manufacture of a tight cask may be divided into the following stages:

Preparing the staves. The staves are either placed in a shaving horse or clamped to a hook on the cooper's block and shaped with a series of draw knives. In a cask the staves are wider in the centre than at the top and bottom and the required taper is obtained with the broad-bladed side axe, followed by the straight-bladed draw knife.

The sides are then bevelled according to the radius of the cask on the long jointer plane.

Raising the cask. The staves are arranged inside an iron raising hoop until a complete circle is formed. An ash truss hoop, again the product of woodland craftsmen, is driven down temporarily to hold the staves in place. The roughly assembled oak at this stage has the appearance of a truncated cone; the staves being held in place at the top by the iron raising hoop, and splaying outwards to be held in place at a lower level by the ash truss hoop. The cask is now said to be raised.

Trussing up. This is probably the most complicated of all the stages, since the straight staves have to be bent to the typical barrel shape. In the larger workshops it is placed in the steaming chest for some twenty minutes at a temperature of approximately 200°F. The more usual method, however, is to moisten the staves with water and place the cask over a fire of wood shavings. This softens the fibres of the wood and enables the staves to bend. The cooper and his assistant, each armed with a heavy hammer, go round and round the barrel, beating consecutively smaller ash truss hoops into place until the splayed staves are drawn closely together. Since the staves used in making wine casks are thinner than those used in beer casks, a slightly different method of trussing up is employed. In this case the staves of pliable Mediterranean oak are drawn together by a rope and tackle known as a Dutch band or Spanish windlass, which is passed round the stave ends.

Firing. The cask is again placed over a small fire and kept there to set for some fifteen minutes. The moisture absorbed in trussing is now dried out, the fibres of the wood shrink so that the strain placed on the staves in bending is greatly reduced. After firing the staves are rigidly set, so that when the truss hoops are removed, there is no tendency for the staves to spring out of position.

Topping. The cooper first of all trims the top of the cask with an adze in order to form what is known as a chime or bevel. The stave ends are then levelled with the semicircular sun or topping plane. Some two inches below the edge, a broad but shallow channel is cut with a special type of plane called a chiv. A deeper and narrower groove into which the cask head fits is then cut with the narrow-bladed croze.

Cleaning down. Since the staves are now well set, all the truss hoops, with the exception of the two iron end hoops, are removed to provide a clear surface for the various shaves used in cleaning and smoothing the cask. Both the inside and outside of the vessel are cleaned by a number of small shaves, all resembling the carpenter's spokeshave.

Bunging. Before the heads are fitted, the bung hole is bored with a conical auger and afterwards smoothed with a burning iron.

Heading. The head of a barrel consists of three or more pieces of oak held together by dowel pegs and caulked with dry rush placed in between the joints. To obtain the approximate radius of the head, the craftsman adopts a trial and error system of stepping the compass around the top of the cask, until the distance between the compass points is one sixth the diameter of the cask top. This gives the radius of the head. After shaping the head is inserted in the cask, the end hoop having been first removed.

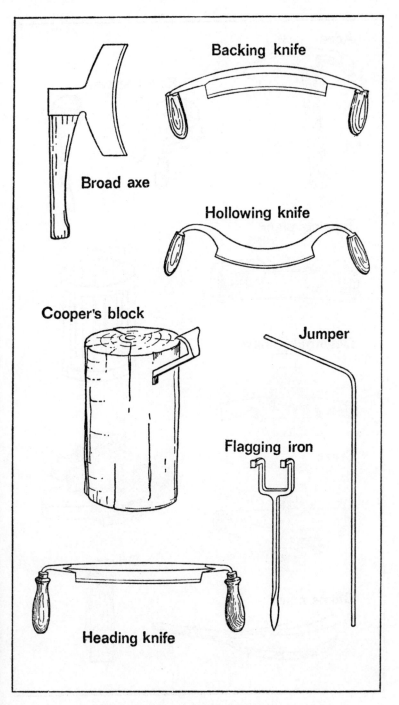

Fig. 21. The Cooper's Tools: I.

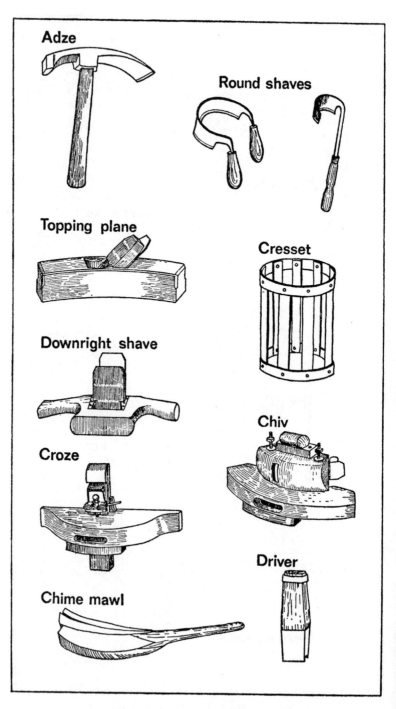

Fig. 22. The Cooper's Tools: II.

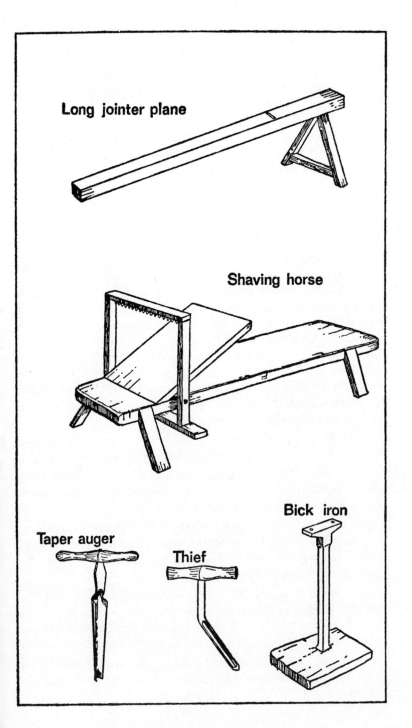

Long jointer plane

Shaving horse

Taper auger

Thief

Bick iron

Fig. 23. The Cooper's Tools: III.

Hooping. The iron hoops are cut, beaten into shape and riveted on the T-anvil or bick iron. They are then driven into place with a hammer and iron-tipped, wedge-shaped driver.

The cask is then stamped, checked to see whether it is completely watertight, whether it is able to bear pressure of up to forty pounds per square inch, and also checked to see that it will hold the correct volume of liquid.

TOOLS

(a) *Stave Shaping Tools*

Broad axe. The broad axe has a blade as long as twelve inches, which is set at a slight angle to the handle to facilitate the downward chopping of the staves. It is a side axe, that is the blade is sharpened on one side only, and having no poll it cannot be used for hammering. It is used by the cooper for two distinct operations. Firstly it is used for splitting the staves and shaping them ready for bevelling on the jointer plane. Secondly, the broad axe is used for the rough shaping of the head. The head is rested on the splitting block, being supported by the craftsman's body and left hand. The head is then shaped with the axe held well up the haft with the right hand.

Draw knife. The straight-bladed, two-handled draw knife is used after the broad axe for smoothing the staves, prior to bevelling.

Backing knife. The backing knife is a two-handled draw knife with a slightly concave blade for shaping the back of the staves; that is the outer surface of the cask.

Hollowing knife. This is similar to the backing knife except that the blade is convex. It is used to shape the inside of the staves, while each stave is either held in the shaving horse or in the hook on the cooper's block.

Cooper's block. This is a heavy log some two feet high and one foot in diameter on which the staves are split. A hook is fitted to the top of this block, and the staves for the larger casks are held in this hook while they are being shaped with draw knives.

Shaving horse. This is used for shaping all staves designed for casks of less than nine gallons capacity. The workman sits astride the horse, the stave being clamped on the sloping table in front of him. The pressure on the clamped stave is regulated by the feet, leaving the craftsman's hands free to shape the stave with the various draw knives.

Jointer plane. This very long plane, with a stock as long as six feet, is used to bevel the edge of each stave, so that they fit together exactly when the cask is raised. The jointer is the largest of all planes, but, unlike all others, it is used upside down, and remains stationary in the planing process. It stands on a pair of straight legs some two feet high, which are socketed loosely into a mortice in one end of the plane. This elevates the plane towards the craftsman and enables him to smooth each stave end as he slides it downwards over the blade.

(b) *Trussing Tools*

Truss hoops. These wooden truss hoops of various sizes are made of ash, and are produced by woodland craftsmen. In trussing a thick iron raising hoop is also used.

Hammer. The type of hammer used by coopers is a short-handled four- or five-pound sledge hammer.

Cresset. This is a small iron grate no more than twelve inches high and eight inches in diameter, in which a fire of wood shavings is lit. It is generally made up of pieces of old hoop iron. It is used in the trussing process, the staves having been first moistened, and is also used for setting the staves of the completed cask.

(c) *Topping Tools*

Adze. Cooper's adzes differ from carpenter's adzes in that their blades are far more curved. Their cutting edges are generally sharpened on the inside only, while the handle is no more than nine inches long. The short handle is necessary so that the craftsman can swing the tool within the radius of the cask.

The adze is used to shape the end of the cask on the chime, to produce a flat surface for the croze to run in.

Topping plane. The topping or sun plane is used to finish off the stave ends. This provides a level surface on which the fence of the chiv and croze will travel when the groove is cut. In its mechanism the tool is similar to the carpenter's trying plane, possessing a flat blade and central shavings discharge. It differs, however, in that the stock is semicircular, in order to conquer the narrow, circular margin of the stave ends.

Chiv. This is a convex-bladed tool and is used for cutting a broad but shallow channel – the howel – some two inches below the top of the staves. It provides a bed for the groove which will be cut with the croze at a later stage. In general appearance the croze and chiv are similar except that the convex blade of the chiv is some two inches wide while that of the croze is no more than half an inch in width.

Before the introduction of the chiv, and also in cases where the cooper does not possess the right size for a particular barrel, the channel is cut with a hollow-bladed howel adze.

For repair work the channel is cut with a curved, hollow-bladed knife known as a jigger.

Croze. The groove for the head is cut with the croze, a tool which is similar in general outline to the chiv. It differs from the chiv in that it has a very narrow blade, which may be a simple router ('hawksbill') or of the saw-tooth type. The most common type of croze consists of a square wooden peg which carries the blade, connected to a large semicircular wooden fence. The fence, which guides the blade in its channel is placed horizontally on the cask rim, and the blade set at the required distance below it. As the instrument is pushed around the inside of the cask, the circular groove to receive the head is cut.

(d) *Cleaning Tools*

Downright shave. This is the cooper's form of carpenter's spoke-shave used to clean and smooth the outside of the cask. All the truss hoops are removed, and the shave is used by pushing it downwards, away from the craftsman. The blade, which is generally about three inches wide, has a slightly concave edge to allow for the curvature of the cask.

Buzz. After the outside of the cask has been cleared with the downright shave, a small scraper shave called a buzz is used to finish off. The blade of this tool is almost at right angles to the stock.

Inside shave. For smoothing the inside surface of the cask, a tool similar in shape to the downright shave is used. In this case, however, it has a slightly convex blade.

Round shaves. A series of single or double-handled round shaves are used for smoothing the joints inside the cask. By pulling the tool along the joints, the craftsman smooths away any roughness on the inside of the cask.

(e) *Bunging Tools*

Taper auger. This is used for boring the bung hole in the cask. It consists of a tapering blade set at right angles to a wooden handle. Where necessary the hole is smoothed afterwards with a burning iron, a tool similar in shape to a soldering iron.

Thief. This is a small knife, similar in shape to a gimlet, but with a sharp edge almost at right angles to the shank of the tool. It is used for paring away the jagged ends on the inside of the bung hole.

(f) *Heading Tools*

Brace and bit. The large cooper's brace with a fixed spoon bit of small diameter is used to bore the dowel holes in the various sections of the head.

Compasses. To obtain the radius of the head, the cooper steps the compasses around the croze mark at the top of the cask, until the distance between the compass points is equal to one-sixth the circumference of the cask. This gives the radius of the head.

Heading knife. After shaping with the side axe, the head is bevelled along the sides with a bowed draw knife, called a heading knife. This differs from the ordinary draw knife in that the blade is much thinner, and is distinctly bow-shaped.

Heading swift. This is a heavy shave, similar in general shape to the downright shave, used for the final smoothing of the head. It has a two-and-a-half inch cutting iron, and the head is planed against the grain.

Chincing iron. This is used to push in the dried rushes or flags into the joints between the separate sections of the head and between the head and the croze cut. The chincing iron is a small chisel, no more than two inches wide, which is often made of old hoop iron.

Jumper. This is a steel or iron bar about three-quarters of an inch in diameter, which is bent at one end. It is used to lever heads into position, and by pushing it through the bung hole it is used to lever the head if it falls below the level of the croze channel.

Flagging iron. In repair work and occasionally in making new casks, rushes are inserted between the staves. A fork-like tool called a flagging iron is used to twist each stave in turn, to open the joint sufficiently for the insertion of rushes.

(g) *Hooping Tools*

Bick iron. This is the tall but narrow cooper's T-anvil known also as a beak iron or cooper's stake. At each extremity of the T, a hole is drilled where the rivets are beaten into the hoop as it rests on it. The hoop-cutting chisel, similar to a blacksmith's hardy, can also be stuck into one of these holes.

Driver. The driver or drift is made of steel and is fitted with an oak handle. The narrow end is grooved to prevent the driver from slipping off the hoop. Its main use is in driving the iron hoops into place on the cask, and due to constant hammering, the wooden handle has to be replaced at frequent intervals. A driver generally measures some six inches in length, while the steel edge is some three inches wide.

Chime mawl. This is a piece of wood, some two feet long, used to beat down the end hoops of the cask.

Coopering remains one of the few crafts where hand methods have not been superseded by machinery, and where those methods have not changed substantially since the Cooper's Company received its Charter of Incorporation in the first decade of the sixteenth century.

Another feature of the cooper's work has also persisted from early times and that is the initiation ceremony at the end of a worker's apprenticeship. Many of the medieval trade guilds practised some form of initiation ceremony, which had to be undergone by apprentices at the end of their time. In coopering, the traditional ceremony is still performed whenever a craftsman ends his five-year apprenticeship. In 1962 I witnessed this ceremony in a Cardiff brewery. The apprentice first of all makes a headless fifty-four gallon hogshead, as evidence that he is a qualified craftsman. With due ceremony this is rolled to the centre of the workshop, the apprentice is grabbed by a number of colleagues and lowered into the cask. Wooden truss hoops are then beaten on, followed by a red hot iron end hoop. Soot, flour, wood-shavings, water and beer are poured into the cask, and on the apprentice as he squats at the bottom. The cask is turned on its side and, with the apprentice still inside, is rolled three times round the workshop floor. The young craftsman then emerges to receive his indentures from his master. Undoubtedly this ceremony is a survival from medieval times, for the ordinances of the Cooper's Company suggest that some form of ceremony had to be undergone by apprentices, before the wardens of the Company presented them to the Chamberlain of the City of London, as fit and proper persons, qualified to take up their freedom.

10. The Coracle Builder

The coracle, which is a keel-less, bowl-shaped boat, has been known for many centuries in Wales, and those in use today on three west Wales rivers may be regarded as the direct descendants of the small, skin-covered vessels described in detail by Caesar, Pliny and other Roman writers. It seems, however, that the vessels described by Roman writers, as well as those mentioned in the *Mabinogion*, were sea-going, keeled boats, similar to the curraghs of Ireland, rather than to the keel-less fishing coracles of Welsh rivers, that were specifically designed for operation in swiftly flowing streams.

The use of the coracle as a fishing craft on Welsh rivers has declined very rapidly in recent years and today coracle fishing is limited to three Welsh rivers – the Teifi, Tâf and Tywi. The Salmon and Freshwater Fisheries Act of 1923 put an end to coracle fishing on many rivers such as the Severn and it severely restricted the use of coracles on many others. Subsequent river authority bye-laws have caused an even more rapid decline in coracle fishing and in some districts the coracle is on the point of disappearing. For example, at the village of Cenarth on the river Teifi, long regarded as a centre of coracle fishing, legislation in 1935 prohibited the issue of licences to new fishermen in the non-tidal section of the river above Llechryd Bridge. Consequently the number of coracle licences issued has declined to such an extent that today no coracle fishing is practised at all at Cenarth. In 1861 it was estimated that there were over 300 coracles in use on the Teifi, with about twenty-eight pairs of full-time coracle fishermen operating above Llechryd Bridge. Below that bridge, however, where the river is classified as tidal, there is no such restriction and five pairs of coracles are licensed to fish in the picturesque if notorious Cilgerran gorge. There they use both the traditional, armoured coracle net and the now illegal set nets for catching salmon.

Coracles are also used on the river Tywi, where twelve nets are licensed to fish for salmon below Carmarthen town. The twelve pairs in use today between Carmarthen Bridge and the sea represent a considerable reduction in numbers since the 1920's, when, in 1929, twenty-five pairs were licensed to fish from coracles. By 1935 the numbers had declined to thirteen pairs, under stringent regulations and, although in the 1930's an attempt was made to abolish coracle fishing, as on the Teifi, it was agreed that coracle fishing could be tolerated on the Tywi as long as the number of coracles did not exceed a total of twelve pairs. In the 1860's, no fewer than 400 men supported themselves on the salmon and sewin fisheries on the Tywi.

On the Tâf, a short, swift river that flows into Carmarthen Bay near the village of Laugharne, two licensees are allowed to fish from coracles. The fishermen based on the village of Lower St Clears are part-time workers and operate at night during the months of June and July only. In the early nineteenth century, the Tâf fishermen were regarded as very efficient and one observer 'saw for the first time those feats of dexterity which are required in the management of such a capricious craft'.

In the summer of 1975, therefore, it seems that the total number of licences for the whole of Wales amounted to nineteen only – twelve on the Tywi, five on the Teifi and two on the Tâf. In the 1920's and 30's, coracles were to be found on many other rivers such as the Dee, the eastern Cleddau and Severn, while in the nineteenth century other rivers such as the Wye, Usk, Conwy, Dyfi, Nevern and Loughor, had coracle fishermen.

The design of coracles and the methods of using them varied considerably from river to river. They varied according to the physical nature of each individual stream, whether it be swiftly flowing or slow moving, whether it had rapids and much rough water or whether it was shallow or deep. Design varied too, according to the preferences of the individual fisherman and whether the fishermen preferred a heavy or light coracle. A Teifi coracle for example, can weigh as little as twenty-five pounds and as much as thirty-six pounds, while length can vary from fifty to sixty inches. The actual size and weight depends almost entirely on the preferences of the fisherman. Again, on the Dee, two-seater coracles were commonplace in the Llangollen district until the 1950's and these coracles, weighing as much as forty pounds, were widely used by anglers for reaching otherwise inaccessible sections of river.

It seems that coracles varied according to the ingrained traditions of the various rivers of Wales, for remarkable homogeneity in the design of coracles occurred in the various rivers and distinct regional types were in existence for many centuries. For example, although the coracle of the Tywi and the nearby Tâf are somewhat similar in shape, the Tâf coracle, designed for use in a fairly narrow, swiftly flowing stream, is heavier than the Tywi variety. Instead of the wattled gunwale of the latter, it has a planked gunwale. The Tâf coracle is sharper at the fore-end and flatter at the stern and weighs about thirty-three pounds, compared with a maximum weight of twenty-eight pounds in a Tywi coracle.

Methods of construction also vary considerably from river to river. Some coracles, like those of the Teifi and Tywi, have plaited hazel gunwales, others have single or double lath gunwales. To build a Tâf coracle, for example, a naturally curving branch of a tree, usually an apple tree, was cut and split in half to form the fore-part of the gunwale. Another branch was treated in the same way to form the rear gunwale. Unlike the other coracles of west Wales, it was the gunwale of the Tâf coracle that was formed first. This was bored with a series of holes to receive the fourteen laths of the coracle frame. In Teifi coracles, seven longitudal and seven cross-laths of cleft willow were steamed, weighted and bent into shape to be inserted in a plaited hazel gunwale, while in Tywi coracles sawn ash laths were generally used. In most types of coracle the number of longitudal laths varied from six (as on Conwy coracles) to ten (as on Severn coracles). Cross-laths varied from six (as on Wye and Usk coracles) to as many as sixteen (as on Upper Dee coracles). The laths could be of ash or willow and carrying straps could be of leather, as in most types or twisted oak saplings, as on the Teifi coracle.

The following were the principal regional types of coracle in existence:

(1) Teifi, (2) Tywi, (3) Tâf, (4) Cleddau, (5) Severn – Ironbridge type, (6) Severn – Welshpool type, (7) Severn – Shrewsbury type, (8) Conwy, (9) Upper Dee – Llangollen type, (10) Lower Dee – Bangor–Overton type, (11) Usk and Wye, (12) Dyfi, (13) Loughor.

The process of building a Teifi coracle begins with the selection of suitable willow trees which will form the frame of the vessel. These are cut in the autumn and winter when there is no sap in the branches. The best quality willow is the pollard variety seven to ten years old. In the past, the demand for willow, which grows profusely on the banks of the Teifi, was considerable, for there was a constant demand, not only from coracle builders, but from basket makers, tool handle makers and many others who lived and worked in this picturesque valley. In those days willow trees were lopped at regular intervals, but today most of them are overgrown and useless for the craftsmen's requirements.

After willow has been cut each rod is carefully split in two with a billhook and, as in most other cleaving crafts such as spelk making and wattle weaving, great care has to be taken to ensure that the two sections are cleanly cut along the grain. To make one coracle, ten longitudinal laths, each seven feet six inches long are required, together with another nine a foot shorter to be fitted at right angles. Each lath must be no more than an inch wide and as little as a quarter of an inch in thickness; yet they must bear considerable stress and strain in the finished coracle. Each lath is then placed in the jaws of a shaving horse and smoothed to the required thickness with a two-handled draw knife and spokeshave. The shaving horse is somewhat similar to that used by other woodland craftsmen such as the chair bodger, and consists of a low bench some five feet long on which the craftsman sits astride, pressing the pair of foot holds so as to hold fast the piece of willow under the projecting clamp block.

When he is satisfied that each lath has been reduced to the required thickness, they are immersed in a tub of boiling water until they are pliable enough to be bent to the bowl shape of the coracle. After the laths have been prepared in this way, the complicated process of assembling the frame begins. The longer laths are arranged on a flat surface, each one some five inches from the next. These are temporarily tacked to the board and the nine shorter laths interwoven at right angles to them. A pair of diagonal braces are also tacked to the framework, and with heavy weights and stones placed at the intersection of the laths, the sides are bent upwards. Thin hazel saplings are next required and they are woven to form the upper rim of the coracle, much in the same manner of wattle hurdle weaving. The willow laths are then inserted in the hazel gunwale and tacked in place.

Before the framework is complete however, the seat, usually a piece of deal planking, has to be cut to size and firmly inserted in the gunwale. Finally, the carrying strap, known on the Teifi as *wden*, has to be prepared. Although today leather straps are used, the traditional carrying handle is of oak. It was customary for the coracle maker to choose an oak sapling some five feet long and without cutting, this was twisted to the roots, tied and left in position for many months before cutting. It was then fixed firmly to the seat.

The final process in making the coracle is to tack the un-bleached calico to the frame. Some five yards are required for each vessel, and this work is often undertaken by the women. After the calico has been firmly strained over the frame and tacked to it, coat after coat of boiled linseed oil and pitch are painted on until the coracle is completely waterproof.

Finally, an ash or larch paddle some fifty-four inches long is cut and shaped and the coracle is ready for the river. The method of paddling a Teifi coracle is in itself an art, for the paddle is held in one hand, its top resting against the fisher-man's shoulder. It is inserted in the water along the waist of the coracle, a figure eight motion being described in the water.

On the Teifi, the coracle still remains a fishing craft. The season starts in March, and the greatest number of salmon are caught in May and June. Two coracles with a long net stretched between them slowly drift downstream, so that a considerable width of the river is covered, and any fish that may be around are caught in the fine mesh of the net.

On the Severn, coracle fishing is illegal, but in the town of Ironbridge a coracle builder still practises his craft. Ironbridge is a stark, bare town and the iron bridge thrown across the murky river in the late eighteenth century is a monument to the engineering skill of the day. But nestling in the shadow of the bridge is a small wooden hut near the water's edge, where for over three hundred years the members of one family have practised the ancient craft of coracle building. Harry Rogers is the last of the long line of craftsmen, but today he only makes the odd coracle for a museum or private collector.

It is surprising that not many years ago Harry Rogers's father held a school for coracle men at Ironbridge, and at that time there must have been a considerable demand from the inhabitants of Severnside to learn the intricate skills of coracle paddling. To paddle and steer the light Severn coracle is a task of no mean achievement, for unless the paddle is inserted in the

62. (*Top right*) Smoothing the rake handle with a draw shave. The handle is clamped in the jaws of a clamping horse.

63. (*Left*) Ernest Sims of Pamber End, Hampshire shaping rake tines.

THE RAKE MAKER

64. (*Below left*) Tining the rake head.

65. (*Below*) Drilling the rake head with brace and fixed bit.

66. Ernest Sims pointing rake tines.

67. Finishing the rake.

THE RAKE MAKER (continued)

68. (*Left*) Harry Wells of Bucklebury, Berkshire, on his home-made tining horse.

69. (*Right*) Ernest Sims bending scythe sneads

o. L. A. West of Baughurst, Hampshire. litting a willow log with beetle and froe.

71. Pointing an upright rail with billhook.

THE GATE HURDLE MAKER

73. Marking mortices on uprights.

72. (*Left*) Removing the bark with a draw knife.

74. The hurdler's monkey being used by Charles Baldwin of Hollybush, Herefordshire.

75. The Midland variety of morticing kn used by Raymond Russell of Whitchur

THE GATE HURDLE
MAKER (continued)

76. (*Left*) L. A. West finishing a gate hurdle.

77. (*Right*) The finished gate.

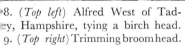

8. (*Top left*) Alfred West of Tad-
ey, Hampshire, tying a birch head.
9. (*Top right*) Trimming broom head.

THE BROOM SQUIRE

0. (*Right*) Making a handle.
1. (*Below left*) Inserting the handle.
2. (*Below right*) Alfred Birch of Wyre
Hill, Worcestershire, using cane to tie
a birch head.

83. Bevelling stave sides on a long jointer plane at a Reading Brewery.

84. Hollowing a stave.

THE COOPER

85. Head making.

86. The raised cask with raising hoop a truss hoop in place.

87. Trussing up. Wooden truss hoops are beaten on the cask. The cresset fire can be seen in the foreground.

88. Levelling the stave ends with the Sun or Topping Plane.

THE COOPER (continued)

89. Crozing.

90. Cleaning down.

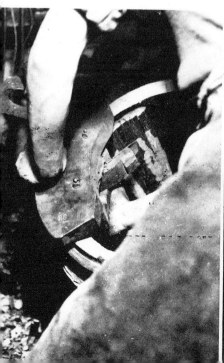

91. John Thomas of Cenarth, Dyfed,
preparing the ribs with a draw knife.

92. (*Right*) Inserting the woven gunwhale of
a Teifi coracle.

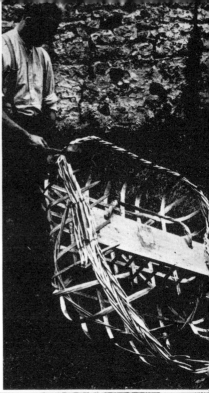

93. Sewing calico on to the frame.

THE CORACLE BUILDER

94. Raymond Rees of Carmarthen with his
Tywi coracle, 1974.

95. General view of a wheelwright's shop. The craftsman on the right is using the spoke dog for felloeing, and the one on the left is shaping a spoke.

96. (*Left*) Fixing spokes.

THE WHEELWRIGHT

97. (*Below left*) Measuring hoops with a traveller.

98. (*Below*) Tireing a wheel at Ardington, Berkshire.

99. H. E. Goodchild of Naphill, Buckinghamshire, adzing a seat.

100. Boring a seat for the legs.

THE CHAIR MAKER

101. Stacks of completed seats.

102. Shaping the backs of Windsor chai

103. Some examples of Windsor chair legs and stretchers.

104. Assembling a chair.

THE CHAIR MAKER (continued)

105. The completed Windsor.

106. Staining.

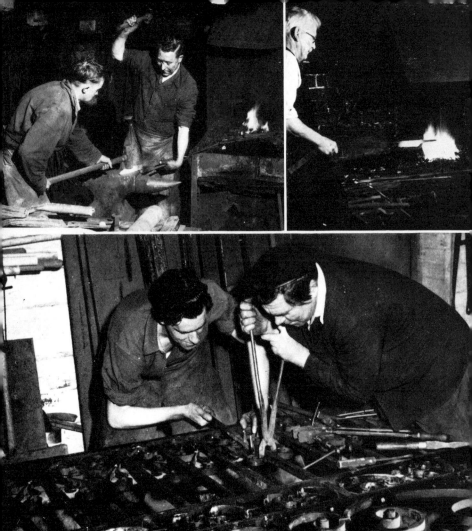

107. (*Top left*) Forging iron in a Berkshire smithy.

108. (*Top right*) The hearth.

109. (*Above*) Shaping a wrought iron gate.

THE BLACKSMITH

110. A completed gate at a Pangbourne, Berkshire, smithy.

111. C. J. Harry of St. Nicholas, Glamorgan, preparing a horse for shoeing.

112. Griff Jenkins of Cwrtnewydd, Dyfed, shaping a horseshoe.

THE FARRIER

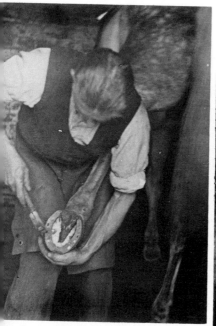

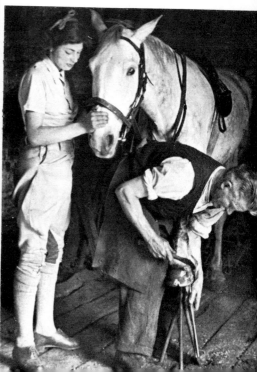

113. Nailing a horseshoe.

114. Nailing and clinching the nails.

115. Cottages being thatched with reed by Peter Slevin at St. Fagans, South Glamorgan.

116. (*Right*) Inserting thatching spars.

THE THATCHER

118. (*Below right*) Using a leggat for trimming reed.

117. (*Below left*) Trimming a long-straw roof with eaves knife

119. Harvesting Norfolk reed.

120. Preparing reed bundles for thatching.

THE THATCHER (continued)

121. (*Left*) Peter Slevin on the roof of a Warwickshire cottage.

122. (*Right*) A completed long-straw roof with straw decoration.

123. (*Top left*) Benjamin Evans of Bwlch-llan, Dyfed, splitting bramble.

THE LIP-WORKER

124. (*Left*) Close-up of splitting process.

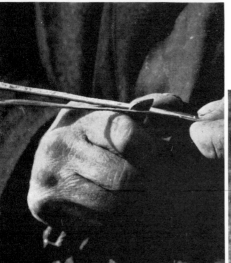

126. Making a seedlip. The rolls are form by a section of cow horn.

125. (*Left*) Tying straw rolls.

water just behind the bow and made to describe an S-motion in water, the coracle either turns over or spins round, out of control.

Although on the Severn, as on other rivers, the coracle was primarily a fishing craft, it was also used for other purposes. Since the bridges on the Shropshire section of the river are few and far between, in the past the coracle was used by the inhabitants of Severnside as an easy means of crossing the river. This may explain to a certain extent why the oval-shaped coracles of the area are so light and manoeuvrable, compared with the heavier and larger vessels of west Wales. The Ironbridge coracle weighs no more than twenty pounds while the average Cenarth coracle is some twelve pounds heavier.

The framework of the Severn coracle consists of sixteen laths of equal size which are usually made of ash. Each one is one-and-a-half inches wide and a quarter of an inch thick and is cleft with a froe. As in Cenarth, they are smoothed with draw knife and spokeshaves and interlaced on a wooden board. An oval ash hoop which forms the gunwale is prepared and the laths are bent up in turn and tacked to its hoop at a height of some fourteen inches above the ground. The frame, to which is added two or three diagonal laths, is left in this position for several days to become set in position. The frame is then trimmed, calico is strained over it and the whole vessel coated with pitch. The deal seat and carrying straps are inserted and the vessel is ready for use. The paddle differs from the Teifi variety in that it is a spade-shaped implement of ash, which is used by grasping with both hands and inserting in the water near the bow of the coracle.

11. The Wheelwright

In the past, the wheelwright was an essential member of all village communities, but today, with the disappearance of horse transport, very few still remain at work. Those that still practise the craft tend to spread their activity over a much wider field and many who still describe themselves as wheelwrights are more often than not carpenters, joiners and undertakers. Constructing a wooden wheel is a lengthy task which demands great exactitude and craftsmanship, for although in many respects wheelwrighting is similar to hardwood joinery, the wheelwright relies completely on tightness of joint to hold the work together and not on glue. He must possess considerable knowledge of stresses and strains; his measuring must be extremely accurate, while in addition he has to be dexterous in the use of a wide range of hand tools. All the timber used in the manufacture of a wheel must be well seasoned, a process that may take ten years or more. The central hub, nave or stock, which varies in diameter from twelve inches to as much as seventeen inches is usually of elm or oak, while the spokes which radiate from it are of cleft oak. The felloes, the curved members forming the rim of the wheel are usually made of ash, although beech and elm are occasionally used.

The whole wheel is bound together with an iron tire or a series of crescent-shaped pieces of iron called stakes. The process of tireing is perhaps the most spectacular of all in the wheelwright's trade, for although the work is strictly speaking the concern of the blacksmith rather than the wheelwright, in the past most wheelwrights were capable of carrying out work both in metal and wood. Indeed, in some of the larger workshops that employed two or more men, it was customary for one craftsman to specialise in metal work while others were primarily woodworkers. In this way a complete wheel or even a complete cart or wagon could be built entirely in a single workshop.

The wheelwright was of course responsible for building complete vehicles, a task of great complexity which has been described elsewhere[7] but perhaps the most intricate of all processes was that of making a wooden wheel. This task falls into five distinct stages:

   (a) Hub making and morticing
   (b) Spoke making
   (c) Felloe making and assembling
   (d) Tireing
   (e) Boxing.

Hub making. After sawing elm or oak trunks into lengths of fourteen or fifteen inches a hole is bored through the centre of each block to assist the seasoning process. They are then stored, with the bark still on, until they are thoroughly dry. Every three or four months the wheelwright visits the store to inspect the timber, and the mildew that appears on the elm as the sap is slowly exuded is brushed off with a hard brush. If this is not done, then fungus will appear and the wood will gradually rot. For a hub twelve inches in diameter at least six years are required for seasoning, while for the older type of hub, fifteen inches in diameter, the seasoning period was as long as ten years. In some parts of the country, it was customary to place the roughly sawn elm butts in a running stream, so that water replaced the natural sap in the wood. The drying process was consequently hastened considerably.

When the seasoning is complete, and the bark has been chopped off with an axe, the perfectly dry naves are placed in a lathe and turned to the required shape and diameter. More often than not this lathe is hand driven and is of a special design and shape. The driving power is a large wheel six feet or more in diameter. This is entirely detached from the lathe bed and it rests firmly in a framework some distance from the lathe, and at right angles to it. The lathe bed may be anything up to twelve feet in length, and it is firmly fixed to the ground by a set of thick wooden struts at each extremity. Running along the centre of the bed is a crack, and into this crack the puppets for pivoting the hub run. These may be adjusted anywhere according to length by a pair of bolts on the underside of the bed. The driving wheel is connected to the pulley wheel of the lathe mandrel by a strap, and while one craftsman turns the wheel by means of the iron crank, the other with his lathe gouges and chisels works on the revolving hub. In turning a wheel only two types of lathe tool are required – a gouge, some one-and-a-half inches in width for the first rough turning and a chisel of approximately the same width for smoothing and cutting the line where the iron hub-bands will be later fitted. As the material revolves, the wheelwright continuously checks it with his calipers to ensure that not too much is being taken off. These calipers, with semicircular, in-curved arms, are generally large and are indispensable when turning.

The hub is now placed on a low stool called a morticing

cradle, and is held there by two pairs of wedges, a pair on either side of the nave. A pair of compasses is taken, and the arms are set at roughly the required distances apart in order to prick off the centre of the spoke mortices.

A spoke is now required to mark out the mortices on the hub, and the outline of each marking is accurately traced. This is the exact size of the mortice to be made.

The mortices are then bored, the wheelwright using a twelve-inch or fourteen-inch sweep brace with a one-inch bit. Three holes are bored, one at the front, one at the back and one in the centre of each mortice mark.

The next step is to chisel out the spoke mortices, but before this is done, the spoke set gauge is prepared. This consists of a piece of hardwood two feet nine inches in length, two-and-a-half inches wide and one inch deep. A hole is bored four inches from one end large enough to take a seven-sixteenths-inch coach screw comfortably. At the other end a series of three-eighths-inch holes, each one inch from the next are cut, and a piece of whalebone nine inches in length is passed through the required three-eighths-inch hole and firmly wedged there. The exact position of the whalebone depends on the actual size of wheel being made. For example, to make a wheel four feet ten inches in diameter, the whalebone should be two feet one-and-a-half inches from the coach screw pivot; that is, the position of the whalebone should be at half the diameter of the wheel (two feet five inches) minus the depth of the felloes (three-and-a-half inches). The whalebone must, of course, be adjusted to the shoulder of the spoke, rather than to its top. With the spoke set gauge prepared the next step is to plug up the central auger hole that runs through the hub. With a pair of compasses the exact centre of the front end of the hub is found, and at that exact point, the plug is bored to a sufficient depth to take the coach screw pivot comfortably. The coach screw is screwed up tightly to the face of the hub, screwed up so that it is just possible to turn the stick without turning the hub. The main purpose of the spoke set gauge is to measure the dish of the wheel, and since the spokes in a dished wheel emerge from the nave at an angle, slanting outwards from the centre, the spoke mortices too have to be cut at a slight angle.

A number of tools are required to prepare the mortices. The first of these is a morticing chisel or bruzz, a long socket handled V-shaped tool with a blade five-eighths inches wide. This is used for cleaning the corners of the mortice, while a three-quarter-inch and a one-inch heading chisel are used for the delicate shaping of the back and front ends of the mortices. While the bruzz and the firmer or forming chisels are used by pounding with a mallet, the more delicate heading chisels are never struck but worked by hand pressure. Great care is required when using the heading chisel, for even the smallest paring in the mortice makes a great deal of difference at the whalebone gauge, which is kept in position during the whole operation. In addition to all these tools, the wheelwright requires a small inside caliper which is used constantly to check on the size of mortice as the work proceeds.

Spoke making. No other part of the wheel bears a greater pressure than the spokes, and for that reason, only well-seasoned cleft, heart of oak is suitable for spoke making. Although some modern wheels have been made of sawn oak, they are far from satisfactory, for the grain must be unbroken, and the cleavage must follow that grain. Oak cleaving must be done during the summer months, when the oak is full of sap and the cleavage will run cleanly from end to end.

On arrival at the wheelwright's yard, the cleft pieces of oak are roughly dressed with the axe to the required shape and size. They are then stacked in the wood store to season for four years or more. When required, the craftsman takes the spokes and planes them down to a diameter of three-and-a-quarter inches or three-and-a-half inches. The foot that fits into the hub is tapered with tenon saw and broad chisel until the tenon measures some three inches long and one inch wide. With the foot being prepared, the exposed part of the spoke is shaped, first with the axe, then with the draw knife and spokeshave, and finally the back is rounded with a hollow bladed plane known as a jarvis. Since the chief strain will be felt at the back of the spoke, great care must be taken not to reduce it too much. The final trimming of the spokes will of course take place when the whole wheel is assembled.

The hub is next placed over the wheel pit in order to drive in the spokes. This wheel pit is rectangular in shape, and measures some six feet in length and ten inches in width. The sides are bricked or lined with timber to make a solid frame for the hub when the spokes are hammered into place. While one person holds the nave steady, and keeps the spoke in an upright position the other swings a fourteen-pound hammer to drive the spokes into place. After each two or three blows, the spoke set gauge is pushed into position to make sure that the spoke is being driven in at the right angle. Since the spoke tenons are tapered, each blow of the sledge makes the spokes tighter in the hub and therefore progressively more difficult to correct. If the spoke is being driven in at the wrong angle despite the wheelwright's efforts to correct it by placing his hammer blows carefully, then it must be left until the adjacent spokes have been fitted.

To correct the alignment of a spoke, a bridle or crooked stick is used. This as its name implies is merely a piece of curved ash two feet six inches long, and it is placed behind the spoke that is to be driven forwards, with its ends in front of the adjacent spokes. In this way the front spoke is pushed forwards to touch the whalebone gauge as it is hammered with the sledge. When all the spokes are in place, the wheel is measured with the spoke set gauge to ensure that it has the right dish.

The next step is to set out the tongue of the spokes. When it was customary to tire wheels with a series of strakes, spokes were generally square tongued, the square tongue being much stronger but more difficult to shape than the round-tongued variety. A scribe which consists of a piece of ash two feet long and three-quarters of an inch square is taken, and a bradawl inserted to produce the gauge tooth for scribing the shoulder on the face of the spoke. The scribe is placed along the spokes, its foot resting firmly at a point where the spoke enters the hub. The shoulder mark is then scribed on each spoke. In a wheel with a diameter of four feet ten inches, the shoulder will lie one foot seven-and-a-half inches up the spoke from the hub, that is from half the height of the wheel (two feet five inches) deduct half the diameter of the nave (six inches) and the depth of the felloe (three-and-a-half inches). First of all the front shoulders are cut with a tenon saw, and split with chisel and mallet, and then the process is continued for the back shoulder, the saw cuts being continued all the way round the spokes. The tongues are then trimmed to a slightly oval shape; a thin slice of oak or ash with a hole in it is carefully tried over every tongue to make sure that it will fit into the auger hole in the felloes. Through the centre of the tongue a notch is cut, and when the felloes have been fitted on with the end of the spoke appearing through its lower end, a wedge is hammered into the notch to tighten the spoke in the felloe.

Felloe making. In Britain, early spoked wheels had one-piece ash felloes, steamed to the correct shape and held there by an iron clamp. Although one-piece felloes continued in use until the close of the Middle Ages, there is no evidence to suggest that they were used in this country during the last four hundred years. From the sixteenth century onwards the practice has been to allow two spokes for each felloe, thus one finds an even number of spokes on all wheels.

More often than not ash is preferred for felloe making, due to its great flexibility and strength, but less satisfactory wheels have been made with elm or beech felloes.

After sawing, the wheelwright shapes the blocks, while still green, before stacking them for seasoning. Although today felloes are shaped with band-saws, in the past the work was carried out entirely by axe and adze. The block was held in a felloe-horse, a low bench into which the block was wedged, and the craftsman standing astride the horse would adze out the belly of the block to the correct shape. Each felloe would be some thirty inches long, and some three-and-a-half inches square.

More recently felloes were sawn with a thin-bladed frame saw, each felloe conforming to one of the many patterns kept by the wheelwright in his shop. After facing up the felloes, the pattern is laid on and the felloes marked for any inequality or unevenness. They are planed with the jack plane, the belly trimmed with the adze and the sole with the axe if necessary.

The wheel is laid face downwards on the low wheel stool and, with the bevel, the right angle for the ends of felloes is obtained and cut to the required size. The felloe is then placed on the wheel, resting on two spokes close to the shoulders. The position of each spoke is then marked on the felloe, and the holes bored with a one-and-a-half inch auger. The dowel holes at the end of each felloe are then bored, each boring being some

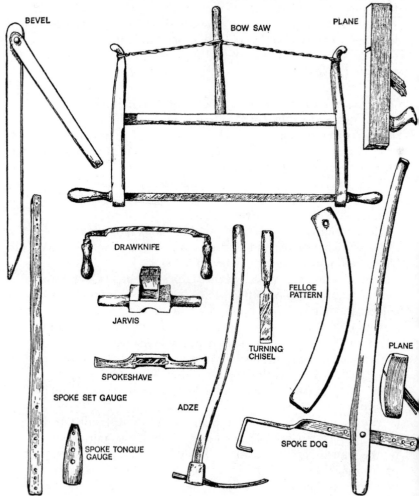

Fig. 24. The Wheelwright's Tools: I.

two-and-a-half inches deep, square and at right angles to the end cut of the felloe. As these dowel holes are being bored endways to the grain, it is extremely difficult to keep the point of the auger or twist bit from running with the grain. With all the holes bored, the felloe is trimmed with the draw knife, compass plane and spokeshave. A hard chamfer is taken from the back of the felloes between the spoke holes, for that part of the wheel

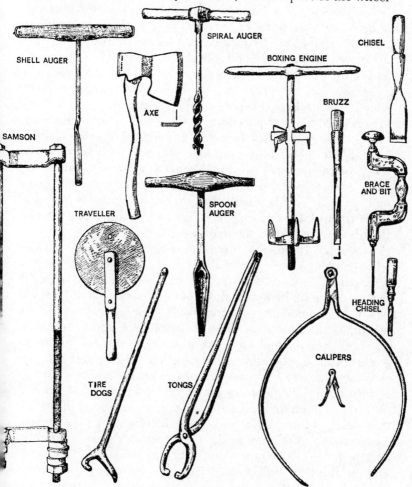

Fig. 25. The Wheelwright's Tools: II.

117

is regarded as superfluous weight, where no great pressure bears. A smaller chamfer, some one-eighth of an inch deep, is taken off the front but great care must be taken not to remove too much of the front of the felloe as it might weaken the spoke shoulders which bear heavily at that point.

With the felloe complete, the next step is to make the dowels that bind the felloes together, and the wedges that close the gap between each felloe. The dowels are four-and-a-half inches long and one inch in diameter, cleft out of dry, tough oak with an axe. Old spokes are frequently used for this purpose, and they are driven in, one in the end of each felloe, with a light hammer, and left protruding two inches from the end of the felloe.

The wedges are prepared out of the larger pieces of waste split off the backs of the spokes when making the tongues. They are chopped to the required size of three-and-a-half inches long, seven-and-a-half inches wide and five-eighths of an inch thick.

With the wheel fully prepared, the next step is to fit the felloes on the spokes. The wheel is placed face downwards on the stool, and a felloe tapped in some three-quarters of an inch on to one spoke. It will be found that the second spoke is too wide apart to enter the felloe. This is due to the radial character of the wheel which causes the spoke tongues to be wider apart than the shoulder. In order to bring two spokes together, so that the felloe can be slipped on easily, a tool called a spoke dog is required. This consists of an ash stick three feet or more in length. Some six inches from the bottom of this handle is a slit which accommodates an iron hook some twenty inches in length. On this iron hook there are eight holes, and by selecting one of these holes and fitting an iron peg through it to form a wrench, the wheelwright is able to adjust the dog to the size of the wheel on which he is operating. With the wooden handle against his left shoulder, and the other end of the stick behind the already fitted spoke, the iron hook is placed around the spoke that needs drawing. He presses the handle of the spoke dog forwards and as he does so the two spokes are drawn together and the felloe can be tapped on. When all the felloes have been fitted in this way wedges are driven into the spaces in between each felloe. All that now remains is to level the projecting wedges with the draw knife and spokeshave.

The outer edge of the spoke tongues that appear at the sole of the felloes are gouged out one-eighth of an inch below the sole so that they will not leave the tire when it is fitted. The whole wheel is placed on the wheel stool and finished with jack plane and spokeshave, each joint being tested with a straight edge.

Tireing. The process of tireing a wheel with a hoop begins by taking a sixteen-foot bar of metal and laying it flat on the ground. The craftsman then takes the measuring wheel, or traveller, and makes a chalk mark on its rim. Another mark is made on the surface of the untired wheel and, with the chalk marks as starting points, the traveller is pushed around the wheel rim and the number of turns noted. It is then run along the bar of iron in order to ascertain the correct length of metal required for the tire, allowing an extra couple of inches at the end for welding the loose ends together and for the expansion of the tire when it is heated. With cold chisel and sledge hammer the iron is cut to length.

The next operation is known as scarfing down and consists of flattening each end of the bar with a sledge hammer. The bar is then heated and passed through the rollers of the tire bender to the required shape. The two loose ends are strained together and the joints welded. Two or three nail holes are punched in the hoop and all is now ready for the process of tireing the wheel.

An open fire of wood shavings or straw is made in a corner of the yard and the tires are heated until they are almost white hot. In some yards, a brick oven, which takes up to half a dozen hoops at a time, is used for heating. Meanwhile, the untired wheel is screwed face down on a heavy iron tireing platform – which is a permanent feature in a wheelwright's yard – by means of a threaded rod which passes through the hub of the wheel. All is now ready for the tireing process. Two or three men with long-handled tireing tongs grasp the white hot tire from the fire, throw it on the ground so that all pieces of fuel adhering to it are knocked off; they grasp it again, they drop it in position over the wheel and, with long-handled U-shaped tireing dogs and sledge hammers, it is knocked and levered to the correct position. The whole wheel rim may burst into flames, but, before the flames can do any damage, water is poured on. There are terrific cracking noises as the tire shrinks and the wheel is tightened under the enormous pressure of contraction.

In the past, cart and wagon wheels were built to a saucer shape, that is, they were dished. In a dished wheel, the spokes slant outwards from the hub. The amount of dish on a wheel can be controlled by adjusting the central screw of the tireing platform. If a great deal of dish is required, the central screw is loosened so that the hub is set free from pressure, and rises up to be tightened by the great force of the contracting tire.

The final process in tireing a wheel consists of hanging it over a shoeing hole. This narrow pit is always kept full of water, and the wheel is hung on an iron bar in its back wall and swung round until the whole tire is cool. With glass and sandpaper, the wheel is cleaned; two or three large nails are knocked into it to ensure that the tire does not become loose in dry weather and finally the whole wheel is painted, usually in an ochrous red colour.

It seems surprising that, although this method of tireing a wheel was known in Britain in prehistoric times, a more primitive form of tireing, known as straking, held its own in some parts of the country until recent times. In Shropshire, for example, wagon wheels were equipped with strakes as recently as 1939, while in Somerset, too, most vehicles were equipped with straked wheels. The process of straking a wheel is completely different from that of tireing it with a hoop.

Strakes are cut off while cold from an iron bar with sledge hammer and hard chisels. They are heated, hammered to a convex shape over the anvil and half a dozen or more square nail holes are punched at either end of each strake.

Before fitting the strakes to the wheel rim, a number of nail holes have to be bored, for strake nails are too large and blunt to enter the felloes without preparatory boring. Great care has to be taken, therefore, to ensure that the nail holes in the strake correspond to those in the felloes.

The strakes are placed in the fire of a strake chimney, a closed-in brick fireplace a little distance from the shoeing hole. The wheel itself is hung through the hub on a post at the back of the shoeing hole, its bottom resting in water. Nearby in a bucketful of water are the long, square nails, while close at hand is the heavy cranking gear known as a samson. The samson is used to bring the ends of adjacent felloes, or sections of the rim, so close together that the strakes can be nailed on. Seizing the red hot strake with a pair of long handled tongs, the wheelwright rushes over to the wheel and places it in the correct position. Nails are knocked in at each end and, before the wheel catches fire, it is turned around so that the newly fitted strake lies in the water at the bottom of the hole. The cooling causes contraction and the whole wheel is tightened. The second strake is fixed directly opposite the first one and the whole process is continued until the entire wheel is shod.

One nail in each strake fitted is driven in firmly but not driven home. The reason for this is that, when the whole wheel is shod, the felloe joints have to be brought closer together with the samson. One end of the samson is hooked around a spoke while the other end is hooked over the projecting nail. The nuts on the samson are then gradually tightened until the intervening felloe joints are close together. The process is repeated for every joint around the wheel; all the nails are driven home and the wheel is complete. When one considers that the craft of tireing wheels with hoops was well-known in prehistoric times, it seems surprising that the more primitive method of straking was still widely practised in twentieth century Britain. Straking is, of course, a far easier process than tireing with a hoop and a relatively unskilled man could be entrusted with the work. In hilly districts, too, where wagon wheels have six- or eight-inch tires, it was customary to shoe those wheels with two or even three lines of strakes. If those vehicles were equipped with hoop tires, the process of shoeing would be very difficult indeed. According to Shropshire craftsmen, straked wheels were always preferred in hilly districts, since they slipped less in traversing an inclined bank, and, of course, when a strake wore out, it could be replaced by a farmer himself rather than call on the services of a specialised craftsman.

Boxing. The final process in the manufacture of a wheel consists of fixing the cast iron box in the centre of the hub to take the wear of the revolving wheel.

A large tapering hole is cut through the centre of the nave with heavy boxing chisels and gouges. In the past the central auger hole was first of all enlarged with the V-shaped morticing chisel and shaped with a wide gouge. More recently a tool known as a boxing engine was used. The engine consists of a round bar of iron two feet or three feet long, screwed down half its length with three pronged grips to hold the nave. Half-way up the stem, there is a small cutter, which can be adjusted according to the width of boring required. The boring bar is passed through the centre of the hub, and is turned by the cross handle at the top, and while the three prongs hold the nave steady, the cutter bores out the hole to the required size. The hole itself is made a little too large for the box, for it is extremely important to have the pivoting true, and this can only be done by trial and error.

The axle arm is temporarily fitted to the bench, and the wheel with the box in position is hung on it so that it swings just clear of the ground. A small block of wood is then placed on the floor underneath the wheel, just touching the tire.

Slowly the wheel is turned around and, as it swings clear of the block, small wedges made of heart of oak are hammered into the end grain of the hub. The process is continued until the box is firmly wedged and centred in the hub. The iron hub-bands prevent the elm of the hub from spreading outwards, and only by spreading inwards can it make room for the wedges. It is important that the wedges themselves do not touch the brittle cast iron box, and for this reason they are driven into the elm itself, a place for them being started with a broad iron wedge. As soon as the box is made immovable, all that remains is to chisel off the ends of the tightly fitting wedges to be finally smoothed with the spokeshave. The wedges are so tightly fitted that only the difference between the grain of elm and oak shows where they are.

Finally a block of wood at the outer end of the hub is cut out, in order that the lynch pin holding the wheel to the axle arm can be removed when required. In the past this block of wood was lined with a little straw or piece of sacking so that it kept its position on the moving vehicles. A clasp and staple are fitted to the hub in order to prevent the lynch pin falling outwards.

12. The Chair Maker

The craft of chair making is concentrated in the Wycombe district of Buckinghamshire. Until recently in High Wycombe and the surrounding villages, all the evolutionary stages in the craft, from the itinerant craftsman working in the solitude of the beech glades to the highly mechanised factories employing hundreds of specialists could be seen. Villages such as West Wycombe, Stockenchurch and Naphill possessed small factories, some employing no more than half a dozen specialised craftsmen; other villages had framing shops where the various parts of the chair made by other independent craftsmen were assembled. Even in the smallest factory, each workman still has his own set of duties and never concerns himself with the specialised tasks of his fellow workers, for the chair making industry is by tradition a trade where division of labour is widely practised. Throughout its history in Buckinghamshire, there have been few craftsmen able to make a Windsor chair from start to finish. One of the last and best known was the late H. E. (Jack) Goodchild (1885–1950) who in his Naphill workshop combined the tasks of bodger, benchman and framer to produce chairs of outstanding quality and workmanship.

While the chair bodger (see pp. 15–22) was responsible for making the turned parts of the chair, the craftsmen who made the remainder were factory workers and in the hey-day of hand craftsmanship there were a number of these.

(a) Benchmen who cut out splats, side rails, arms and other sawn parts.
(b) Bottomers who adzed chair seats.
(c) Benders responsible for boiling, bending and trimming bows for backs.
(d) Framers who assembled chairs.
(e) Finishers and polishers.
(f) Caners, often women out-workers who made the rush, cane or willow seats for certain types of chairs.

In some of the smaller factories, one craftsman would be responsible for more than one process, for example, benchmen often adzed chair seats, while framers were responsible for polishing as well as assembling. Nevertheless, the basic division of the labour force into benchmen and framers has continued to the present day. While benchmen are responsible for the rough shaping of chair parts, the framer is always responsible for assembling those parts and finishing them after they have come from the benchman's shop.

The benchman. The benchman is responsible for cutting the sawn parts of the chair using beech for the legs, stretchers, banisters and many other parts, yew for bow and elm for the chair seat. The timber that he requires is delivered in the form of planks to his workshop and in the past these were cut by specialised pit sawyers, well known in the Buckinghamshire woodlands. The benchman's traditional tool is the bow or frame saw known in the Wycombe district as a Betty saw, dancing Betty or a Jesus Christ saw.[8] These vary in size from a large up and down saw, with a blade some thirty inches long for sawing the larger parts, to a small bow saw with a blade no more than seven inches long for cutting out the intricate pattern of a wheel-back Windsor. The latter process is long and laborious 'for every piercing – and some banisters had as many as twenty – meant boring a hole, dismantling a bow saw, threading the blade through the hole, reassembling the bow saw, cutting out the piece, dismantling the bow saw, and so on until the whole pattern had been completed.'[9]

The bow saw itself is a tool of great antiquity with a blade strained along the margin of a frame tightened by means of a rope at the other side. Its great advantage lies in the fact that the blade can be adjusted to any angle. For the benchman's work of cutting out a great variety of shapes and sizes, the frame saw is therefore far superior to the open hand saw used by most other woodworkers. A great deal of material for a chair has to be sawn at a cant while the intricate patterns of banisters and splats can only be cut with highly adjustable tools.

The bottomer. While the benchman's characteristic tool is the bow saw, the bottomer's essential is a long-handled, razor-sharp, hollowing adze. This has a curved wooden handle some twenty-eight inches long and a blade some three inches wide

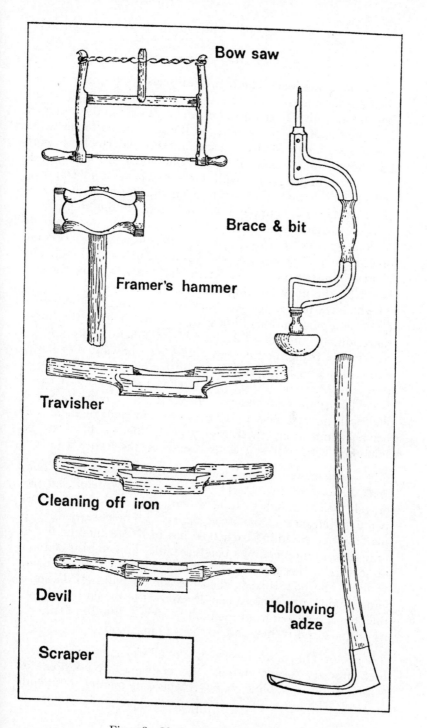

Fig. 26. Chair Making Tools: I.

and nine inches long. The blank elm seats, each some eighteen inches square and two inches thick, are sawn to shape by the benchman with a large up and down bow saw, but the bottomer is responsible for their shaping. In the past the bottomer was a specialised, highly skilled workman, who undertook no work but the adzing of chair seats. The smoothing of the seats was left to the framer who, with his spokeshaves and scrapers, reduced the bottomer's work to a smooth finish. H. E. Goodchild's father, for example, was a bottomer and nothing else.

Today, modern routing machines are able to complete bottoming very quickly, and the ancient adze has become obsolete in an industry where it was once such a vital tool. The method of using the adze is for the bottomer to place the seat blank on the floor, holding it firmly in place with both feet. The blank is then quickly reduced to the correct shape with a quick chopping motion of the adze, at right angles to the run of the grain. In some cases the seat blank is held in position for working by being mounted on a base – an unwanted or faulty seat with four screws projecting and piercing the underside of the seat. After the adzing is complete, the seat is a maze of irregular ridges and hollows. At one place it is perhaps two inches deep, at others it is no more than half an inch, and before completion, these ridges and hollows have to be smoothed with spokeshaves and scrapers, the framer's task.

The bender. The chair back is framed with a bow of which both ends are fixed in the seat. The best bows are made of cleft yew or ash stakes, roughly squared with the draw knife before bending, but most chairs are equipped with bows sawn out of a plank. After trimming each bow has to be steamed or boiled until pliable and bent on a bending table. This consists of a low table with a block of wood and wooden pegs screwed to its surface. The bow is wedged to the correct position, the loose ends bound with twine. When dry and set to the correct shape, the bow is removed from the table, a strut is fitted to maintain its position and is then sent to the framing shop.

The framer. One of the most skilled of all workmen in the furniture industry is the framer, the craftsman responsible for finishing and assembling chairs. It is his duty not only to smooth

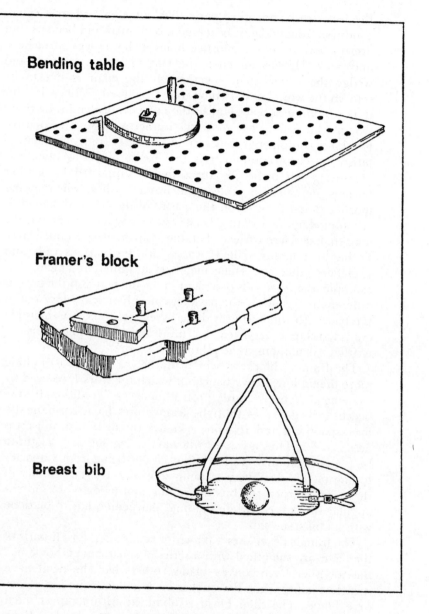

Bending table

Framer's block

Breast bib

Fig. 27. Chair Making Tools: II.

the legs, seats and other parts that come to him in a rough condition from bodgers, benchmen, bottomers and benders, but also to bore dozens of mortice holes in bows, legs, stretchers, and seats. He has to tenon the various parts and glue and wedge the whole chair together. If the chair is not to be sold 'in the white' or passed on to a specialised polisher, it is his duty to stain it as well. Unlike the other craftsmen in the trade who use but one or two tools, the framer possesses an extensive tool-kit of equipment rarely seen in any other trade. His characteristic piece of equipment is the breast bib, a wooden bar measuring ten inches by three inches supported by leather harness, designed to protect the framer's chest when boring mortice holes. A recess in the centre of the bar is designed to accommodate the rotating heads of the wooden braces and the long-shanked screwdriver that the craftsman constantly uses. Boring is a highly skilled process, for the various rails and stretchers enter the other members at different angles. For example, the back rails of a chair enter the seat and the bow at different angles, while the back legs of a chair must slope out at the back. All the boring is done by eyesight and considerable craftsmanship is required, for the framer uses no pattern or written calculations to help him in his work.

The framing block on which the boring is done is nothing more than a low, heavy bench on which the work is secured by wedging it between three protruding pegs. Traditionally the beech-stocked braces that the framer uses have permanently fixed spoon bits and each one is known by the type of work it is designed for. Thus a framer will have a 'legging bit', 'a stump bit', 'a bow bit' and 'a stick bit', each one being from a quarter to one inch wide. Every framing shop has a large number of these. To sharpen the bits a scraping tool made of an old triangular file is used, while the final sharpening has to be done with an oil stone slip.

The framer never uses a plane for smoothing, for all parts of the chair are smoothed with a series of spokeshaves. Some like the travisher have convex blades, others like the devil have straight blades, while the smoker back hollow knife has a concave blade. The final finish is obtained with scrapers often ground down from pieces of old, broken saw blades. Each scraper is first of all sharpened with an oil stone and then turned in the manner of a currier's knife (see pp. 212-15) with a ticketer – an old cobbler's awl. Scratch tools, somewhat similar to the scrapers, are used to produce the shallow mouldings found on some chairs. In addition the framer uses a number of two-handled draw knives, morticing and firmer chisels, gouges, a steel-faced framing hammer, calipers for setting out, screwdriver and reamers. A stove is essential for drying out wedges and tenons as well as for drying out the various parts of the chair, for the parts cannot be assembled until they are bone dry and fully seasoned.

Finally with wedges and glue the chair is assembled and although some are sold 'in the white' others are taken to the staining or polishing shop.

The finisher and stainer. Today, finishing and polishing is a mechanical process and the craftsman uses spray guns and other pieces of modern equipment to complete the work very quickly. In the past, however, hand staining and polishing was a lengthy process and for the more expensive chairs it demanded considerable skill and craftsmanship.

Chairs were first of all cleaned down with nitric acid, an undesirable task, usually performed by young boys. Each chair was then immersed in a heated tank containing a solution of wood chips and water until it was completely stained. A variety of combs were then used to add grain decoration.

Some of the cheaper chairs were polished by oiling with linseed oil 'some were waxed, some had a coat or two of shellac polish slapped on with a brush, while the best work had the full french polish treatment or was highly polished and then dulled to a satin finish with pumice powder or similar abrasives'.[10] The polisher's equipment consisted of no more than a quantity of rag and wadding, half a dozen grades of sandpaper and a length of horsehair rope used for rubbing down the more inaccessible parts of the chair. The craftsman always worked at a low bench in a well-heated workshop, and in most cases the craftsman in question, like others in the chair making industry, was a specialist who undertook staining and polishing for a large number of framers.

The caner. Although a large proportion of the chairs made by Buckinghamshire craftsmen in the past were all wooden, cane- or rush-bottomed chairs were equally well known. By tradition, the actual caning was carried out by women, who were often 'out-workers' carrying on the trade at piece-work rates in their own home. The actual preparation of the cane, however, was man's work, and the 'marker-off', as he was known, split canes with a knife blade and wedge and finished them on a marking-off board. This consisted of nothing more than a plank some fifteen inches long and five inches wide with sets of razor-sharp blades piercing its surface in V-shaped pairs. The distance between each blade could be regulated by turning a screw to contain the width of cane required. In addition, each marking-off board had a horizontal blade, so that the pith could be removed by pulling the cane beneath it.

The actual caning, a simple process though a great variety of patterns was evolved, was carried out by women and children with the minimum of equipment. This consisted of nothing more than an old knife for cane cutting, a small mallet to drive in the wooden pegs used to attach the cane, and a few awl-like pegs for clearing holes.

Rush matting was also used for seat bottoms, but the actual sorting and plaiting of rushes was hard and dirty work, demanding considerable skill. The inside of the seat had to be stuffed with broken rushes, but before they could be used they had to be soaked in water to make them pliable. The women who carried out this work carried out their tasks on a workshop floor and the work was considered so unhealthy that Wycombe matters had to have a monthly medical examination. The matter's tool kit was again simple – an iron peg, a wooden rubber, a knife and a stuffing stick.

IV

Metal and Straw Crafts

1. The Blacksmith

THE GREAT CHANGES that have taken place in the countryside have affected the blacksmith more than any other craftsman. In the past, when the horse provided the only motive power on the farm and the equipment and machinery of the farmer remained simple, the blacksmith was a vital member of the rural community. Not only was he concerned with shoeing horses, but he was also responsible not only for repairing but also for manufacturing a wide range of farm and domestic equipment. Blacksmiths were responsible for making such things as plough shares and harrow tines, they were responsible for tireing wheels and making edge tools, cooking pots and fire backs; indeed no rural community could exist without its smithy. Since the beginning of the present century, and particularly since 1939, the whole character of British farming has changed; the tractor has almost completely replaced the horse; mass-produced machinery of considerable complexity has replaced the traditional local ploughs, harrows and other implements. A great deal of the old business of the rural blacksmith has disappeared, and those that have survived to this day are those craftsmen who have been able to meet the challenge of changing circumstances, becoming agricultural engineers rather than true blacksmiths. Others, however, have been able to adapt their work to modern conditions by specialising in making decorative wrought iron work, but nevertheless only a very small proportion of existing smithies have specialised in this work, despite the fact that the demand is heavy.

To give some indication of the changed conditions in country smithies, let us take the example of one particular craftsman in a north Ceredigion village. Fifty years ago he began a two-year apprenticeship in a west Wales smithy. At that time the workshop was manned by a blacksmith, a journeyman and two apprentices while almost every village in the region had its blacksmith's shop. After a further two years assisting another blacksmith as an improver, the craftsman started on his own in a village in north Ceredigion in 1927. In the twenties and thirties he was a creative craftsman; he built gates, ploughs and harrows; he tired wheels, shod horses and undertook decorative wrought iron work. All these tasks were done with the minimum of machinery; the forge fire had to be blown by hand, iron had to be drilled, welded and filed by hand, and the craftsman had to work long hours, not only to complete his work but also to make ends meet. Today, as in other smithies, machinery has replaced handwork; the forge fire is blown with an electric fan; the craftsman has electric drills, electric grinders, oxy-acetylene welding equipment, and a great deal of other machinery that has helped to make his life less strenuous than in the past. The character of the work has also changed, for no longer is the Dyfed craftsman concerned with making farm and domestic equipment, but being the only blacksmith within a radius of twenty miles, he is fully occupied with the maintenance and repair of factory-made commodities.

The working of iron is, of course, a craft of great antiquity and the blacksmith by tradition has been regarded as society's chief craftsman. In medieval Wales, for example, the smith took his place of honour with the poet and the priest in the Prince's Court. The techniques of the craft have not changed in general principles since prehistoric times, for the modern smith uses the same method of forging as was used thousands of years ago. Forging is essentially a moulding process; just as the potter moulds or models plastic clay, until he gets the shape he requires, so the smith by means of the hammer, anvil and other tools, forms the hot iron into shape, not by cutting, but by causing the metal to flow and spread in the way he wishes.[1]

The main processes of the smith's work are drawing down,

upsetting, welding, bending and punching. When metal is red hot it may be bent and twisted easily, when it is white hot it may be beaten to any shape and when it is even whiter, presenting a dazzling white appearance, it may be welded. The process of drawing down or fullering means reducing the thickness of a piece of metal, and while such pieces are beaten on the anvil with a hammer, the fuller has to be used for heavier pieces. The piece of iron then has a wavy appearance and it has to be smoothed with the flatter, a convex faced hammer.

The process of upsetting or jumping is to get more metal at one part of the work than the other, as, for example, in the making of a head for a rivet. One end of a rod is heated and then beaten down on the anvil or with a hammer until the desired shape is made. To weld two pieces of metal, they are first heated to welding temperature, which is just below melting point. The two white hot pieces are then beaten together with considerable speed.

The wrought iron smith depends very largely on the process of bending, a process that has provided countless examples of the malleable qualities of iron. The smith, too, punches a great deal of his work using tools that vary from a small hand punch to heavy power drills. Punching is a process that strains metal very considerably and great care is essential in judging which work is suitable for punching.

In the past blacksmiths were responsible for making a wide variety of farm and domestic equipment and the smithy was an essential element in all rural communities. With intense competition from large-scale manufacturers, however, thousands of shops have been forced to close within the last hundred years or so. Among the many products produced by the country blacksmiths in the past were agricultural hand tools, billhooks and sickles, scythes and spades, axes and turf irons. As most of these craftsmen produced goods for a specific district, a considerable variation of tools between one district and the next came into existence. Some workshops, like that at Aberaeron in Ceredigion, attained considerable fame for their shovels, which were shaped on a primitive water-driven trip hammer, while others attained fame for billhooks and spades. Towards the end of the nineteenth century, when the work of the country

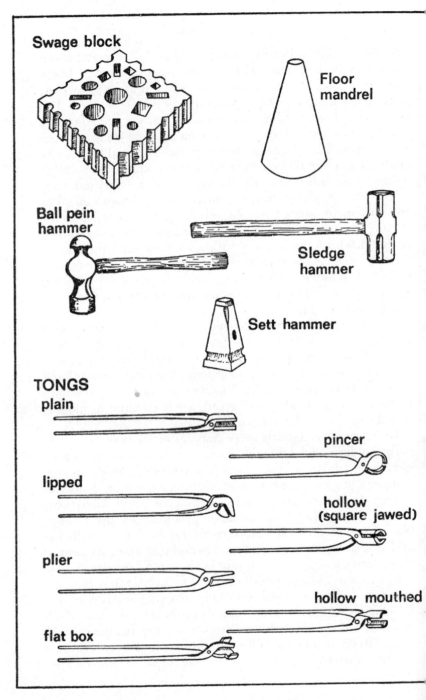

Fig. 28. The Blacksmith's Tools and Equipment: I.

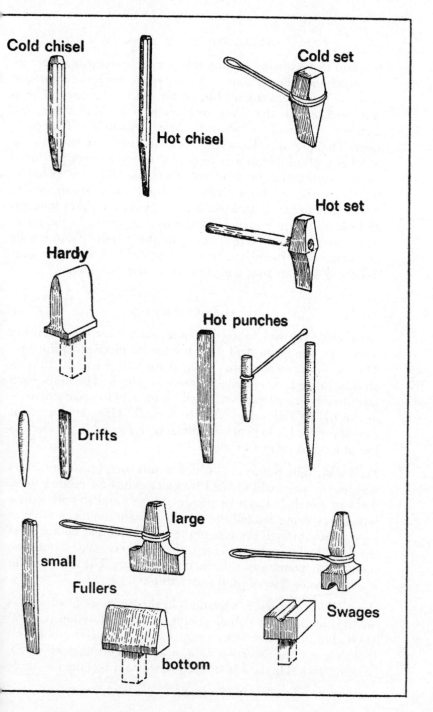

Fig. 29. The Blacksmith's Tools and Equipment: II.

blacksmith was being rapidly taken over by large-scale manufacturers, those manufacturers took over the designs and patterns of the old rural craftsman. Indeed the old local names for tools still persisted, so that even recently a large Midland manufacturer[2] still made a 'Somerset Marsh Spade', a 'Caergwrle Gorse Hook' and a 'Kettering Billhook', together with dozens of other tools of the same pattern and design as were produced by blacksmiths hundreds of years ago. In 1899, for example, the catalogue of Isaac Nash of Stourbridge shows ninety billhook patterns, sixteen slashers, forty-six axes and hatchets and ninety-four hooks and sickles made by them. In the metal trade, even though it is largely in the hands of large-scale manufacturers, there has been a continuity of tradition over hundreds of years that has persisted to our own day.

TOOLS AND EQUIPMENT

Beam drill. In the eighteenth- and early nineteenth-century workshops the beam drill was an essential piece of equipment. The cutting bit was triangular in shape and it was fitted to an all-iron brace twelve inches or more in length. The brace itself was fitted below a heavy weighted beam, kept in place when not in use by hooking on to a rafter or wall. This gave sufficient weight for the bit to penetrate metal of appreciable thickness as the brace was turned by hand.

Pump drill. The pump drill which is still used by stoneworkers was, in the past, widely used by blacksmiths for cutting small holes in metal. It has a wooden cog wheel and spindle with a handle revolving around the spindle at right angles. A piece of rope passes through the tops of the spindle joining both ends of the handle. The rope is twisted, the fly wheel revolves and the pointed bit penetrates thin metal with ease. The action is an intermitten backwards and forwards one.

Anvil. There are many variations in the design of blacksmith's anvils, but the most popular is the so called 'London pattern' anvil. This has a flat face equipped with a punching hole and tool hole for the insertion of a swage or cutting tool at the hanging end. The face is stepped down to a rectangular table and this continues in the form of a heavy pointed projection known as a 'bick'. The whole anvil either stands on a block of elm or an angle-iron stand. The face of the anvil has a hardened steel top, while the table and bick are of steel or wrought iron without a hard steel cover. The main reason for this is when the blacksmith cuts iron with a chisel, the work is moved to the table before the final blow is delivered. This is to avoid damaging the chisel edge. The anvil is a vital piece of equipment, for 'working on a bad anvil is like jumping on a heap of sand, whereas working on a good anvil set on a proper foundation is like jumping on a springboard – the rebound from one blow helps towards the next'.[3]

The hearth. A great deal of the blacksmiths' work is carried out in and near the hearth. This is made of stone, brick or cast iron and it has a large rectangular container for the fire. In front of the fire is a water trough to cool pieces of iron while the tue iron of the bellows or blower enters the hearth either at the side or back. The old hand bellows, some of which were as much as seven feet long, were fixed at the side, while the handle, often with a horn tip, projected over the front of the hearth. This could be operated by the smith's left hand while his right hand held the tongs in the fire. Nowadays, most workshops are equipped with electrically driven blowers.

Vices. The blacksmiths' shops are equipped with work benches, with tool racks above and one or two vices attached to the end of the bench. Heavy bending or hammering is done on a heavy leg vice, so that the strain and shock on the jaws are taken by the leg which is usually set into a steel socket set in a concrete floor. In addition, a small engineer's vice is also necessary to hold the lighter work.

Swage block. This is a heavy square or rectangular cast iron block with different sizes of half round and V-shaped notches on all four sides and different shaped holes in the face. It is used to shape heated metal and is often placed on a metal stand to lift it to a convenient height for working.

Floor mandrels. The smith usually possesses a number of these ranging in size from twelve inches to as much as four feet. The floor mandrel is a hollow cast-iron cone and is used for rounding up hoops and rings. For example, a mandrel was essential for shaping the hub-bands of a wheel.

Ball pein hammer. For most forging tasks the blacksmith uses a ball pein hammer varying from one-and-three-quarters to three pounds in weight. The handles vary in length according to the craftsman's preferences. In addition a sledge hammer for heavier work is essential, while a number of specialised hammers, such as set hammers with square flat heads for shaping iron may also be necessary. In the past blacksmiths made their own special hammers often from old cart springs, but nowadays most of those that they require are made by large-scale manufacturers.

Tongs. Tongs are used to handle hot metal during forging operations. There are a large number of different types adapted to the special requirements of forging, for unlike any other craftsman, the blacksmith is able to make his own tools. No one set of tools is therefore like any other. The universal tongs are the plain tongs which are constantly required by the blacksmith for holding iron, while a few of the varieties found in any smithy are shown in Fig. 28.

Cold chisels. These are used for cutting iron while cold and they are made in various widths with thick points. Each one is a short, thick tool and is used in conjunction with the ball pein hammer. They are made of steel containing 0.875 per cent cast iron.

Cold sets. These are the sledge hammer versions of the cold chisel. Each one is either equipped with a wooden handle or with a handle of twisted hazel or wire. They are very short and thick.

Hot chisels. Chisels for cutting hot iron are longer and more slender than cold chisels, so as to keep the smith's hand well clear of the hot iron. It has a much narrower point and as the chisel becomes hot it is quenched in water after every three or four strokes. They are made of steel containing 6.75 per cent carbon.

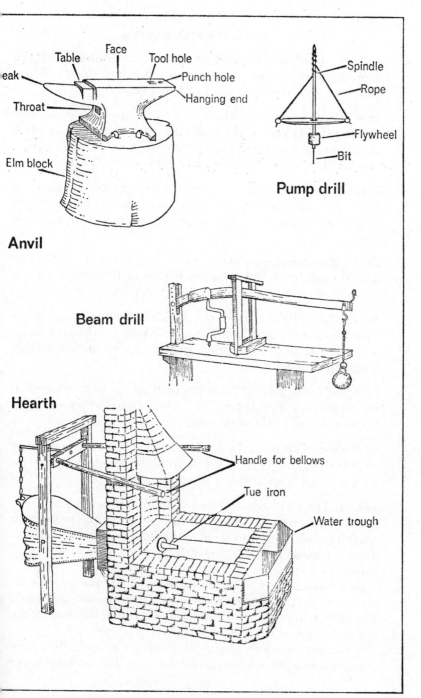

Anvil — Table, Face, Tool hole, Punch hole, Hanging end, eak, Throat, Elm block

Pump drill — Spindle, Rope, Flywheel, Bit

Beam drill

Hearth — Handle for bellows, Tue iron, Water trough

Fig. 30. The Blacksmith's Tools and Equipment: III.

Hot sets. These are sledge-hammer versions of hot chisels. As they are used for precision cutting they are nearly always equipped with wooden hafts like hammers.

Hardy. This is a heavy chisel that fits into the square tool hole at the hanging end of the anvil. The iron that is to be cut is placed on the hardy and beaten down with the hammer until it breaks off.

Punches. For hot work, the blacksmith requires a variety of punches which are long enough to keep the craftsman's hand well clear of the work. The larger types are rodded like cold sets.

Drifts. These are pieces of steel with a long taper at one end and a short taper on the other for driving through punched holes in order to enlarge, shape and smooth them.

Small fuller. This is a hand tool similar in shape to a chisel but with a rounded nose. They are mainly used for drawing metal in one direction, for forging special shapes or for making shoulders in metal.

Large and bottom fullers. These are used for the same purpose as the small fuller. The large fuller is rodded and the bottom fuller fits into the tool hole of the anvil.

Set hammer. This has a flat or slightly convex face with sharp or rounded edges and it is struck with the sledge hammer for flattening hot metal.

Swages. These are top and bottom tools for working metal to shape. The top swage which has to be struck with the sledge is rodded, while the bottom swage fits into the anvil tool hole. They are made by the blacksmith himself from tool steel, in a variety of designs and shapes.

In addition the blacksmith possesses a number of tools for managing the fire. These are a shovel, a poker, a rake and swab. The swab is a tool for placing kindling stakes in the heart of the fire in order to start it.

A blacksmith who undertakes decorative wrought iron work requires a number of other specialised tools. The main ones are:

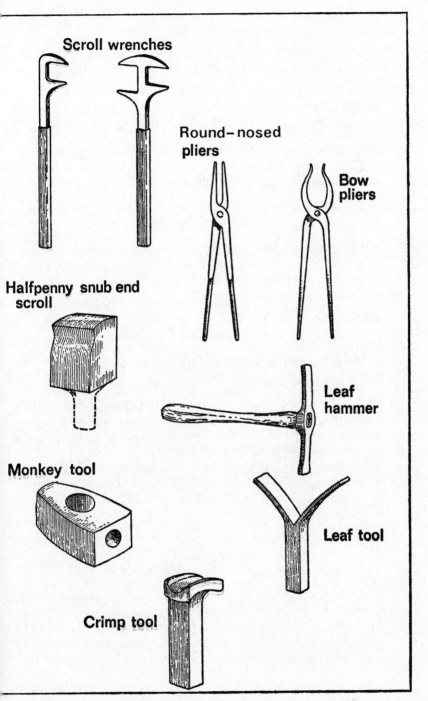

Fig. 31. Wrought Iron Tools.

Wrenches. These are long-handled tools with pairs of parallel noses for shaping scrolls. They are made in many different sizes and shapes.

Monkey tool. This is used for squaring the shoulders of round tenons and it works on the same principle as the nail heading tool.

Round-nosed pliers. These are used for gripping the tips of a scroll as the scroll wrench is used for shaping and also for fitting collars or adjusting the curve of a scroll.

Bow pliers with long, straight noses are used for fitting collars without damaging them.

The halfpenny snub end scroll is a tool with a one-inch-groove on its side for finishing a piece of wrought iron with a rounded tip or snub. It fits into the anvil tool hole and the iron is shaped by beating it into the ground.

Side set. A handled hot set with one edge of the blade handled at an angle of seventy-five degrees for squaring shoulders.

Butcher. A handled hot set for cutting metal, particularly the shoulders.

Leaf tool. A forked iron stake with the inner edges slightly rounded for shaping wrought iron leaves. In addition for leaf making a crimp tool, somewhat similar to a bottom swage and a long-headed leaf hammer are required.

In addition to all these tools, the blacksmith does need a large number of files and rasps of different shapes and degrees of coarseness as well as a number of specialised tools such as those for tireing wheels (p. 119).

2. The Farrier

The craft of the shoeing smith or farrier is one of great antiquity, for since Roman times it has been the custom to equip horses with shoes for the protection of hooves, particularly on hard surfaces. The farrier is something far more than a manual worker for his craft demands a considerable knowledge of the anatomy of the horse's foot, its diseases and the methods of curing those diseases. The Master Farriers' Association has at the present time a national apprenticeship scheme, in which apprentices learn as much as possible about the anatomy and health of the animal as well as the practical aspects of shoeing. The Rural Industries Bureau, until recently, provided elementary farriery instruction but now maintains a panel of qualified farriers capable of instructing men who desire to sit for one of the qualifying examinations of the Worshipful Company of Farriers.[4]

The craft has changed but little since Roman times and a farrier still practising his art in the countryside uses the same techniques, the same tools and equipment that have been used for many centuries. All his requirements, nails, hammers and other essentials are kept in the shoeing box, a handled box measuring some eighteen inches long, ten inches wide and ten inches high. The equipment must never be taken from that box for any other purpose but shoeing.

When a horse is brought to the smithy for shoeing, the farrier first of all examines the hooves, fore feet first. In most cases the craftsman lifts each foot and grasps it between his knees, but in some cases, when the horse is particularly nervous, the animal has to be fettered, its legs tied and the shoeing performed while the horse is on its back. With horses that are being shod for the first time the latter process has to be adopted very often.

After examination, the old shoes have to be removed and in the past this was a task often undertaken by apprentices. The nails are cut off with a piece of metal called a buffer and the whole shoe removed with a pair of pincers. In some smithies the old shoes are again forged into new ones, a task that demands considerable hammering and heating.

When the old nails have been taken out, the hoof is cleaned and smoothed with knife, rasp and hoof parers, until it is flat enough for the shoe. Although many farriers at present buy shoes which they can adapt for the needs of each horse, some still make their own shoes and nails. They first of all take a measurement across each hoof and calculate the amount of wrought iron that will be required for each shoe. With a cold

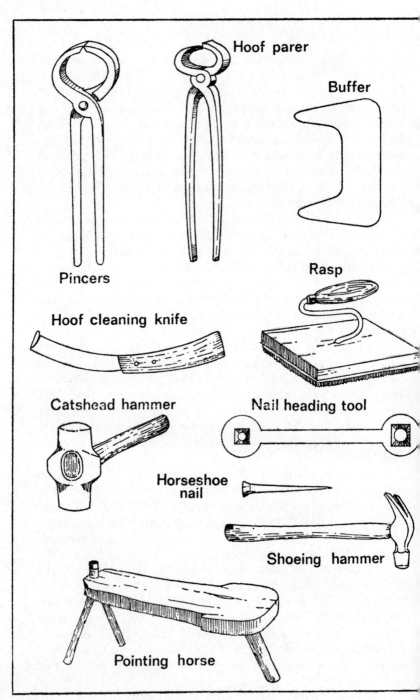

Fig. 32. The Farrier's Tools.

set weighing three pounds or more, the required length is cut from a rod of iron on the anvil. For this purpose a heavy sledge hammer is required.

The shoe is next marked in the centre, heated in the fire and bent to a V-shape. It is again heated and shaped to fit the horse's hoof. For this purpose a heavy catshead or shoe-turning hammer is required. This is double-headed, one end being flat, the other slightly convex. On each side of the handle are protruding small heads or webs used for drawing the clip on the front of a shoe.

In the old days, too, the special nails for fastening shoes were also made in the smithy. A rod of iron some eighteen feet long was heated and cut into the required size on the cutting edge of the hardy, which was inserted in the anvil orifice. It was then inserted in the nail heading tool, which consisted of a flat metal bar fitted at each end with a perforated knob. The perforation complied with the size and shape of the nail shank and was also countersunk to correspond to the nail head. After inserting the red-hot piece of metal in the nail hole, the tool was placed over the anvil orifice and the head hammered into shape. All that now remained was to point each nail either with a rasp or on a pointing horse. After filing off the sharp edges, the tapering nail holes are punched with the pritchell or punch and the shoe is held to the hoof in order to 'seat' it. The seating produces clouds of smoke as it burns the insensitive horny substance of the hoof.

After several reheatings, filings and hammerings, the farrier is satisfied that the shoe fits, and all that now remains is to nail it firmly in place. Great care has to be taken that the nails point outwards so as not to damage the sensitive flesh of the foot. The shoeing hammer weighs between ten ounces and sixteen ounces and in addition to a flat head it has a V-shaped projection at the other end for clinching the nails as they emanate on the side of the hoof.

3. The Thatcher

The art of thatching is one of great antiquity and from time immemorial man has used the material growing around him to provide a weatherproof roof over his home and crops. Not only do the style and techniques of thatching vary tremendously from one part of the country to the other, but the material used by the countryman varies according to the raw material available locally.

Whatever material the craftsman uses for thatch, he certainly requires a large number of wooden spars. These spars are made in different lengths from eighteen inches to as much as four feet and they are cleft from hazel rods. (See pp. 39–41.)

Straw from wheat threshed in the normal way, though not favoured in certain parts of the country such as Devon, East Anglia and Dorset, has been used by many generations of thatchers, particularly in corn-growing districts. Due to the increased popularity of combine harvesters and balers, however, 'long straw thatching', as it is called, is becoming far less common than in the days when flails and threshing drums were used. Modern machinery tends to flatten the tubular stems, so that the straw lies less compactly and is less waterproof. In many parts of the country in the past, it was customary to cut the wheat close to the ear, thus leaving the stems undamaged by threshing. Even in recent years, it was a custom in some parts of the country to reserve the wheat growing around the edges of a harvest field for thatching. This was generally cut either with a sickle, or scythe and cradle in order to open the field for the reaper or binder.

Threshed long straw has to be thoroughly prepared by moistening and ensuring that all the straws are parallel with their butts level. Slightly green straw is preferred and before using it is tied into bundles or 'yealms', each some eighteen inches wide and five inches thick. The yealms are tied with straw rope and each yealm is applied to the roof, tied with spars and hazel rods, with the process continuing from the eaves to the ridge until the whole roof is covered. The butts of the yealms are never dressed with the bat or leggat as is usual with combed straw, while a long straw roof is easily distinguishable by the way in which the eaves and barges are decorated with a pattern of liggers and cross rods. A roof gives the impression 'that the roof covering as a whole has been poured over the underlying structure . . . it is thus given a plastic quality enabling it to follow the irregular planes in the roof, without giving rise to any sense of rupture or stress'.[5] The main body of the long straw roof is not clipped in any way although the eaves may be trimmed with shears and a long-handled thatching knife, the latter being an old scythe blade fixed to a wooden handle. The smooth finish of the roof is done with a side rake which is used with a beating and combing action, while the thicker covering for the ridge, with its maze of liggers and cross rods, may also be trimmed with the knife.

Besides the threshed long-straw method of thatching, there is another way of using wheat straw. It is not threshed in the usual manner, and the material is known as 'reed straw', 'combed wheat reed' or 'Devon reed'. The craft may be seen at its best in the villages of Devon and Dorset, where generations of craftsmen have been masters of the technique. In the past, to obtain reed straw, the grain was beaten over a threshing frame, a semi-circular construction some three feet wide and two feet high with a number of parallel cross-bars. In Devon flails were less often used for threshing, since their beating action tended to bruise and flatten the wheat stems. A small sheaf of wheat was taken and beaten against the bars of the threshing frame or 'webble', so that all the ears were knocked out and the straw kept free from damage.

A slightly more advanced method of beating out the ears without damaging the stalks was to employ a small threshing drum. The grain was beaten out by the revolving arms within the drum and the straw was pulled out without damage. The much larger combing machines, which may still be seen occasionally in the south-west, are attached to the mobile threshing machines. Selected wheat is fed through this machine which strips all the ears and flag from the wheat without the straw going through the drum. The combed wheat reed thus comes from the machine undamaged and is bundled with the ends lying in one direction. The traditional bunch of Devon reed is known as a 'nitch' and weighs some twenty-eight pounds.

A roof thatched with straw reed has a somewhat different appearance to that thatched with long straw. The object is to present a brush-like surface to the weather, a coarse but plush-like texture, produced by the outward facing butts of the stalks.

Few liggers and cross-sticks are to be seen, while the spars, tarred cord and straw rope are concealed by the butt ends of the straw. A combed wheat reed roof differs from the Norfolk reed roof in that the gables and eaves of the wheat reed are cut to shape, rather than tapered as in Norfolk reed thatching.

A roof thatched with Devon reed generally lasts some fifty years on a forty-five degree pitch, while that thatched with Norfolk reed has a life of a hundred years or more. Norfolk reed (*phragnites communis*) is an aquatic plant that grows in many parts of the country but more especially in the vicinity of the Norfolk Broads where it is harvested annually. Reed, the most expensive of all thatching materials, is not grown especially or cultivated in any way, although the best reed comes from beds which are regularly cut. In some cases reed mixed with bulrushes and the stalk of the wild iris is preferred by some thatchers; the material being known as 'mixed reed'. When cut with a scythe or sickle, often in the most difficult marshy conditions, the reed stands from three feet to eight feet high. It is tied into bundles some twelve inches in diameter. Unlike straw, Norfolk reed quantities are calculated by the fathom rather than by weight. 'When the bundles are neatly stacked together a string passed around the stalk at butt level should measure six feet or one fathom.'[6]

For ridging a reed roof another marsh plant – sedge (*cladium mariscus*) is used. This, unlike reed, is pliable and has a life of twenty-five or thirty years, and is kept in place on the roof with hazel cross-sparring.

TOOLS

The tools the thatcher uses vary from district to district. Many of them are made by the craftsman himself to suit his own particular needs. The principal ones are:

Leggat. A square or rectangular block of wood used by thatchers for beating reed or Devon reed into position. For true reed, the leggat may have a number of holes in its surface or is equipped with rows of iron pegs or nails. For combed wheat reed the leggat has a number of parallel grooves. The latter may have a long handle, or may be equipped with a handle at

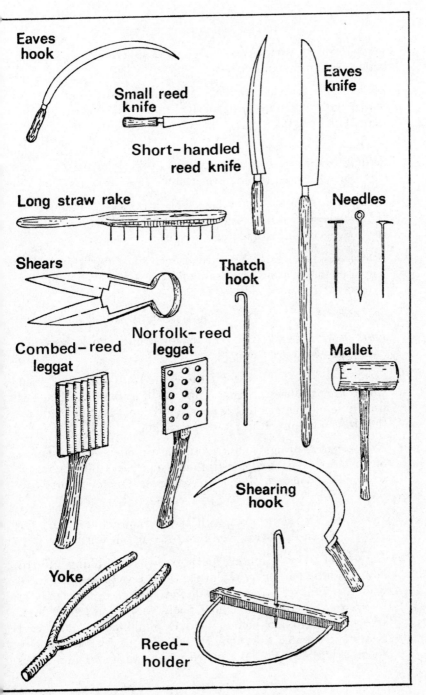

Fig. 33. The Thatcher's Tools.

the back of the wooden block for use in difficult places such as between windows and valleys.

Mallet. The thatcher requires a round headed beechwood mallet with a handle some twelve inches long for driving in spars. For iron spikes a claw hammer is required.

Needles. Various sizes of needles are required by thatchers for holding yealms of thatching material in place on the roof and for inserting tarred twine in the thatch.

Reed-holder. A home-made hazel bow attached to a batten at right angles which is hooked on to the roof to hold a bundle of reed in place while thatching.

Bow, jack, yack or yoke. A forked branch some thirty-six inches long used for carrying yealms up to the roof and for holding the long straw in place ready for use.

Spar hook (see pp. 39–41) for splitting and pointing hazel rods.

Eaves hook. A gently curving, narrow-bladed hook, used for trimming wheat reed thatch.

Short-handled knife. Used for cutting the tops of Norfolk reed where they protrude over the apex of the roof. The blade is usually some eighteen inches long and the tool may be made by the craftsman himself from an old scythe.

Eaves knife. A straight-bladed knife, again often an adaptation of an old scythe, used for trimming the eaves in long straw work. The whole tool may measure as much as forty-two inches long.

Side rake. A straight rake with ten or more tines, used for dressing down long straw work and raking out waste.

Hand shears. For trimming purposes when finishing off. In addition a thatcher may require knee pads to protect his knees while working on a roof; he will certainly need a quantity of tarred rope and iron thatching hooks varying in length from seven inches to ten inches, used in conjunction with hazel sways to fix thatch to rafters. He will also need ladders, one of them a short ladder of the spiked variety with two long spikes at one end which anchor it to the roof. In the west of England the thatcher's horse replaces the spiked ladder. This is a rectangular wooden frame some three feet long and eighteen inches wide and it has two spikes which penetrate the thatch.

4. The Lip-Worker

In the past a great variety of objects for farm and domestic use were made of straw bound into rolls with bramble, cane or some other binding material and coiled into a receptacle. This category of work was known as lip-work, the word *lip* being a derivation of the Scandinavian *lob*: coiled basketry. In Scandinavia as well as in Western Europe generally the craft was widespread and objects ranging from seedlips to cradles and from chairs to bushel measures were made from coiled straw. It has persisted until recently in western and northern Britain, where a number of notable craftsmen still practise the trade on a part-time basis. In the Orkneys, for example, a barrel-shaped straw receptacle for carrying grain is known as a *luppie*, while a larger version of it, known as a *cubbie*, is well known in the islands. Although the majority of these receptacles are made of straw, a more open version known as a *caisie* is made of the ripened stalks of the common dock.

In Wales, the craft was widely practised as a leisure activity in many parts of the country, and there are still one or two craftsmen in west Wales that practise it. The most notable perhaps is an elderly smallholder and stone mason in central Cardiganshire who is able to make baskets and seedlips of exquisite workmanship and design using the minimum of equipment.

To make a straw basket, the craftsman requires a quantity of wheat, which has to be unthreshed and not bruised or bent in any way. Winter wheat is preferred, for it is considered much harder than the spring-sown variety. The heads are cut off and the stalks are cleaned thoroughly with the penknife. Before the straw can be used it must be very dry. The bramble for binding the coils has also to be selected with great care, the best type growing in sheltered positions under trees in forests and plantations. Due to the number of off-shoots it possesses, hedgerow bramble is less satisfactory. The bramble has to be winter cut for if there is sap between the bark and the core, it is not suitable for the craftsman's needs.

The tools required for the work consist of nothing more than a sharp pocket knife, an awl and a shaping horn. The awl is a piece of bone from a horse's hind leg, for metal awls similar to those used by osier basket makers are too hard and pointed and tend to break the delicate wheat stalks. Wooden awls, on the other hand, tend to break easily if they are sharpened to a thin point. One particular type of bone suits the craftsman's needs perfectly; it need not be sharpened or flattened in any way; it is thin, straight, pointed and strong enough, and it is a solid bone some seven inches long without any marrow. It is said that the older the horse, the better the bone. The device used for shaping the straw coils is a section of a cow horn, three-quarters of an inch to one inch in diameter, although in some cases craftsmen use a small leather cylinder for the purpose.

To make a basket, the bramble is split into four sections with the knife; the craftsman splitting against the line of growth from the thin to the thick end. Holding the knife against the thicker butt end of the bramble the pith is removed by drawing the section back under the knife. Next, each bramble is reduced to the correct width by drawing the knife along its edges, again starting at the butt end. This is then pointed and the bramble binding is ready for use.

The actual weaving then commences. A bunch of wheat stalks is passed through the horn to form a coil. The bramble is drawn tightly around this; more wheat coils are added and as the work proceeds the bramble binding is attached to the end of the stitch below it. The cow horn remains in place throughout the whole process of construction, for not only must the bramble 'stitches' be equidistant throughout, but the coils must be of equal thickness.

The centre of the basket may be in one of three forms. Firstly it may be snail-shaped with the coils running from a central point; secondly it may be rosette shaped with radiating stalks, or the centre may be in the form of a cross. There is also a variation in the pattern of weave, the usual method being to pass the strip around a coil to pierce the edge of the coil below. In addition a strip may penetrate the actual strip of the coil below so that all the stitches are in a straight vertical line throughout the basket. In addition there may be variations of this, such as two stitches around the coil with one piercing the stitch below. One particular aspect of the trade that was widely distributed throughout the British Isles was the making of straw bee skeps. For this task, rye straw was preferred because of its length and toughness, but wheat straw was also used. Work on the skep commenced at the centre of what would become the top of the dome and the straw coils were then sewn round and round until the whole skep had been completed. In southern England in the nineteenth century it was common for the farm labourer to make his own skeps from straw supplied by his employer, but there were also craftsmen who spent all their time making skeps for those who could afford to buy them. Bedfordshire, the centre of the straw hat industry, was noted for its straw hives. The association of the weaving techniques with straw skeps was so well-known that the lip-work chairs, so common in country households in the past were known as 'beehive' chairs.

5. The Straw Plaiter

The technique of weaving rush, grass or straw is one that goes back to prehistoric times and there is evidence to suggest that by the fifteenth century the craft of straw plaiting and hat making flourished in many parts of Europe. By 1575, for example, the straw hat merchants of Tuscany had been formed into a corporation and that region, with Leghorn at its centre, later became the world's most important centre of plaiting. In Saxony, too, the tradition of straw hat making goes back to the sixteenth century, while in the Liège district straw hat making is said to date from the Middle Ages.

Straw plaiting was introduced into Britain in the sixteenth century by the Lorraimers and the industry became established in Bedfordshire, Buckinghamshire and Hertfordshire. As time went on and straw hats gained in popularity, plaiting together with lace making became one of the most important industries of the south-east Midlands and by 1851 eighty per cent of the total workers in the hat trade lived in the region.[7] Straw plaiting dominated home life in Luton, Dunstable and the surrounding villages, plait schools flourished, weekly plait markets drew thousands of people to the market towns of the region and the whole economy and social life of the south-east Midlands was tied up with the straw plaiting trade. Other specialised craftsmen, such as hat block makers and box makers were entirely dependent on the plaiters and hat makers. Although plaiting was primarily a female occupation, most boys were also taught plaiting 'and attended plaiting schools until they took up farm work at about fourteen or fifteen. Even the men did plaiting as a spare time occupation'.[8]

Until the second decade of the twentieth century the straw hat industry flourished and the plaiters working in their own homes found a ready market for their plait in the dozens of hat factories in the region. In most cases, however, the plait was first of all sold to middlemen, the straw dealers who travelled from village to village. Plait makers were also extremely important, and raw material was bought and the finished plait sold at these markets. On Mondays, Luton had its market, on Tuesday Hitchin, Wednesday Dunstable, Thursday Hemel Hempstead, Friday Tring and Shefford, while on Saturday a market was held at Toddington. For years there were open air markets, and in some towns they continued to be so, for as long as they existed. The plait makers set up their stalls in the streets, but in the 1860's and 1870's, at a period when the plaiting industry was on the wane, Luton, Dunstable and Hitchin had their special plait halls. Here all dealings in straw, the buying of raw material and the selling of finished plait to the middlemen were carried out. The plait was in time sold by the straw dealers to the dozens of hat factories located in the region, or it was sold to the hundreds of 'makers up' who carried out their task in their homes. The latter were mainly concerned with making the cheaper variety of hats. Again, some of the makers up did work for the large factories and until the 1920's home work was an essential feature of the hat making industry.

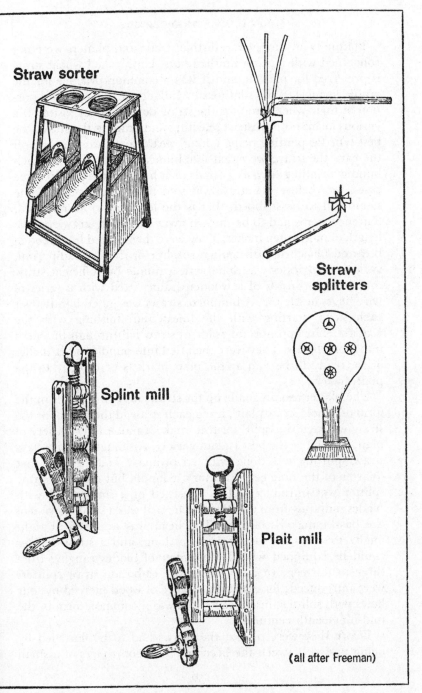

Straw sorter

Straw splitters

Splint mill

Plait mill

(all after Freeman)

Fig. 34. Straw-plaiting Equipment.

Plaiting was, however, a distinct trade and plaiters were not concerned with making finished hats. Unthreshed wheat straw is preferred for plaiting and it was a common practice for the arable farmers of the south-east Midlands to reserve a proportion of their wheat crop for the straw dealers. They visited the various farms of the district selecting and grading the straw, the best type for plaiting being a long, clean stem. After cutting off the ears, the straws were tied into bunches by the dealers, each bundle weighing fifty-six pounds or a hundredweight. In some cases, too, before the straw was sold to the plait makers, the stems had to be stripped, that is the leaf had to be removed, flattened stems had to be thrown away and each straw cut to a length of nine or ten inches. They were then placed in a wooden box and bleached with molten sulphur or dyed. Grading into various thicknesses was done with a simple but efficient straw sorter. This consists of a wooden frame fitted with a series of wire sieves at the top. A bundle of straws was jolted lightly over each sieve, starting with the finest and finishing with the coarsest. The appropriate grade of straw fell through the mesh into a box below. They were then tied into bundles of six inches or so, ready to be sold at the plait markets or directly to the plait makers.

The plaiter usually made up the straws into plait either in the form of 'whole straw plait', using each straw in the round, or the straw was used in 'split' form to make a much finer variety of plait, as good as the best Italian variety. Although in early days straw splitting was done with an ordinary knife, in the first quarter of the nineteenth century a simple but effective straw splitter was introduced. This consisted of a small head with blades radiating from the centre. The tool was a small version of the basket maker's cleaver. The head was attached at right angles to a handle some six inches long, and a straw splitter could be equipped with any number of blades ranging from three to thirteen. In later days more elaborate straw splitters were introduced; for example, a piece of wood pierced by four holes with splitters inside each hole was a common form in the mid-nineteenth century.

Before they were plaited the straws had to be flattened by being passed between the beech or boxwood rollers of a small mangling device known as a splint mill. These were screwed to cottage doorposts and children were often given the boring task of operating it. In some districts, too, an ordinary rolling pin was used for flattening straws and splints.

The plaiter, armed with a bundle of whole straws or splints under her left arm, worked at great speed, drawing out each straw from the bundle as it was required, moistening it with the lips and plaiting a number simultaneously. The straws in use at the same time were known as 'ends' and they ranged in number from three to seven. A great variation of pattern could be made by varying the weave. The ends of the straws that projected from the plait had to be cut off with the knife and the work had to pass through the rollers of a plait mill. This was similar in shape to the splint mill, but the rollers in this case were grooved to take the various widths of plait.

The plait was then coiled into scores, coils of twenty yards, and sold at the markets. It is said that one source of great loss to the hat manufacturers in the first half of the nineteenth century was the widespread practice of giving short measure. In 1852 the *Straw Hat Manufacturers Association* was set up to combat this and it continued to operate for over twenty years.

V
Stone and Clay Crafts

1. The Brick Maker

CLAY WAS USED for making bricks long before man had discovered how to harden it in the heat of the fire. Bricks made in ancient Egypt were sun baked, but however hard they became after exposure to the rays of the sun, they softened again in the wet, for hardened clay has the property of absorbing moisture into its particles. It was a great technological step forward therefore, when around 300 B.C. the technique of firing bricks was evolved in the Middle East.

It was the Roman conquerors who first introduced the craft into Britain and during their occupation a large number of brick works were set up throughout the country. When the Romans departed, however, the art of brick making died out and did not return on any scale until the fifteenth century. There were, it is true, one or two brickyards in Suffolk as early as the thirteenth century, but the majority of brick buildings of pre-fifteenth-century date in East Anglia were built of bricks imported from the Low Countries. They were extremely expensive and were only used to build noblemen's castles, manor houses and churches. In the late fifteenth century in East Anglia and other regions where building stone was scarce and the timber of the forests was running short, the craft of brick making took root and workshops were set up wherever suitable clay occurred. Nevertheless during this early period the new building material was still limited in its use; limited to building stately homes like Mapledurham in Oxfordshire;

castles like Hurstmonceaux in Sussex and colleges like Queens in Cambridge.

It was not until the end of the seventeenth century that bricks became the common material for building homes of ordinary people, and it was not until then that the craft spread very quickly to all corners of Britain. In the eighteenth and early nineteenth centuries, it was a common practice for brick makers to travel around the country, visiting places where houses were required. They tested the clay of the locality, decided on its suitability for brick making and often blended and treated it. Their techniques and processes were adapted to suit the nature of the local clay. In this way a vast number of small brickyards came into existence, while in addition many of the larger country estates had their own brick works.

The eighteenth century was the flourishing period of the small brickyard in Britain, for in the nineteenth century the craft, like many others, became greatly mechanised. Many of the small yards were forced to close down in the face of new competition from the large firms. In the miles of red, yellow and grey brick work of nineteenth-century industrial Britain there is a dull monotony that was completely absent from earlier work. Whereas in the factories the clay is extruded from a machine in lengthy strips and cut up into bricks by another machine, in country workshops each brick was moulded individually; each one was slightly different from the next and so had character. The small brickyard contributed in no small measure to the architectural harmony of a region, by providing building material made from the clay that occurred locally. Not until the middle of the nineteenth century were bricks of the same kind sent all over the country from the vast, highly mechanised brick works of London and the Midlands. These machine-made products certainly destroyed the old local harmony of colour and style that characterised the earlier brick buildings. Although the majority of the old rural brickyards were forced to close down, here and there one may still find a small yard in operation, clinging to the techniques and methods of past centuries, despite competition from large-scale manufacturers. The country yards concentrate on the manufacture of sand-faced, hand-moulded bricks, of a quality that no machine can equal. Although this type of brick is three times as expensive as the machine-made variety, they are still greatly valued for wall facings.

Finished bricks vary in colour according to the quality of the clay and the degree of firing to which they are subjected. If water is present in the clay, for example, then the colour produced at a moderate heat will be red, but a much brighter clearer red is produced from the shales of coal measures. Staffordshire bricks again are red in colour, but by longer firing at a greater heat the bricks become blue in colour. The addition of lime to the clay makes a cream-brown brick, while the presence of magnesia produces a yellow brick. For brick making a proportion of sand is mixed with clay, but there are many parts of the country where sand and clay occur in the right consistency, and there are others where sand is found in close proximity.

Clay for making bricks is dug in the autumn before the winter rains set in, making the clay beds impossibly waterlogged. For some four months the nearly dry clay is left in large heaps so that it experiences the mellowing influence of frost, snow and ice. During the winter months the masses are broken up and turned constantly so that the atmosphere can penetrate in every direction. To do this the traditional clay spades are used. These spades made of willow and shod with metal sheeting have an advantage over metal spades in that the clay does not stick to the blade to the same extent as it does to metal. They are also much lighter, a very important point when dealing with heavy material, and since the spade is shaped from a single piece of wood there is no danger of it cracking at the joints.

After clay has been broken up by natural forces, it is broken up even further in the pug mill. In the early days of brick making the grounding of clay into paste was done by allowing horses or barefooted men to walk on it until it was fully broken up. It is said that the puggers' feet were so sensitive that they were able to pick up the smallest pebble from the mass of clay. Later, most brick works installed a horse-driven pug mill in the form of a gigantic coopered churn within which were a series of revolving knives. The horse, very often a blind one, was hitched to a horizontal shaft, and led by a young boy, it was

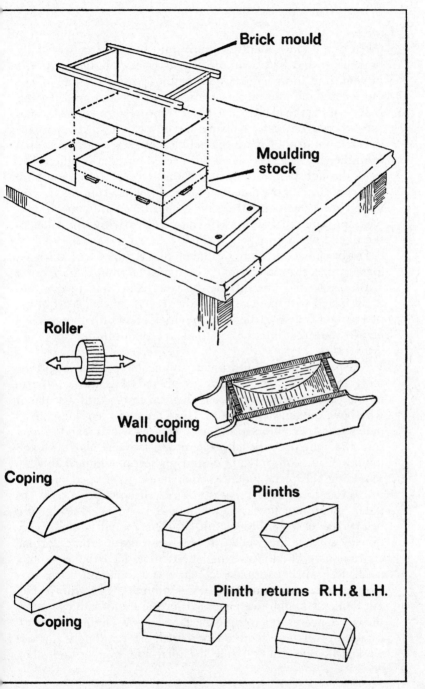

Fig: 35. Brick Making Equipment: I.

taken round and round the churn until the contents were fully broken up and had acquired the necessary plasticity. At the present time, however, brickyards either possess a rolling mill or more commonly an oil or electrically driven pug mill. In this type of mill, the clay is first of all tipped into a conical metal tub, where a series of revolving knives break it up. It then falls into a large drum, where the pebbles and stones are separated from the clay. The clay itself is squeezed out in a spaghetti-like mass through perforations in the wall of the drum. The pure clay comes out of the mill at its lowest level in a continuous strip some twelve inches square. This is cut into slabs by means of a wire bow and the slabs are placed on a low barrow and taken to the moulding shops.

For brick making a proportion of sand is mixed with the clay, for pure clay shrinks and warps on drying, forming a hard outer crust before the interior moisture has had time to dry out. Sand mixed with the clay not only prevents shrinkage, but the presence of coarse particles in the brick allows the free passage of air into the interior, so that the moisture escapes and evaporates.

The process of moulding is very simple and consists of nothing more than throwing a piece of tempered clay into a box-like mould. The superfluous clay is then taken off with a strike or wire bow, the finished brick is placed on a wooden slat called a pallet and lowered on to the hack barrow which stands alongside the moulder's bench. There are two methods of hand moulding – slop moulding and pallet moulding. In slop moulding the rectangular wooden mould is dipped in water from time to time to prevent the clay from sticking to it. In pallet moulding, however, the mould is sprinkled with sand before the clay is thrown into it. The moulder works very quickly so that the whole process has the appearance of one continuous motion. An experienced moulder, who is usually paid piece work, can make as many as a thousand bricks in a working day, or twenty-four in five minutes. As a craft it does not demand a high degree of skill in the use of hand tools for the whole process is a routine mechanical one. In the nineteenth century it was quite common for a small brickyard to be run and worked by one family; while the men and women undertook

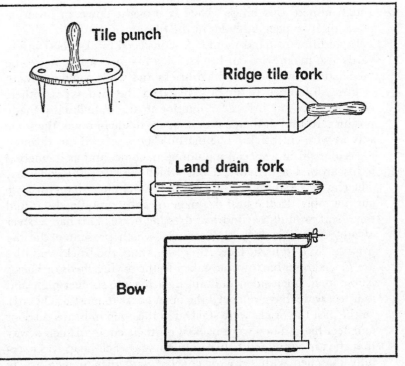

Fig. 36. Brick Making Equipment: II.

moulding, children were expected to supply the moulders with all the clay that they required and ensure that they had a plentiful supply of water and sand.

In addition to making ordinary bricks, the small brickyards specialise in odd shapes that are still required in the modern building industry. For example, some specialise in making round-edged brickettes, others in making pantiles, but for all the specialised bricks and tiles, the process of hand moulding is virtually the same. For making ordinary red roofing tiles, for example, the equipment consists of a mould in which the clay is shaped, and a special type of bow. One side of this has a wire for cutting away superfluous clay, while on the other it has a flat slab of wood for smoothing the surface of the tile. The back of the mould is hinged to a square iron frame which has two prongs some four inches apart. After the tile has been moulded and trimmed, this hinged back is brought down in order to make the two pegging holes in the tile.

In addition to hand-moulded, sand-faced bricks, most brick-yards also make wire-cut bricks. Clay for this variety has to be much stiffer than for moulded bricks and while some say there is little difference in quality between the two types, others consider wire-cut bricks far inferior to the individually made product. Round drainage tiles, too, are made in much the same way as wire-cut bricks. The plastic clay is pressed out through a circular slit in a special moulding machine, and as it emerges it fits around a cylindrical bar which supports the soft clay. The clay sets and the tiles are cut to the right length on the wire cutting table. In the past drainage tiles were moulded flat and then bent around a cylindrical dressing horse. This had a cover of moleskin or in later days canvas which prevented the tile from sticking to its surface. After moulding, the bricks and tiles are placed on a barrow and taken to the drying sheds or hacks. These long, open-sided buildings, each some six feet high and four feet wide, have replaced the open hacks in most brickyards. In the past the bricks were stacked in the open in heaps three or four feet high. They were packed on their edges in such a way that the air circulated between them, and each heap was care-fully thatched with straw or covered with tiles in such a way that they dried gradually without being exposed to the direct rays of the sun. In modern brickyards, however, bricks and tiles are artificially dried in specially heated buildings. Before firing, bricks are generally dressed with a beater to correct any warping or twisting that may have taken place during the first stage of drying.

Although today bricks are burnt in kilns, in the past clamp drying was widely practised. Clamp burning has advantages over kiln burning in that it is possible to burn just as many bricks as are required, whereas a kiln has to be filled completely. In addition clamps can also be built anywhere where bricks are required. K. S. Woods describes how brick clamps are con-structed in a country yard near York.[1] 'A floor of roughly dried bricks with channels for thorn and rough coal. Round it is built a wall of old spoilt bricks called "scovers" to a height of about four and a half feet. These are laid lengthways and across alternately, with a flat surface on the outside of the wall, but leaving space inside into which the green or "raw" bricks to be burnt will fit closely. These are also built lengthways and across alternately to clamp together in layers. Between each layer of bricks is spread a thin layer of slack. Above the surrounding wall the clamp rises stepwise in a dome which is covered in with a shell of scovers.' The principle of clamp burning is somewhat similar to that employed for charcoal burning, for the close packing ensures the exclusion of air. Great care must be taken not to overheat the clamp or the bricks will fall into one shapeless mass.

Nevertheless for many centuries, specially made kilns have been used and there are three broad classes of these. The first group are rectangular kilns with fire walls in the sides. This type has narrow doorways at each end and narrow archways on the sides almost exactly opposite one another. The doorways are bricked up and plastered so as to prevent cold air entering, while the top is covered so as to retain the heat. The second type is the rectangular kiln with arched furnaces running under the floor, while it has numerous holes in the floor to allow heat to ascend. In some districts the circular kiln or cupola with fires in the side walls is widely used. With each group of kiln types there are numerous variations in shapes and design, but the brick maker is concerned with arranging the draughts in such a way that there is the minimum of spoilt products. Both the modern circular down-draught kiln and the continuous and semi-continuous rectangular kiln, each with its chambers and fire-places, are far superior to the traditional up-draught kilns.

The colour of the finished brick not only depends on the raw material available, but also on the amount of firing they receive. Much of the variety of colour in old brick work is due to the unequal heat the bricks received when they were burnt in clamps or up-draught kilns.

2. The Potter

One of the oldest crafts of mankind is that of making pottery, for since the dawn of civilisation wherever there was suitable clay, men used it for decorative as well as for utilitarian objects. Throughout the ages, the techniques of pottery making have not changed in any important detail and the methods adopted at modern studio potteries at the present time differ little from those employed in prehistoric times.

Potteries of old standing are always found near beds of local clay, for the difficulty of transporting such heavy and bulky material determined their site. In Wales, for example, the potteries at Ewenni near Bridgend, at Rumney near Cardiff and at Buckley in Flintshire came into existence due to the availability of clay. A second pre-requisite is fuel to fire the kilns, for although today electrically fired kilns are found in almost every pottery, in the past it was an advantage for the potter to site his workshops within easy reach of coal supply. Nevertheless, the availability of coal was less important than the availability of clay. In Devon, for example, the famous Barum ware of Barnstaple was produced in a district far removed from the nearest coal deposits, as were the potteries at Poole in Dorset, at Hailsham in Sussex and Weatheriggs in Cumberland. Although a large number of old-established potteries still exist, the new demand for hand-made earthenware has led to the establishment of a vast number of studio potteries in all parts of Britain, particularly in those districts that are centres of the tourist trade. The craft is perhaps more flourishing than it has ever been and although many of the craftsmen produce goods of excellent quality and design, the market has also been flooded by vast quantities of inferior material.

The methods adopted by potters are simple, for the art of the potter arises in his ability to treat and shape clay rather than on any elaborate pieces of equipment and tools. The preparation of the clay is extremely important, for it must be smooth and of the same consistency throughout. Great care must be taken in the choice of clay, too, for in some districts such as the Vale of Glamorgan, the local clay contains limestone which tends to act as a flux when the pottery is fired, and for this reason the raw material has to be washed thoroughly before it can be used. Clay is dug in the autumn before the winter rains set in, making the clay beds impossibly waterlogged. The methods of weathering and pugging have already been described in the previous section, indeed pottery can be made from the clay from any brickyard, provided that it can be made into 'slip', the name given to it when mixed with water to a creamy, smooth consistency. This is usually passed through a silk gauze, the water squeezed out leaving it stiff enough to be shaped into balls and thrown on the wheel. For heavy, large pots the clay has to be considerably stiffer than for small pots so as to prevent them from sagging with their own weight before they are dry enough for firing.

The potter's ability as an artist and craftsman is exhibited most clearly in the age-old task of throwing, for the potter must make sure that the pots are strong yet light, and he must allow for shrinkage in firing. The potter's wheel, which in itself is a very ancient piece of equipment, consists of a revolving wheel driven by foot or electric power. It must be heavy enough to revolve steadily and to ensure that the pots are symmetrical it must balance accurately. The thrower sits on a seat fixed to the framework of the wheel, while at the top is a tray containing the prepared balls of clay. After pressing or 'wedging', to get rid of air holes, the ball is thrown with considerable force on to the revolving disc. Wetting his hands at frequent intervals the spinning mass is shaped into a tall cone, flattened, raised and shaped with fingers and thumb. Gradually the wall is thinned, the height is checked with a home-made gauge and the pot is removed from the wheel with the help of a wire cutter. It is then placed on a board, ready to be taken to the drying racks. At this stage the pots are described as 'green' and after drying under artificial heat or in the open air they are trimmed with a scraper as they revolve on the potter's wheel and all the marks are removed with a wet sponge. Before they can be fired, however, they have to dry out thoroughly and evenly.

Other methods of making pots are practised in some country workshops, the most common being the semi-automatic process of jollying. It is particularly useful when large quantities of the same product are required. The jigger and jolly machine consists of a plaster cast of the inside of a pot firmly pegged to the revolving surface of the potter's wheel. A cast of the outside of the pot is made and this is carefully shaped to a metal template fixed to a movable spring arm or spreader of the machine.

While the revolving plaster cast ensures the correct shape for the inside of the pot, the spreader and its template shapes the outside. Once again they have to be turned, that is with a metal strike and wet sponge, they have to be cleaned on the potter's wheel. For objects of an irregular shape, plaster moulds are used and the casts can be used time and time again to produce objects that are exactly the same in all details.

Green pots have to be thoroughly dried, preferably under natural conditions before they can be fired. If they contain the slightest amount of moisture, they may explode under the terrific heat of the kiln. The correct firing of pottery needs a great deal of skill, for the quality of the finished product depends as much on correct firing and keen judgement as it does on skilful throwing. The old type of kiln which may be coal, gas or wood fired, has to be carefully filled with the saggars containing green or glazed pottery. The saggars themselves are large round or rectangular containers of coarse pottery, often made of clay and pieces of broken crockery. The heat of the kiln is raised to a very high temperature, then allowed to cool before the pots are removed.

Pottery is fired either once or twice according to the nature of the clay and the use to which the pottery is to be put. Unglazed ware and stoneware is fired once only and the products are known as 'biscuit' whilst most glazed ware has to be fired twice. The glaze is applied after the first firing and in the second firing it is fused with the body of the pot. Great care has to be taken in stacking glazed pottery in the kiln for no two pots must touch, while in order to see what is happening inside a burning kiln removable bricks are built into the kiln wall. Within sight inside these small peep holes are placed small glazed, fireclay cones. When their tips begin to bend over, the potter knows that the glaze is fusing and that the heat must be reduced.

3. The Stone Mason

In the past, the stone mason and the quarryman who supplied him with his raw material were vital country craftsmen in almost every district. Today, with the advent of other, simpler building materials, he is a rarity except in those districts such as the Cotswolds where the local stone is still used for building. Every type of stone has its own characteristics and in the past the methods of shaping and dressing the different types varied very greatly from district to district. The hard Cornish granite, for example, had to be dressed with the heavy scabbling hammer and tooled with chisels, while the softer Bath stone could be sawn with a hand saw and dressed with combs. In Purbeck, again, the stone could only be cut with wedges and hammer, and it took considerable knowledge and skill to know exactly where splitting was possible.

The art of dressing stone is a very old one, for the Romans were well versed in all the techniques of stone cutting. With their departure from Britain the techniques fell into decay but by the seventh century A.D. the oolitic limestone of the Cotswolds was being worked, while after the Norman Conquest the inhabitants of all parts of Britain were well versed in the techniques of quarrying and stone dressing. Nevertheless, domestic buildings in stone were relatively rare in the Middle Ages.[2] 'Even the houses of noblemen were usually built of timber, wattle, plaster and thatch. But the predominance of timber, for constructional purposes in no way diminished the scale of those buildings designed to be of stone such as castles, churches, cathedrals, city walls and a few other constructions.' By the fourteenth century A.D. the mason had become a vitally important craftsman, for the master mason was almost equivalent to the modern architect, designing and supervising the erection of buildings. Under him worked a number of freemasons who were 'qualified to carve freestone or fine grained sandstone and limestone. . . . In his work there were many possibilities for individual artistry'.[3] With the freemasons worked the rough masons who carried out the less skilled operations of dressing stones, while under them were gangs of labourers who were expected to carry and heave.

The art of building in stone is one that demands great skill, for unlike the bricklayer who uses uniform blocks, the mason deals with irregular shapes of many different sizes. Since there is such a variation in dressing stone as well as in the method of arranging dressed stone in buildings, in this section some of

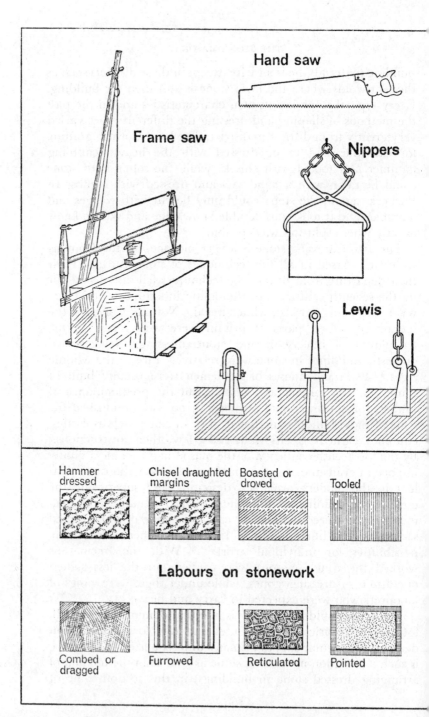

Fig. 37. The Stone Mason's Tools and Equipment: I.

the terms used in masonry will be given, for it would be impossible to describe in detail all the variations of work carried out by traditional stone masons. The principal terms in stone dressing are:

Scabbling. Taking off the irregular angles of the stone with a hammer. This is usually done at the quarry and the stone is then said to be quarry pitched or hammer faced.

Chisel-draughted margin. To ensure good fitting joints in hammer faced stones a smooth surface about one inch wide is cut with a chisel.

Rubbed work. To make stones as smooth as possible a piece of harder stone with sand and water is rubbed on.

Polishing. Granite and marble, in particular, are polished by rubbing turpentine, beeswax or putty applied with a soft flannel.

Droved work. This consists of making a number of parallel chisel marks across a stone with the boaster. The marks are not kept in continuous rows over the surface of the stone.

Tooled work. In this case the boaster marks over the surface of a stone are kept parallel and in a continuous line. Again a two-and-a-half-inch boaster is used.

Furrowed work. This consists of tooling a number of grooves in the surface of a stone and also cutting a deep margin along its edges.

Dragged work. By using a comb on soft stone, irregularities are removed. The comb is drawn over the surface of the stone in all directions until it is smooth.

Pointed work. The surface of the stone is worked to a smooth surface by means of a pointed punch.

In addition to these dressing processes, there are many others which are less common, such as vermiculated work with a number of irregularly shaped channels cut into the surface of the stone.

The methods of building are equally varied as are the terms used in designating particular sections of walling. The following are examples of those more commonly used.

Bond. The method of arranging each stone so that it laps over the stones with which it is in contact above and below it.

Through stones. Stones which extend through the entire thickness of a wall to tie or bond it.

Headers. Stones laid across a wall for some three-quarters of its thickness in order to bond it.

Grout. The mortar poured over the stones to bring them level or to fill in spaces between stones or in the heart of a wall.

Quoins. In rough rubble walls, quoins are pieces of large carefully shaped stones inserted to give it strength.

Apex stone. The highest stone of a gable end of a building.

Lacing course. Owing to absence of bond in flint walls similar to those of East Anglia, courses of bricks are inserted at intervals to give the wall strength.

Ashlar. Stones that are carefully dressed and usually over · twelve inches in depth.

TOOLS

The mason's tools have not changed in any important detail since medieval times; indeed, the hammer, square and plumb bob, which are the symbols of his trade, are three tools that go back to prehistoric times. In Ancient Egypt, for example, stone was shaped with stone hammers and finished with copper chisels, while about the only hand tool that became common in post-medieval times was the spirit level, invented in the seventeenth century as a replacement for the clumsy prehistoric water-table. The tools and equipment of a modern mason may be divided into five distinct classes.

    (a) Hammers and Mallets.
    (b) Setting out tools.
    (c) Cutting tools.

(d) Saws.
(e) Hoisting equipment.

(a) *Hammers and Mallets*

Mallet. The mason's beechwood mallet, with a head varying in diameter from six inches to eight inches is in the form of a truncated cone with a handle. It is used for shaping stone in conjunction with the flat, mallet-headed chisels and boasters.

Dummy. This is a smaller version of the mallet and is mainly used in conjunction with chisels for carving. In the past they were always made of beech, but in more recent times metal-headed dummies became popular. These have heads up to four pounds in weight.

Iron hammer. The older type of dressing hammer has a head similar in shape to a carpenter's mallet. They weigh four pounds or more and they usually have handles some eight inches long. This type of hammer is usually used for carved work.

Waller's hammer. This sledge hammer has one square flat face and a straight or cross pein head for roughly squaring stones, mainly in rubble work.

Mash hammer. This is a heavy, stone-handled hammer with round faces used on hammer-headed chisels for dressing stone.

Pick. This has a long head, pointed at both ends, used for the rough dressing of hard stone such as granite. It weighs sixteen pounds or more.

Axe. This has a head weighing some twelve pounds in the shape of a double wedge and is mainly used for the final dressing or decorating granite or some other hard stone.

Spalling hammer. A heavy sledge hammer with two square or rectangular faces for the rough dressing of stones.

Scabbling hammer. A heavy sledge hammer with one square face and pointed pein is used for the rough dressing of hard stones.

(b) *Setting Out Tools*

Square. Made of iron and often graduated along both arms. It is set to an angle of ninety degrees and each arm is eighteen inches or more in length.

Set Square. A triangular iron square set to an angle of forty-five degrees or some other fixed angle as required.

Bevel. Consists of two metal blades slotted and fastened with a thumb screw. The bevel is essential for marking out work and measuring angles.

Spirit level. A seventeenth-century invention of great delicacy. The mason's spirit level is at least eighteen inches long.

Plumb rule. This consists of a wooden slat some thirty-six inches long which is used as a straight edge, while a plumb bob is supported from the top and hangs in a hole near the bottom of the rule. This, like the ordinary plumb bob, a tool known in prehistoric times is used to test verticality.

Compasses. Used for marking the ever recurring arcs and circles in the mason's work.

(c) *Cutting Tools*

The mason's chisels are divided into two distinct classes. Firstly those for use with hammers which have their striking ends made small to lessen the amount of burr. Secondly there are mallet-headed chisels with broad striking ends to avoid injuring the wooden mallet or dummy.

Punch. A hammer-headed tool with a cutting edge one-quarter of an inch or less for rough dressing.

Point. Has an edge similar to a punch but is used with the mallet for dressing hard stone.

Hammer-headed chisels. These have heads one-quarter inch to one-and-a-quarter inches wide for dressing stones, but not for smoothing or tooling.

Boaster or Bolster. A mallet-headed chisel one-and-a-half inches or more wide for tooling surfaces.

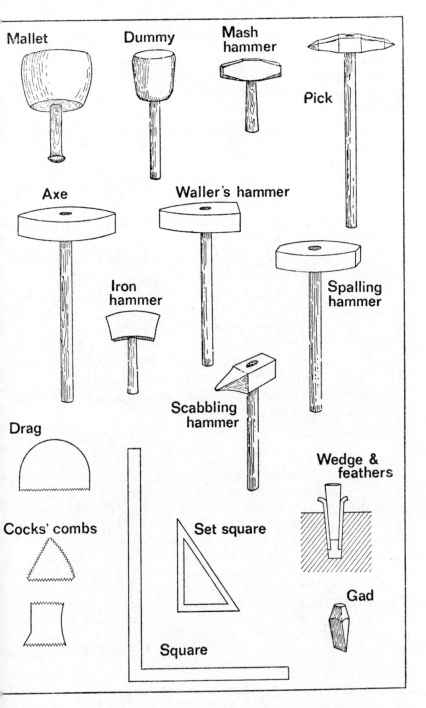

Fig. 38. The Stone Mason's Tools and Equipment: II.

Claw bolster. Has an edge with a number of teeth from one-eighth of an inch to three-eighths of an inch wide and is used for dressing the surface of granite or some other hard stone after the point or punch has been used.

Pitching tool. A hammer-headed tool with a thick point similar in general outline to the boaster. It is used with the hammer for reducing stone.

Wooden-handled chisel. Used in conjunction with a mallet for shaping soft stone such as Bath stone.

Drag. A piece of steel with a saw edge for reducing the surface of soft stones to a uniform level.

Cocks' combs. Specially shaped drags, triangular, round or some other shape for moulded work in soft stone.

Wedge and Feathers. To sever hard stones such as granite, the flat edge of a special plumb known as a 'jumper' is hammered into the stone to bore holes along a specific line. A pair of curved steel feathers are then inserted into each hole and a conical wedge is hammered in between the feathers, driving them apart and splitting the stone.

Gads. These are small iron wedges inserted into holes made with the pick, for splitting soft stone.

(d) *Saws*

Saws may be used to cut up stone, particularly the softer variety. Although today power saws are used for stone cutting, in the past a number of hand saws and a number of ingenious devices for their operation were widely used. For Bath stone and stones of a similar nature a hand saw, similar to a carpenter's rip saw was used while the cross-cut double-handled saw with a blade five feet or six feet long was equally well known. For cutting large blocks of stone, however, the frame saw attached to a system of pulleys was used. The blade was one-tenth of an inch thick and four inches wide and the cutting action was assisted by coarse sand and water. With the help of the pulleys which gave the saw the required amount of vertical play, it could be operated by one man.

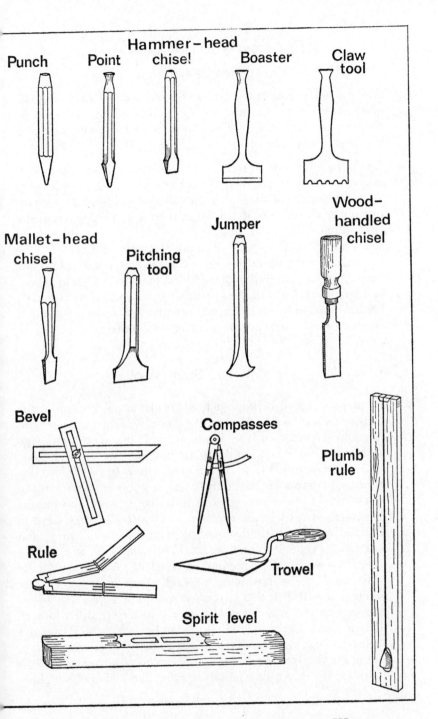

Fig. 39. The Stone Mason's Tools and Equipment: III.

(e) *Hoisting Equipment*

Nippers. These consist of two curved and pointed arms rotating on a pivot and fitting into notches cut in the sides of stones. As the nippers are raised by block and tackle the points bite into the stone and it can be lifted with ease.

Lewis. In cases where stones are too heavy to be lifted with nippers, a hole is bored in the surface of a stone and lewises, an arrangement of dovetailed metal blocks, inserted. A chain can be attached to an iron loop at the top of the lewis and the stone lifted.

In addition to these tools and elaborate equipment, the mason, of course, needs trowels of various sizes and shapes. They vary from the large diamond-bladed mortar-spreading trowel to a small, similarly shaped pointing trowel and a rectangular-bladed margin trowel. He also requires a series of straight edges and hods for carrying mortar and cement.

4. The Dry Stone Waller

In many parts of Britain such as the Dales of Yorkshire, the Cotswolds and North Wales, dry stone walls are a very conspicuous element in the landscape. A hundred years ago agricultural writers were complaining that efficient dry stone wallers were difficult to find; today they have almost disappeared completely and only a few are able to carry out the work apart from repairing existing walls. Although no mortar or cement is used in the erection of these walls, they have to be solid enough to withstand the strong force of winds and storms on exposed upland farms. The waller's art arises in his ability to work with irregular material of many sizes, for he must size up the possibility of each stone knowing exactly whether it will fit into a particular gap. The true stone waller does not cut his raw material to size if he can possibly help it. This is particularly true in Wales and the North of England where the native stone is hard and difficult to cleave cleanly, but in the Cotswolds where the stone is softer, the heavy waller's hammer is often used. This is a short-handled tool weighing some ten pounds with two cutting edges. One edge is very sharp and is used to cut the stone, while the blunter edge is used to crack the stone to the requisite shape.

The first task in building a stone wall is to mark out its base line with pegs or string. A shallow trench is then cut and the stones are carried in heaps on both sides of the trench and as near as possible to it. A wooden frame corresponding to the exact shape of the wall to be built is inserted firmly in the ground and another with plumb bob attached some distance away from it. Lengths of string which will act as a guide in building are strained between the two frames and the task of building begins by laying the foundation stones. These are the

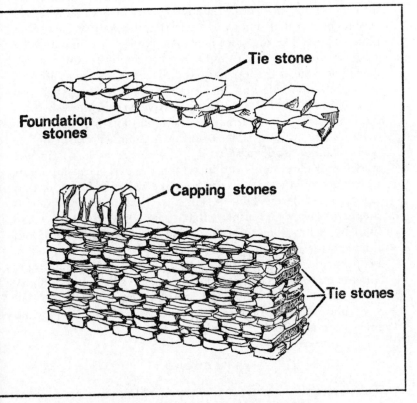

Fig. 40. The Method of Dry Stone Walling.

larger, more regular stones, and are laid in such a way so as to provide a solid basis for the wall. The width may be as much as thirty inches at the base and particular care has to be taken in laying the corner piece or 'scuncheon' at the corner of a gateway. A large, carefully dressed boulder is laid at the corner and this must be strong enough to carry the bottom hinge of a gate.

After the base has been laid, in some districts a line of tie stones, with the stones laid lengthways in the form of a bond is inserted, but in others the wall is built up to half its height before the tie stones are inserted. In good-quality stone walls, the raw material is laid in such a way that each stone is slightly inclined downwards from the centre. This inclination causes rain which may have found its way through the wall to be thrown off to the sides. In addition to large stones, small pebbles of irregular shape are inserted in the body of the wall to fill all spaces. The top is levelled with large, flat stones and the coping is completed by using pointed or gently rounded stones placed on edge at the top of the wall. Heavy copestones are laid at regular intervals and the thinner stones wedged between them. Finally small stones are firmly wedged in the wall with the hammer wherever room can be found for them.

Dry stone walling is by tradition a summer craft, for the waller cannot work in wet or cold weather as handling wet stones with bare hands is difficult. In the past, farm labourers were often competent to carry out the work. It is a task that demands a different kind of skill from that of masonry, for as Stephens says, 'We suspect that many dry stone dykes are built by ordinary masons who being accustomed to the use of lime mortar are not acquainted with the proper method of bedding down stones in a dry dyke as firmly as they should be, and are therefore unfitted to build such a dyke. A builder of dry stone dykes should be trained to the business, and with skill will build substantial dykes at a moderate cost which will stand erect for many years'.[4]

5. The Slater

The attractive character of domestic buildings in Britain is due in no small measure to the craftsman who slated or tiled the roofs. Slating is a craft that not only demands considerable skill in the positioning and nailing of slates, but it also demands considerable knowledge of roof geometry. Knowing exactly how to cover a roof economically, taking into account the awkward angles of dormers and valleys, needs both training and experience.

In the past, slating was a specialised occupation, though in some districts such as the Cotswolds, the slatters as they were called, combined roofing in the summer with whitewashing and plastering.

Roofing slates are usually dressed in the quarry by specialised 'strikers' or 'knappers'. After repeated splitting along the bedding planes, the slates are shaped ready for use. Good roofing slates should be hard, yet fine, their grain should run the whole length of the slate; they should cut easily without splintering or becoming jagged at the edges. In some districts, notably the Pennines and North Wales, greater care is taken in trimming slates than in such districts as the Cotswolds. The Cotswold slatter is quite prepared to place slate fragments called 'gallets' beneath broken slates and to fill any gaps in the roof with gallets. This in itself is a task that demands considerable skill, though it has been said that Cotswold slating is similar to dry stone walling on account of its relative crudity and necessity of packing.

In the past, slate quarries were common in many parts of the country, particularly in the north and west and though the advent of other roofing materials has meant the disappearance of many quarries, a certain amount of demand still exists. The principal types of slate are the following:

Wales. Bangor slates – colours range from blue to purple.
Dinorwig slates – colour range includes blue, green, grey, red and green mottled.
Penrhyn slates – colours include blue, grey, red and grey mottled.
Ffestiniog slates – blue grey in colour.
Prescelly slates – rougher and thicker than North Wales slates. Usually grey or grey-green.

Cornwall. The important slate quarry in Cornwall is Delabole which produces durable slates of grey, grey-green and reddish tints.

Westmorland. These are considered to be of excellent quality and the colour varies from a light grey to deep olive green. They are rough in texture.

Burlington slates from north Lancashire, of igneous origins are rough and stout and are of excellent durable quality.

Scotland. Scotland possesses a large number of slate quarries, particularly along the Great Glen Fault. They are usually dark blue or grey, while those of Banff and Aberdeen are dark grey.

In addition to the slates proper, in lowland England there are the so-called 'stone slates'. These differ from slates in their mode of splitting, for whereas slates split along lines of cleavage at angles to the bedding planes, stone slates, which range in character from limestone to true sandstone, split along lines that are parallel to the bedding plane. The following are the principal stone slates:

> Horsham stone – a flaggy sandstone from the Weald clay used throughout south-east England.
> Collyweston slate – occurs in limestone from Oxfordshire to Lincolnshire, the best quality occurring in Northamptonshire and East Leicestershire.
> Stonefield slate – occurs at the base of the limestone from Dorset to Gloucestershire and Oxfordshire. It is quarried in blocks and often split by frost action.
> Elland flags – carboniferous slates that occur in west Yorkshire, east Lancashire (Rochdale flags), Derbyshire (Wingfield flags) and north Staffordshire (Alton rock).
> Rough Rim flags – occur near Halifax and Huddersfield.
> Yorkdale and Pendleside slates – these sandstone slates occur widely throughout northern England but quarrying, as in Wensleydale, has always been on a small scale.

Slaters know the different qualities and sizes of slates by specific names, many of which are picturesque names handed down over the centuries. The Cheshire slater, for example, had his 'Haughattees' and 'Widetts', his 'Jenny why gettest thou' and 'Rogue why winkest thou'. Bangor slates are still sold

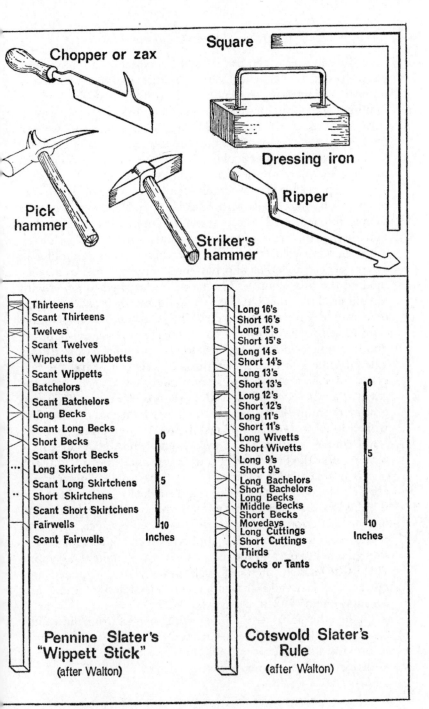

Fig. 41. The Slater's Tools.

according to size which are named 'Duchesses' and 'Viscountesses', 'Broad Ladies' and 'Narrow Ladies' together with many other names referring to female rank. In the Cotswolds and the Pennines the old names have persisted and slates are measured with 'slat rules' or 'wippett sticks'. These have no written measurements of any kind but the carved symbols on their surface designate a particular size of slate which will have its own specific place on the roof of a house (Fig. 41).

The appearance of roofs varies greatly from one district to the other. Cotswolds roofs with dormers and valleys are very steeply pitched, while those of the Pennines with stone gutters and absence of dormers are very gently sloping.

In the Cotswolds the roof framework consists of stout oak rafters pegged together and battened with split oak to accommodate the slate courses. The laths are fastened to agree with the material that the slatter has on hand and their exact position is measured with the slate rule. The 'Cussome' or under-eave slate is bedded in mortar directly on the wall of the building and it is tailed under the first batten to prevent it from tilting. The cussome is nearly horizontal and between it and the first course of slats a number of stone wedges are placed, with the result that the edge of the roof is slightly concave. The slates gradually diminish in size as one goes towards the ridge, but while stone wedges are placed between the rafters and the lower courses to support the extra weight, no wedges at all are present after the first three or four courses have been laid. Each one is fastened with either an oak peg or nail. The ridge or cresting is separately sorted out and stacked at the quarry and it is bedded in mortar and jointed and pointed together with one or two courses immediately below. The eaves are either pointed or a mortar coping is applied over the slates that project some six inches beyond the line of the walls. Unlike the Pennine slater who makes valleys of overlapping slates, arranged as a gutter, the Cotswold craftsman cuts his slates to shape and arranges them to produce a swept valley.

Finally the joints are pointed with mortar from the inside. In the past, however, the insides were often stuffed with moss to provide a weatherproof roof, and mossing was recognised as a distinct trade in the eighteenth century.

VI

Textile Crafts

1. The Wool Worker

THE CRAFT OF SPINNING wool and weaving cloth was, at least until the end of the nineteenth century, the most important of all rural industries. It was certainly the most widespread and almost every rural locality had its carders, spinners, weavers and fullers responsible in the main for meeting a regional or local demand for cloth, blankets and knitting yarn. Many of the craftsmen concerned with producing these essentials of life were domestic workers who practised their trade in their own homes. Some, however, worked in factories, for textile mills, especially fulling mills utilising water power, were known in rural Britain from the Middle Ages.

In many parts of the country, the manufacture of cloth went beyond the stage of supplying local, self-sufficient rural communities with essential textiles, for in those areas the textile crafts developed into industries of major importance. Many of those huge industrial undertakings developed from the small workshops of the craftsmen-weavers or craftsmen-fullers and the history of many a well-known firm can be traced back to the simple workshop of a hand craftsman. Although today the woollen trade is dominated by the large-scale, highly mechanised production unit, with a highly developed system of specialisation and division of labour, the processes of textile production themselves have changed surprisingly little; it is merely the tempo of manufacturing that has quickened. Thus, for example, the high-speed, multi-shuttled modern loom does exactly the same work of intertwining warp and weft as the warp-weighted loom of prehistoric times, while the modern carding engine with its complex of revolving rollers does exactly the same work of disentangling and combing wool fibres as the primitive teasel. There is, nevertheless, a vast difference between the large textile mills of Yorkshire and Gloucestershire and the truly rural mills as found, for example, in parts of Wales and Devon. In most country mills all the processes of textile manufacture were concentrated in one building and the highly specialised dye works and spinning mills of industrial Britain were a rarity in the rural districts.

An example of a truly rural industry is provided by the industry in Wales, where textile manufacturing on a greatly reduced scale still persists in a rural setting. The history of the industry may be traced back to prehistoric times, but within the last fifty years it has declined to such an extent that there are fewer factories in production today than at any other time.

In the Middle Ages, woollen manufacture was particularly important in the county of Pembroke, where natives and Flemish immigrants spun yarn and wove cloth in their cottage and farmhouse homes. At that time cloth manufacturing was little more than a domestic activity, and the people of Pembrokeshire worked the wool of local sheep to provide themselves with blankets and rugs, tweeds and flannels. Occasionally there was a surplus that could be sold at one of the many local fairs, or taken by ship from the nearest creek or bay to Bristol. From Bristol, Welsh cloth was re-exported at considerable profit by the traders, to Gascony and Brittany, to Portugal and Iceland. Although Pembrokeshire cloth was an important item of trade, its quality was not high; it was thick, rough and drab, being designed for hard wear rather than appearance. Indeed it was so bad that it was given to the poor people of English cities on Ash Wednesday.

By the end of the sixteenth century, the demand for Pembrokeshire cloth had fallen off to such an extent that the industry itself almost completely disappeared from the county. But as cloth making in West Wales declined, that of Montgomeryshire, Merioneth and Denbighshire grew very rapidly.

By the middle of the eighteenth century, Montgomeryshire in particular had attained pre-eminence as an important centre of flannel manufacture. Towns and villages such as Llanidloes, Newtown and Llanbrynmair, were almost entirely dependent on textiles. In the west of the county, farm labourers were hired at the November fairs as much for their weaving capabilities as for their knowledge of farming. A farm servant was expected to work in the fields during the summer months, but at the loom in the weaving shed in the winter. The products were, until the end of the eighteenth century, sold at the Shrewsbury market, and until that period, flannel making in Powys remained an industry of the scattered homesteads, bringing in extra income to supplement the meagre returns of farming.

After 1790, however, Newtown, the old borough of Llanfair yng Nghedewain, became one of the most important manu- facturing centres in Wales. Indeed it became so important that travellers to the district described it as the Leeds of Wales. A building which is now the town cinema was erected in 1832 as the flannel exchange for the county, and in this imposing build- ing weavers met drapers from Liverpool and Shrewsbury, London and Manchester at the weekly market. A canal to take flannel to England was constructed in 1821, and a cargo could be sent from Newtown directly to Manchester at the cost of two shillings and eleven pence per hundredweight. The population of Newtown went up by leaps and bounds. It drew immigrants from Yorkshire and Lancashire, the Leaches and the Corfields and many others, to work in one of the 82 weaving factories and 35 spinning mills. Welsh flannel was cheap, it was known throughout the world and was worn by the Duke of Welling- ton's army as well as the slaves of North America. Even today, the tall three- or four-storeyed dwellings in Newtown and Llanidloes bear witness to the importance of flannel in the history of Montgomeryshire. A weaving factory, occupying the third and fourth floors of a building, stretched over a number of cottage dwellings, and it could be entered by an outside stair- case at the back of the terrace. A factory of this kind could accommodate anything up to forty looms. In many cases the owner of a weaving factory was also the owner of a shop at the end of the row, and when applying for work, weavers were always asked the size of their families: the larger the family the better were the chances of obtaining the work. At the end of the week the weavers were paid an average wage of eleven shillings for a six-day week and the master would keep an appreciable proportion of this wage in payment for the goods bought at his stores during the week.

Montgomeryshire could have developed into one of the most important textile manufacturing districts in Britain if the road, railway and canal had not led eastwards, almost to the heart of the Lancashire textile industry. If coal supplies had been nearer, if marketing facilities could have been bettered, then Newtown could truly have lived up to its name of 'the Leeds of Wales'. As it was, as soon as power looms came in, Montgomeryshire manufacturers made a mistake from which the industry never recovered. They attempted to compete with the textile manufacturers of Lancashire and Yorkshire on their own terms, with the result that there was very little to distinguish Montgomeryshire flannel from Rochdale imitations. By 1860, the industry was in difficulty; bankruptcy was rife, unemployment was common, but in the 1870's there was a slight revival, with the foundation of the first mail-order business in the world at Newtown. Pryce Jones established the Royal Welsh Warehouse on the products of the two flannel mills that he owned, but very soon he found that it was far cheaper for him to buy 'real Welch flannel' made in Rochdale. By 1900, the Montgomeryshire woollen industry was almost completely dead, and Newtown once again reverted to being a small market town.

Woollen manufacturing was widely practised in all parts of Wales but the Teifi Valley in west Wales attained eminence as the new centre of the weaving industry in the late nineteenth century and here it remains as one of the last strongholds. By 1895 the counties of Cardigan, Carmarthen and Pembroke had 325 woollen mills and the whole life of villages like Drefach-Felindre, Pentrecwrt and Llandysul revolved around the factory and the production of flannel shirts, underwear and blankets for the ever-growing industrial districts of south Wales. By 1900 the village of Drefach-Felindre alone had 52 mills in full production.

The golden era lasted until the end of the First World War, but by 1920 the seeds of depression were already bearing fruit, and there followed a period of great difficulty. Government surplus stock of flannel and blankets was thrown on the open market and at ridiculously low prices, so that the woollen manufacturers were forced to meet this unfair competition by cutting their costs and prices. The wages of the workers were cut and hundreds were dismissed in the losing battle of making ends meet. Since 1920, the story of the Welsh woollen industry has been one of contraction, with the number of mills decreasing from 250 in 1926 to 81 in 1947 and to 27 in 1973.

Within the last twenty years, the position has got steadily worse with even the large and modernised mills going out of production. Although the market for Welsh textiles has been extended considerably, particularly with the introduction of double weave tapestry bedcovers, furnishing fabrics and light flannels, the number of craftsmen supplying that demand has decreased greatly.

Before raw wool can be spun into thread, it must be thoroughly cleaned and sorted into qualities. This is a task that demands experience and skill, for not only are fleeces variable in quality, but a single fleece may provide as many as ten different grades. These may range from the fine wool of the back and neck to the coarse 'britch' from the animal's legs which is usually sold for carpeting. The long-stapled wool is reserved for making finer cloths such as worsted, while 'tailings' from the sheep's tails may be sent directly to the saddler for stuffing collars.

In the Middle Ages, sorted wool was washed in lye, while in later days the favourite washing agent was a solution of three parts water and one part urine. Grease, dirt and salts were removed in this way. In many parts of the country, too, the clean wool was placed in large baskets in a stream, the baskets being anchored to the bank so that the wool and all traces of lye or urine were rinsed away by the running water. The wool was then dried on boards or on a hurdle or framework of cords and beaten thoroughly with sticks to open the texture.

Since the eighteenth century, however, a special piece of machinery has been installed in rural factories to carry out this disentangling of raw wool. This machine, which works on the same principle as a barn threshing drum, is known by a variety of names. In some parts of the country it is known as a 'devil', in Wales it is known as a 'willy' or 'willow', while in others it is called a 'tucker' or 'wool mill'. This machine, which may still be seen in constant use in some of the smaller Welsh factories, is not only used to open the close matting of the wool, but it is also used to mix different qualities or colours of wool together. For example, to produce grey, a common colour for many Welsh bed covers, black and white wool are placed together in the willy. The machine, which is usually water driven, consists of a large drum some thirty-four inches in diameter and twenty-four inches wide encased in a wooden box. The drum is covered with rows of iron spikes, each some two inches long. The wool is placed on a canvas table at the front and is drawn into the body of the machine by a pair of small revolving rollers. The thoroughly mixed and disentangled wool may be collected with a comb at the back end of the machine.

When coloured wool is required, dyeing takes place either before or after willying, depending on the craftsman's preferences, and the traditional method of dyeing was to boil the raw wool for some time in a large copper boiler. In the past, vegetable dyes collected from the fields and hedgerows were the only dyeing materials available to the country craftsmen, but for the last sixty years or more most factories have depended entirely on chemical dyes. Nevertheless, the boiling method of imparting dye to the fibre has continued to be practised.

After the willying, comes the real process of disentangling the locks of wool, separating fibre from fibre with the object of producing a thoroughly mixed uniform web of fibres, from which the foundation of the thread is built. This is the carding process and a large number of expedients to ease this work have been used by craftsmen. The simplest is to use teasel or even the heads of thistles to do the work, and in the past teasels were specially grown for wool combing in some parts of the country such as Dorset and Somerset. Teasels are still used to raise the naps of cloths and the harvesting of teasel by women in July and August was quite important in those districts until recently.[1]

By far the most common method of hand carding in Britain was to use carding boards. Each board consists of a handled, metal-covered card each measuring some nine inches by six inches. Cards are always used in pairs and a small quantity of wool is placed on one card and worked 'by pulling it apart gently with the teeth of the other. After a time the wool becomes evenly distributed among the teeth of the two cards; one card is then moved in the reverse direction and so collects the whole of the wool which is released as a spongy roll'.[2]

For making worsted and fine cloth where long-stapled wool is required, carders cannot be used and long-toothed combs are employed. Each comb has two or three lines of teeth, each row some nine inches long, attached at right angles to a wooden handle. The teeth are kept very sharp and straight, a metal pipe being often used to straighten irregularities. To comb a quantity of wool a pair of combs is heated on a stove and the mass of wool is transferred from one comb to the other until nothing remains but long parallel fibres. The shorter fibres which cannot be used for making worsted remain on the combs.[3]

The old method of bowing regarded as an alternative to carding and combing was done by plucking the string or gut of a bow so that the rapid vibrations disentangled the wool placed on a bench below. Nevertheless, despite persistence of hand methods of carding and combing in the wool textile trade, mechanical devices for arranging fibres have been well known for centuries. The simplest is the carding bench consisting of a table some sixty inches long and thirty inches wide equipped with a surface of card brushing. The wool was dragged against this and removed with a comb; the whole process resembling that of flax retting. A carding machine was patented as early as 1748 and, although that machine was in itself unsuccessful, developments of it became universal in country woollen mills in the first half of the nineteenth century. Early carding engines produced thick rolls of carded fibre which could be more easily drawn out and twisted into yarn. The thick strands had to be pieced together by hand, a job usually undertaken by young children who with bloody hands were employed on piecing in woollen mills from dawn to dusk. A later development was the addition of a piecing machine which delivered continuous slubbings of wool and wound them on bobbins. The familiar condenser carder found in all country mills at the present time was introduced *circa* 1850. It reduced the carded fibres to such a size that they could be spun immediately so that the intermediate process of piecing was unnecessary.

For countless centuries the process of spinning was undertaken by women as a domestic occupation, the only equipment required being a spinning wheel. An account of life in rural Denbighshire[4] in the middle of the last century gives a vivid account of the method of spinning. 'First of all there was a small three-legged bench about two feet high; in the centre of this bench was set a stick also about two feet high, with a small coil or bobbin at its end. The wheel itself was like the wheel of a vehicle with this difference, that the spinning wheel was very lightly built. The rim was some six inches wide and an eighth of an inch thick. At the end of the bench was another post or stick with a forked end and a hole bored through. The whorl was placed in the fork and the spindle was then pushed through the hole and the whorl. A strap or belt plaited from the woollen yarn was run around the wheel and the whorl and the wheel was turned by placing the finger between the threads. Since the wheel's diameter was three feet or more and that of the whorl only an inch and a half, the revolution of the spindle was very rapid. The end of the coil was tied to the spindle and the weaver (i.e. spinner) began work by giving the wheel a quick turn with one hand, while holding the coil in the other. . . .'

Spinning remained a domestic industry for as long as the spinning wheel remained the only piece of equipment to do the work, but by the end of the eighteenth century spinning machines, firstly the jenny and then the spinning billy and jack had been introduced into the Welsh woollen industry. This meant that factories and water power were required to accommodate them. In the last decade of the century therefore, the spinning factory became common in woollen manufacturing districts such as Montgomeryshire, Merioneth and Denbighshire.

The spinning jenny, originally invented for the cotton industry, could spin a number of threads simultaneously and although it was manually driven, it took up a great deal of space

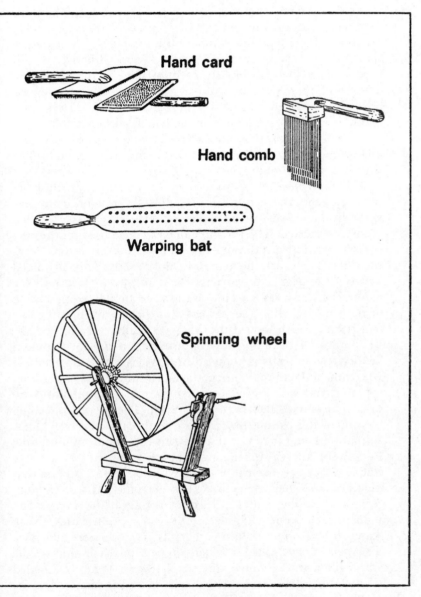

Fig. 42. The Wool Worker's Equipment.

and had to be accommodated in a special building. The slubbing jack, with its complex of moving parts, carried some forty spindles. The billy, a development from the jack, carried more spindles and was driven by water power, although it still depended on the spinner's strength for some of the operation. The hand mule, which again depended on the spinner for assistance, was introduced in the early 1800's; it was soon followed by the self-acting mule which automatically performed all the operations and relieved the spinner of every duty except supplying the carded rovings, the piecing of broken threads and the doffing of the spun yarn.

Weaving, however, continued to be a handicraft until the middle of the nineteenth century; indeed the hand loom persisted in many parts of the country for as long as the woollen industry persisted. The principle of weaving consists of running two sets of spun yarn through one another rectangularly to form the cloth. The warp, the longitudinal yarns, were first arranged between the pegs of a warping frame and transferred into the loom. The wool was woven into the warp by the manipulation of the shuttle, while the pattern was formed by pressing the foot pedals which moved the warp vertically.

The process of fulling was the earliest process to become a factory one and was introduced into Wales by Flemish settlers who came to Pembrokeshire in the fourteenth century. Carding, spinning and weaving continued to be domestic pursuits long after fulling mills had been introduced. The process of fulling consists of the closing together of the threads of woven cloth, so that on being fulled, it thickens. In the Middle Ages fulling mills were known as walking mills, for the earliest form of fulling was to walk on the cloth with the feet, a process that persisted into the twentieth century in some parts of Ireland. A typical fulling mill consisted of a pair of heavy wooden mallets each some eight feet long worked alternately by a water-driven tappet wheel some fifty-six inches in diameter. The pair of iron-lined wooden tappets on each side of the wheel lifted the hammers alternately, so that they descended with considerable force on the cloth placed in the trough beneath. In the traditional process cloth was first fulled with urine, then with fuller's earth and finally with soap.

Finally the nap of cloth had to be raised with teasels and sheared to a smooth finish before it was ready for use.

Today the Welsh woollen industry is very small compared with the highly mechanised trade of Yorkshire. Here and there one may still stumble across the ruins of a woollen mill which bears witness to a very important chapter in the economic history of the Principality, for the woollen industry of Wales possessed the potentiality of developing into an industry of major importance. But due to distance from the markets and the independence of the rural woollen manufacturer, it failed to realise that potential.

2. The Rope Maker

The practice of making rope by plaiting or twisting fibre, strips of hide or animal hair goes back almost to the dawn of man's existence on earth. Like basket making and pottery it is a craft that has not changed in any substantial degree since the dawn of history. Although machinery has been introduced into the ropeyards within the last hundred years, the process of hackling, spinning and twisting has remained substantially the same for thousands of years. An Egyptian rope walker of 400 B.C. could easily recognise the methods employed in country rope-yards at the present time, for in those few yards that still remain open, hand methods still reign supreme.

In Britain the history of rope making can be traced back for two thousand years, and in the City of London alone it has been carried on continuously since Roman times. In the Middle Ages the Corders of the Ropery were among the earliest of the craftsmen to be established as a guild. In the sixteenth century, when Britain reigned supreme as a maritime power, rope making was a vitally important industry and ropeyards were established in almost every coastal town and village. Bridport in Dorset attained pre-eminence as a centre of the maritime rope making industry, for as early as 1211 it was granted a charter to supply the British navy with cordage.

In addition to coastal ropeyards, inland walks were also extremely important and many villages and country towns had their rope makers who supplied a local agricultural market with ropes, nets and halters. Although the country rope maker has virtually disappeared, an old established yard still produces hand-made cordage for the farming population at St. Ives in Huntingdonshire. The celebrated craftsman who spins ropes in Peak Cavern, Derbyshire, still works on a part-time basis. Since the sixteenth century rope had been made in the limestone caves of the Castleton district in conditions of extreme discomfort 'Working in the mouth of a cavern which hangs with icicles in winter and runs with water in summer'.[5]

A variety of fibres may be used for rope making, the most important being hemp. In the past a great deal of hemp was grown in the damp, rich soil of Dorset, and this fact contributed in no small measure to the establishment of the rope making industry at Bridport. Hemp or 'neck-weed', as it was called, was harvested in July and again in September and tied into bundles of thirty-six inches in diameter, threshed with flails and placed in running water for four days or more. The bundles were then dried in the open air ready for use. Today, little home-grown hemp is used and most of it is imported from New Zealand, Mauritius and the East Indies. Manila fibre, sisal, cotton, jute and flax are also widely used in modern rope works, while in the past nettle stalks, willow bark, bramble and dock stalks were equally well known.

The first process in making a rope is to clean the fibres, ensuring that they are parallel, straight and of equal thickness. This sorting process is known as hackling and even in modern rope works it is still done by women. Although machinery working on the same principle as the wool-worker's willy is used in the modern rope works, until recently hackling boards were used for the purpose. The hackle board is a wooden block some sixteen inches long by five inches wide studded with strong, tapered steel pins, each some five inches long. To ensure that the fibre is thoroughly hackled, the rope maker has a series of these boards, with prongs diminishing in size and set more closely together. The hackler takes a handful or 'streak' of hemp, wrapping one end firmly around his hand and distributes a little whale or linseed oil over it, at the rate of one pint to every hundredweight of hemp. Not only does the oil soften the fibres, and facilitate splitting, but it also keeps the hackle pins in good condition. The hemp is struck against the pins and drawn through repeatedly until all the fibres are parallel. First the top half of the streak is hackled, then the bottom half. The hackled streak is then weighed, doubled up to prevent tangling and laid aside ready for spinning.

The actual spinning of yarn takes place in the rope walk, which may be a long, low and narrow building long enough to accommodate a standard rope length of 120 fathoms. Thus the building may be as long as half a mile, although width varies considerably. In most rope walks the building has to be wide enough to accommodate two sets of equipment and two distinct processes, spinning and twisting. In the past many rope walks were open and it was customary to plant trees along its length to give some shelter to the workers who toiled in the rope walk in summer and winter.

The spinner is laden around the waist with the streaks of hackled hemp with the ends at the back. From the middle of the streak he draws out some fibres twisting them between finger and thumb and attaches them to one of the four hooks on the large spinning wheel. This wheel, which is some three feet in diameter to which the whirls are attached, is turned by a crank handle, a job usually done by a young boy. Slowly the spinner walks backwards drawing out more fibres as he does so. He ensures that the fibres emerge equally from both sides of the bundle and with his left hand he makes sure that the yarn is smooth surfaced. As he walks back, the spinner throws the yarn over hooks driven into the beams of the building or over the T-shaped stakes embedded in the ground at regular intervals along the rope walk. When thread of sufficient length has been spun, the boy at the wheel detaches the end from the whirl and fixes it to a winding reel. Slowly the spinner walks forwards along the rope walk, holding the end of the yarn to prevent it unravelling and keeping it taut throughout the journey. The process is repeated until the reel is full with some 250 pounds of well-spun yarn. Spinning is one of the most skilled of all the processes in a ropeyard and a good spinner may walk many miles during a day. 'The whole effect of the spinner moving slowly backwards in the dim light of the rope walk is that of a spider weaving a web in its lair.'[6]

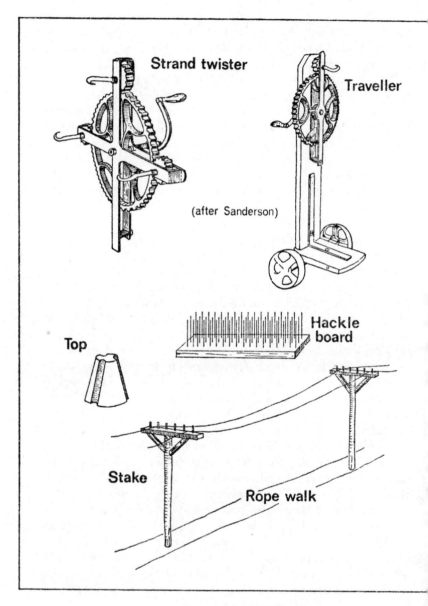

Fig. 43. Rope Making Equipment.

The next process is that of strand making. Spun yarn is unwound from up to twelve reels and stretched along the rope walk in parallel and straight lines. At intervals they are supported by T-shaped posts, with each yarn between the upright divisions of the post. In some yards the yarn passes through a register plate, a round disc pierced with a number of holes along its edges. After the yarns have been passed through this plate, they are drawn through a tube in a fixed or standing part of the rope making machine, known as foreboard. The strand is drawn through the tube and attached to the sledge or traveller, which is a machine furnished with a series of four revolving hooks. Traditionally the yarns were attached to the backs of the hand-operated tackle board at the fore-end of the rope walk. This consists of a heavy and rigid wooden framework with a series of four revolving hooks attached to a wheel at the top. As the hook on the traveller revolves in the opposite direction to those on the tackle board, the double movement ensures that all the yarns are twisted evenly around each other to form a hard, solid strand. As the twisting process shortens the strands, the traveller is pulled towards the tackle board.

Finally the strands are laid; that is the strands are twisted together to form a rope. The three or four strands still attached to the tackle board are fixed to a hook in the centre of the traveller. A cone of hardwood, known as a top is inserted between the three strands at the traveller end. This may be on a special machine known as a top cart. The strands are placed in the grooves of the top and the hooks on the tackle board revolve. This operation causes the top cart to travel in the direction of the foreboard and results in the strands being twisted together to form a rope. According to the speed at which the top cart travels, the lay of the strands in the rope becomes longer and shorter as required. Undoubtedly this method of rope making was well known in prehistoric times and it has continued almost unchanged to the present day. The most laborious process of all is the laying of cables consisting of three complete ropes laid together to provide a strong, elastic cable. In the past this required the strength of as many as eighty men and the use of a large heavy top.

3. The Net Maker

Today, most of the nets used by fishermen in Britain are manufactured by large-scale manufacturers, Bridport in Dorset being
by far the most important net making centre in the country.
Manufacturers are asked to produce a variety of nets that fulfil
conditions of design, size and mesh specified by the authorities
and they may still produce a net that custom and tradition in
various parts of the country have dictated. Although some
fishermen still braid their own nets from one of the bast fibres,
such as hemp and flax, most of the nets in use today are com-
mercially manufactured nets made of synthetic fibres.

The process of making a net by hand is known as 'braiding'
or 'beating'. Ordinary, simple rectangular pieces of netting,
such as are found in drift nets and seine nets, can be made by
machinery, but most of the nets that have to be braided to a
special shape have to be made by hand, although shaped pieces
can be cut from machine-made net and laced together. The
process of hand braiding demands very little in the way of
equipment, but requires considerable dexterity in the manipulation of twine. The twine is first of all wound on a special
hardwood 'needle', which is a wooden shuttle, flat in cross-
section and varying in size according to the size of net being
made. The mesh is regulated by forming each one over a piece
of wood, oval in cross-section and known as 'a spool'. In braiding a net, the twine is wound on the needle by being passed
alternately between the fork or the back of the needle and
round the tongue in its centre, so that the turns of the twine lie
parallel to the length of the needle and are kept on by the fork
and tongue.

The techniques of braiding can vary tremendously, but to
make the simplest form of rectangular net, such as a seine or
drift net, the process is as follows: a length of line is stretched
out taut, usually between two stakes and on to it is set a row of
'bights' or 'loops' of the netting twine. These loops are attached
to the line by a series of 'clove hitches' from right to left, and
they form the first row of half meshes. The second row of half
meshes is then made on to the first, from left to right, the knots
of the second round being made on to the centres of the bights

of the first round, thus completing the first row of full meshes. After the completion of the second round, the process is then repeated from right to left, and thus the third round is made. The completion of the third round closes the half meshes remaining between the bottom halves of the full meshes formed by the completion of the second round, so that two interlocking rows of full meshes are now formed. This process can be repeated indefinitely until the whole piece of net is formed. It is usual, after braiding a few rounds, to remove the original line, thus casting off the clove hitches and leaving free the first row of full meshes, which are then threaded on a line or thin rod.

From the twelfth century, Bridport has been the all-important centre of rope and net making in Britain. Undoubtedly one of the main reasons why Bridport became pre-eminent in the manufacture of cordage was that the soil and climate of Dorset were particularly suitable for the growth of flax and hemp and the early industry was stimulated by the demand of fishermen and boatbuilders, who flourished on the Dorset coast. By the end of the sixteenth century, Bridport, with its superlative hemp and flax and with its long start over other centres, had achieved a virtual monopoly over other centres of production in Britain. Although there was a decline in the industry in the early eighteenth century, the second half of the century saw the return of prosperity, with nets of all kinds, rather than rope, becoming the most important product. At the turn of the nineteenth century, a contemporary writer[7] noted that: 'the manufacture of Bridport perhaps flourishes more than at any other former time and furnishes employment not only for the inhabitants of the town, but for those likewise of the neighbouring villages to the extent of ten miles in circumference. It consists of seines and nets of all sorts, lines, twines and similar cordage and sail cloth.' As in the wool textile trade in Yorkshire, Wales and elsewhere, hemp merchants who organised the manufacturing processes were common in the Bridport district. Samuel Grundy, for example was a merchant and possibly a banker who, as early as 1665, purchased the hemp crop, issued it to families for conversion into yarn and nets in their homes, and then marketed the goods.

Until well on into the nineteenth century, most of the net making was carried on as out-work in the cottages of Bridport and
the surrounding countryside, and methods of braiding by hand
were handed down the generations from mother to daughter.
Net making was organised from a central factory; twine was
delivered weekly and the finished nets were collected when next
week's work was delivered. John Claridge estimated that in
1793[8] there were 1,800 people concerned in the rope and
netting trade in Bridport and a further 7,000 in the surrounding
countryside.

During the nineteenth century imported hemp replaced
the locally grown crop for the manufacture of nets and the
century, too, witnessed the growth of a factory system in the
Bridport industry, with new machines being introduced to spin
and hackle fibres. Hand looms, the early ones known as 'jumper
looms' became commonplace after 1860. The jumper loom,
invented in the 1830's, was so called because of a wooden pedal
on which the operator had to jump. This formed the knots
around three rows of hooks and drew twine for the next meshes
by means of a long needle-like, barb-tipped shuttle. Thrifty
families were able to purchase one and with the purchase of a
second loom and hiring an operator many an individual's
cottage workshop developed into a small factory. By 1900 power
looms were being introduced into the industry, and factory
production of nets was in the hands of fifteen family firms.
Today the industry that supplies most of the netting requirements of the fishing industry is in the hands of one large-scale
manufacturer, although a certain amount of domestic manufacture is still practised. 'Despite looms which tie knots at
unbelievable rates, the net making industry still has to fall back
on outworking skills which are based on pure pre-Industrial
Revolution cottage industry, and has to dispatch vans daily to
take out the raw material, collect the finished nets and pay for
them.'[9]

Traditionally, hemp twine was preferred by all fishermen for
fishing nets, but between the two World Wars low-priced
cotton was widely used. It was regarded as being much lighter
than hemp, despite its inferior strength. Since 1945 synthetic
fibres have become increasingly more important in the netting

industry, although for some nets, such as coracle nets and Dee trammel nets, fishermen still insist on traditional materials. Nets of nylon, terylene, polyethylene and polypropylene, have, according to some, many disadvantages. They are affected by sunlight; some create static electricity and many, being made of very thin twine, can cut off the heads of fish. It is not surprising, therefore, that some fishermen still braid their own nets from hemp and cotton and equip them with headlines of horse and cow-hair, much in the manner of past centuries.

VII

Leather Crafts

1. The Tanner

ONE OF THE OLDEST crafts of mankind is that of the tanner for, even in Palaeolithic times, man knew how to scrape, dry and oil animal skins to produce leather that could be used for a great variety of purposes. The earliest method of tanning was to impregnate hides with animal fats, and Homer describes in some detail how a skin impregnated with oils had to be strained and pulled out in all directions, so that the oils penetrated it completely. This technique of oiling hides, known as chamoising, continued until modern times and the leather produced by it was very flexible and tough. In prehistoric times, too, animal skins were smoked and dried in the sun, while an early discovery was that of applying alum to an animal skin to produce stiff, hard leather known as tawed leather. This, as is depicted in an Egyptian tomb drawing, had to be softened by rubbing or staking against a blunt edge. The alum process of tawing was particularly important in the Middle Ages and like chamoising it persisted until fairly modern times. Throughout the Middle Ages and until the eighteenth century, the great European centre for leather production was the town of Cordova in Spain, where from the eighth to the eighteenth century, the skins of the 'mouflan' – the Sardinian and Corsican sheep were tawed with alum, tanned with sumac and finished with oils to produce leather of unequalled quality. The cordwainers of Spain were primarily concerned with producing leather for footwear and, for well nigh a thousand years they enjoyed a

204

127. Preparing plaiting straws, Pitstone, Bucks.

THE STRAW
PLAITER

128. Sorting straws at Ivinghoe.

129. Prepared clay c[omes]
out of a pug mill at a [?]
shire brick works

THE
BRICK MAKER

130. Moulded, sand-faced bricks placed o[n]
the hack barrow, ready to be taken to th[e]
drying sheds.
131. (*Left*) Stacking bricks in a kiln, read[y]
for firing.
132. (*Below*) Finished bricks.

3. Throwing a flower pot at a Berkshire pottery.

THE POTTER

134. A potter at work.

135. The interior of a pottery kiln.

136. A kiln at Ewenni, Glamorgan, in the early years of the present century.

138. Trimming a block of Portland stone.

137. Quarrying stone at Portland, Dorset.

THE MASON

139. Carving Portland stone.

140. General view Portland stone worksho

141. Building a dry stone wall in the West Riding of Yorkshire.

Inserting tie stones at regular intervals in the wall.

(*Above right*) Placing capping stones.

THE DRY STONE WALLER

144. The completed wall.

146. Slate splitting at a North Wa quarry.

145. (*Left*) A Collyweston slater.

THE SLATER

147. (*Below left*) P. Smith, a Cotswold slater of Stow-in-the-Wold trimming slate at Withington, Gloucestershire

148. (*Below*) Slating a Cotswold roo

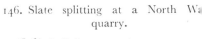

149. The Esgair Moel Woollen Factory from Llanwrtyd, Powys, now at the Welsh Folk Museum, St. Fagans

150. The willy for the initial disentangling of wool.

THE WOOLLEN WORKER

151. Glyndwr Bowen feeding the carding machine.

152. Jenkin Davies of St. Fagans, spinning with a hand mule.

153. Making bobbins on a spinning wheel.

154. Weaving a bedcover

THE WOOLLEN WORKER (continued)

155. The fulling stocks

156. The press.

157. (*Top left*) Drawing out and spinning hemp.

158. (*Top right*) Laying threads at a rope walk in Hawes, Yorkshire.

THE ROPE MAKER

159. (*Left*) The top cart.

160. (*Right*) Crofters making rope on the west coast of Scotland.

161. Harvesting oak bark for tanning.

162. (*Right*) Stored bark ready for grinding.

THE TANNER

163. (*Below*) Grinding oak bark: one of the most unpopular tasks in tanning.

164. (*Below right*) The beamsman scraping away hair at Llanidloes, Powys.

165. The Rhaeadr, Powys,
Tannery in 1895.

THE TANNER (continued)

166. (*Right*) Tan pits in a modern
tannery.

167. (*Below*) Stretching tanned hides
over frames for drying.

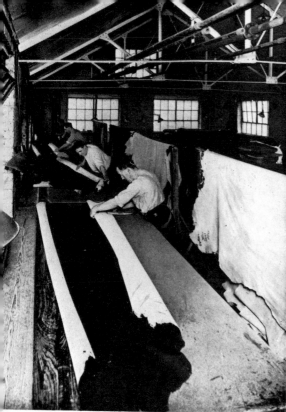

168. (*Left*) Softening leather by staking in a Warwickshire workshop.

THE CURRIER

169. (*Right*) Hand boarding cow hide for upholstery at the London factory of Connolly Bros.

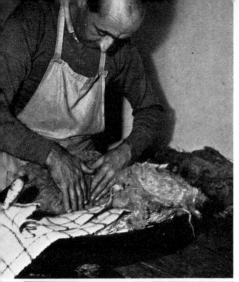

170. Geler Jones of Cardigan making a horse collar. Flock is placed over the straw stuffing.

THE SADDLER

171. (*Middle left*) Straining flannel over the collar stuffing.

173. Thread making.

172. The completed collar.

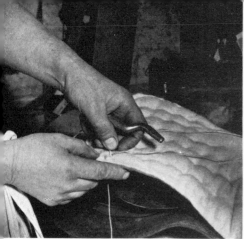

174. Harry Barrett, Feckenham, Worcester-shire using a palm iron for quilting a riding saddle.

175. (*Right*) Cutting leather with a round punch.

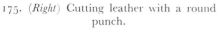

176. (*Left*) Cutting leather for saddles with a half moon knife

THE SADDLER (continued)

177. (*Right*) Geler Jones of Cardigan sewing a harness strap.

179. The stock of bespoke lasts at Long Buckby.

178. A hand bootmaker at Long Buckby, near Northampton, hand lasting a shoe.

THE BOOTMAKER

180. Hammering the seat.

181. Trimming the welt.

182. Thomas James of Solva, Dyfed, shaping a sycamore clog sole with a stock knife.

183. Cutting the channel around the so with the morticing knife.

THE CLOGMAKER

184. Close-up of morticing knife.

185. Assembling the clog.

notable reputation as craftsmen and artists of outstanding capabilities.

Nevertheless, despite the early discovery of oil and alum for treating hides, by far the most common types of tanning agents in Europe were vegetable in origin, the most important and efficient being oak bark. The origins of this method of tanning are unknown, but until recent years oak bark tanneries were extremely common. In Britain they were as ubiquitous as the saddlery and bootmaking trade that they served and many country towns and even villages had their tanneries, where hides from local farms and slaughter-houses were converted into leather. Until the mid-nineteenth century, oak bark tanneries were commonplace in Britain, particularly in the market towns. In Wales, for example, the towns of Radnorshire, Brecknockshire, Montgomeryshire and Merioneth were important centres of the tanning industry. Today the craft in its old rural form has completely disappeared from the Principality. Although some Welsh towns such as Dolgellau, Newtown and Llanidloes possess skinyards where light sheep and goatskins are processed, the production of heavy boot and saddle leather is today a highly mechanised, chemical process concentrated in the industrial regions of Yorkshire and the Midlands.

The old country tanyards obtained their hides from a variety of sources. In some cases they purchased hides from the slaughter-houses of large cities such as Manchester, the Scotch heifer hides being particularly sought after. In other cases they obtained hides from the fellmongers who bought them from local abattoirs or farms. Sometimes, too, the tanner acted as his own fellmonger and bought hides directly from the butchers. All the hides obtained from these sources were known as slaughter or market hides and they arrived at the tannery in a moist, soft condition often covered with blood and dirt. From the mid-nineteenth century, imported hides were widely used by Welsh tanners. These arrived in two conditions: as dry salted hides or as wet salted hides, tightly packed in large barrels, and before they could be tanned, all traces of salt had to be removed. In addition some tanners also used sun-dried or flint hides.

In many Welsh tanneries it was customary to keep one or two large mastiff dogs, and it is said that as soon as market hides were delivered to the tanyard, each one was pegged to the ground so that the dogs could bite off any fats and flesh that adhered to the skins. The mastiffs were, of course, useful to guard the premises and to keep control of the vast number of rats that always infested tanneries. In addition the dogs' excreta when mixed with hot water was essential for treating certain types of soft leather before tanning.

The first process in the lengthy business of tanning was to cleanse each hide in the water pit. Blood had to be removed from market hides as the presence of blood in leather leaves dark stains and bad grain while all traces of salt had to be removed from imported hides. At a tannery in Rhaeadr, Radnorshire, the water pit measuring some seven feet square and nine feet deep received a constant supply of clear water, while the presence of an overflow pipe ensured a gentle movement of the water. In addition to removing impurities, the water bath had the effect of swelling up the fibres of the hide as much as possible, bringing them back to as near as possible to the condition in which they left the animal's back.

After washing, the hides were then placed in one of three lime pits, each one containing a solution of lime and water. The first pit usually contained a weak solution of old lime, highly charged with bacteria, the second pit contained a less mellow solution while the third contained almost new lime. The length of time that hides remained in lime depended entirely on the quality of leather required, for the softer the leather, the longer the hide remained in the pit and the mellower the solution. For example, hides designed for sole leather had to be hard and tough and eight days or ten in fairly new lime was sufficient. Harness leather on the other hand, which had to be much more pliable, required mellow liming of twelve days or more, while soft shoe upper leather required anything up to six weeks in old and mellow lime. The skins were either suspended by chains from the side of the pits or were allowed to float in the lime solution, but the main object of liming was to loosen the hair and epidermis of the hide. These were then removed by special knives leaving the corium, the central layer of skin, which had to be preserved. The craftsman responsible for these cleaning processes was known as a 'beamsman' and he worked in a special building designed for the purpose, known as a 'beam house'. At the Rhaeadr tannery this was a low building measuring some twenty feet long by fourteen feet wide. The tanner's beam is a steeply sloping working table of wood and cast iron, convex in section, over which the hide is thrown for dehairing and fleshing. The unhairing knife is a somewhat blunt, narrow-bladed, two-handled tool which the craftsman used by pushing downwards against the hide. It was considered essential to remove as much as possible of the hair root sheaths and fat glands which could discolour the leather.

After removing the hair, hides were thrown into cold water so that they swelled a little and then underwent the operation of fleshing. This again was done over the beam and the knife used was a double-edged fleshing knife. The concave edge of this was for scraping while the much sharper convex blade was for cutting. Finally fine hairs were removed with a very sharp butcher's knife.

So far the treatment for all skins from the lightest glove leathers to the heaviest sole leathers was similar in principle, but from fleshing onwards there was a great division in technique. Lighter hides for boot uppers, for example, were placed in a solution of hen or pigeon manure and water, to mellow and soften. Great care had to be taken not to leave them in these mastering pits for too long as the solution would rapidly reduce the substance of the hides. Other hides were not mastered in this way, but they were again placed on the beam and all traces of lime removed from them with the slate-bladed scudding knife. Before tanning, too, each hide had to be cut up or rounded with a sharp butcher's knife for the degree of tanning required for the different parts of the hide varied considerably. For example, the butt of a skin is close grained while the offal is loose and coarse. If both are placed in the same tan pit, the best tannin would be soaked up very quickly by the open-pored offal. After mastering, the irregular pieces of hide considered uneconomic to tan, together with the fleshings, were thrown into a pit to be taken away as raw material for glue and gelatine manufacturers.

After scudding and mastering and rinsing through water or weak acid, the tanning process proper began.

To make the tanning liquor, the craftsman needed a vast quantity of oak bark, ground finely and mixed with cold water. In the past oak was especially grown in coppices and the bark was harvested after some twenty-five or thirty years' growth. The coppicing of oak trees for bark was an extremely expensive process, for vast quantities of bark were required by every tannery. Some eighteenth-century farmers regarded the production of oak bark as an essential part of the farm economy and the demand for good quality bark at that time was very large indeed. In more recent times bark was either obtained as a by-product of winter-felled oak trees or those felled during the spring months. It was far easier to remove the bark from spring-felled oak and the method of stripping was to score the tree at intervals of some twenty-four inches with a hatchet or bark knife. Vertical slits were then made with the bark knife and large semicylindrical plates of bark levered off. As tannin is soluble in water, the plates of bark had to be stacked in such a way that the rain did not penetrate them. Barking was a task often undertaken by women and children who sold the bark to the tanneries, and the oaks of Montgomeryshire and Herefordshire were considered especially rich in tannin.

One of the most unpopular tasks in the old tanyards was that of grinding oak bark for the fine dust emanating from the bark mill penetrated everywhere. The large, dried plates of bark were placed in the hopper of the water-driven grinding mill and pushed down between the rapidly revolving cutters of the mill. At the Rhaeadr tannery the bark shed was a very large high building and in the hey-day of tanning it was kept full of ground and unground bark collected from the forests of mid-Wales and the Border counties. The ground bark was carried from the mill in large baskets to the series of leaching pits where the tanning liquid was made by adding cold water to the bark. Occasionally some other vegetable matter such as gambier, valonia or sumac was added to the oak bark in order to hasten the tanning process. The tanning liquor was then pumped from the leaching pits to the others in the yard and tannage began.

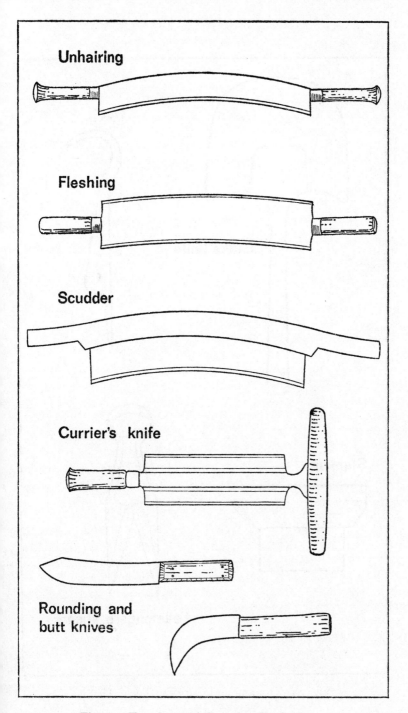

Unhairing

Fleshing

Scudder

Currier's knife

Rounding and butt knives

Fig. 44. ·Tanning and Currying Tools: I.

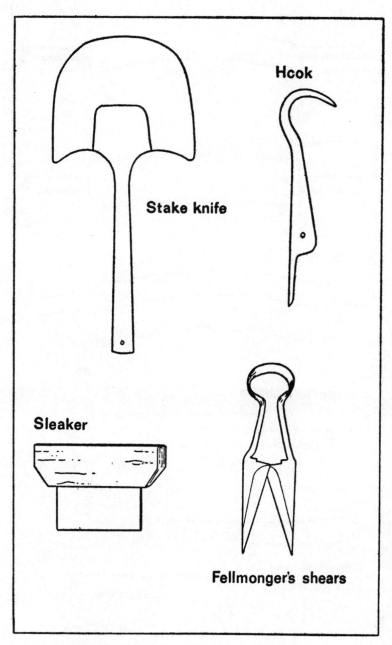

Hook

Stake knife

Sleaker

Fellmonger's shears

Fig. 45. Tanning and Currying Tools: II.

The butts, as unsplit hides are called, were first placed in the
suspender pits, a series of eight or ten pits containing the
weakest liquors in the tanyard. Each hide was tied to a string
and attached to sticks laid across the top of the pit, while a more
modern method was to tie the hides to a wooden framework or
rocker which could be moved gently to and fro to ensure an
even flow of tanning liquids. The hides were moved daily from
one pit to the other; the liquors becoming continuously stronger
from one pit to the other. The tanner had to be very careful
the hides did not touch one another in the suspender pits as
they would display touch marks and be of uneven colour.

At the end of the suspender stage, the butts with all traces of
lime removed would be soft and porous, and they had to be laid
flat to straighten out lumps and creases, before being placed in
the next set of pits – the handlers or floaters. Here the hides
were laid flat rather than suspended and were moved from one
pit to the other at regular intervals of two or three days.
Tanneries had twelve or more of these handlers, and each one
contained continuously stronger liquors. A bucketful of finely
ground bark was often added to the liquor in these pits so as to
increase its strength. A long-handled wooden plunger was used
to distribute the bark dust evenly throughout the pit, while the
spent liquors were pumped back to the suspenders. In the handling pits the hides were moved from one to the other either by
means of long-handled tongs or steel hooks.

After some weeks of moving through the series of handlers,
the hides then passed to the final set of pits, the layers, which
contained the strongest liquors in the yard. Each hide was in
this case sprinkled with finely ground oak bark so that each one
was saturated with tannin as it sank to the bottom of the pit.
Occasionally the liquor in the layer was pumped off, and the
partially exhausted vegetable matter removed for further extraction. The hides were then returned to a new liquor until
they could absorb no more tannin; a process that took anything
up to six weeks.

After the last layer, the fully tanned hides were washed in a
weaker solution before being sent to the drying sheds. Before
drying the hides were very lightly oiled with crude cod liver
oil and allowed to dry slowly and evenly. When half dry they

were laid out in a pile with sacks in between each hide and then pinned with the striking pin. This is a triangular-bladed, two-handled knife designed to remove all irregular marks from the hide. Once again the hides were dried, and in order to knit the fibres together, they were placed under a heavy roller. They were usually rolled three times, with a period of drying between each rolling. The whole process of finishing took at least a fortnight and the craftsman had to take great care with the temperature of the drying sheds.

The tanning of leather was a highly complex chemical process and it is surprising how much of these complexities our forefathers knew. A piece of skin would remain in the tanyard for eighteen months and more before it was converted into leather.

Before a piece of tanned leather could be sold to the saddler or bootmaker, it had to pass through the hands of another craftsman – the currier. His craft was equally complicated, demanding considerable knowledge of the hides and considerable dexterity in the use of hand tools.

2. The Currier

While the tanner's craft is one where considerable knowledge of chemical processes is required, that of the currier is a craft demanding a high degree of skill in the use of hand tools that are entirely different from those used by any other leather worker. The tanner could not complete his work without the assistance of the currier, for tanned leather is stiff and badly coloured, and cannot be used by saddlers, bootmakers and clog-makers without passing through the hands of the currier, whose task it is to make it more supple and highly polished. Although in more recent times tanning and currying were carried out on the same premises by highly skilled, though separate and specialised craftsmen, in earlier times the craft of tanning and the craft of currying were always independent and separate. At the Rhaeadr tannery in the late nineteenth and early twentieth centuries, for example, both crafts were carried out under the same roof, but before 1850 the currier's shop was situated half a mile away from the tannery. Again in South Wales, the mining town of Ystalyfera had its currier's shop until the 1920's, but the nearest tannery was at Brecon, some thirty miles away. These peculiarities of the leather trade in Britain were the result of legislative interference which decreed it illegal to carry on together the two trades of tanning and currying. Thus two operations, which are naturally a part of one process, became separated and leather was dried out by the tanner, taken to the currying shop and then wetted again by the currier.

After delivery from the tanyard the currier's first task is to prepare the leather for dyeing or polishing by removing the 'bloom' and the dried tanning liquor that clog up the grain. The hide is soaked and softened in a hot sumac bath and is then laid on a large mahogany table and scoured with a hard brush, possibly using soap and large quantities of water. To force out the dirt retained just under the hair roots or just below the grain layer, the currier uses a peculiar knife called a sleaker, which is simply a flat steel blade some six inches wide and four inches deep set in a wooden handle. The handle is grasped with both hands and rubbed with considerable pressure against the surface of the hide until all the impurities are removed. In modern tanneries, a striking machine is used for removing bloom. After sleaking and scouring the hides are partially dried or 'sammied' by pressing or squeezing between rollers. The sammying machine, with its pair of heavy rollers pressing against one another with considerable force, was an innovation of the late nineteenth century but the traditional method of sammying, which persisted until recent times in some currying shops, was the heavy brass roller. This is some fifteen inches wide with the roller some eight inches in diameter and it usually required two men to pull and push it over the rolling platform. The platform itself usually some eight feet square had a surface of wood or of sheet zinc and it was a feature of all currying shops.

Perhaps the most skilled and intricate of all the currier's tasks is the hand shaving or splitting of sammied hides. This is done on a heavy upright beam faced with glass or lignum vitae and is undertaken with the peculiarly shaped working knife. This consists of a heavy, rectangular two-edge blade some ten or twelve inches long and six inches deep. It is made of soft steel held by a bar down the centre which carries a handle at each end. One handle is in line with the bar and the other at right angles to it. The knife is first of all ground to a sharp edge and set on a 'Water of Ayr Stone'. It is then placed between the knees, with the cross-wise handle resting on the ground, and the edge is gradually turned to a right angle. This is done by rubbing a smooth steel, held with both hands, with considerable pressure against the blade. This is pressed over the edge, first outside and then down the angle formed by the blade. A thin shaving of leather on the flesh side is then removed and the hide is ready to receive oils and grease.

The process of impregnating leather with grease is known as 'stuffing' and the traditional method is to damp the leather and then apply a thick layer of dubbing to one or both sides. Dubbing itself is a mixture of tallow, preferably that from mountain sheep and cod oil, which in the past was imported from Newfoundland in large casks. These are boiled in a large cauldron and allowed to cool before use. The dubbing is applied with a brush, known as a 'drumming brush' and the hide is allowed to dry slowly at a moderate temperature. As the water evaporates, the fat becomes thoroughly distributed over the fibres, but the harder fat called 'table grease' is left on the surface and has to be removed with a sleaker.

After drying, the flesh side of the hide has to be whitened with a steel sleaker that has a slightly turned edge to remove surplus grease and smooth the surface. The whitening table itself consists of a sheet of plate glass in a wooden frame, which is placed over the currier's mahogany table and, unlike the scouring sleaker which it resembles in general shape, the whitening sleaker is used with a near circular motion rather than in an up and down movement.

The tools for softening leather and for the finishing processes vary considerably. If, for example, the leather as it comes from the tannery is very stiff, it has to be softened on a stake. This consists of a thin half-moon blade some six inches wide fixed to the top of a wooden stake some thirty inches long. The leather is pulled backwards and forwards over this stake until it is soft and all the irregularities removed. For softening white leather made from horse hide and required for thonging, a T-shaped hand staker, again with a half-moon blade is used. Finishing processes differ according to the kind of leather that is being processed. For taking marks out of shoe upper leather and harness leather a stone sleaker is used while for calfskins finishing is done with a sizing pad, a tool some eight inches long that consists of a wooden block with soft leather nailed to it. Again for waxed goods, particularly calfskin, a grain is raised by boarding with a rectangular cork board. This is rubbed lengthways and across the hide for a considerably period of time; it is then passed from corner to corner so that a pebbled grain of no definite form results. For ordinary shoe upper leather the hide is polished and the grain applied with a rectangular mahogany board, which is rubbed over the hide with the fore-arm. Indeed many old craftsmen believed that the best polished surface of all could be obtained by rubbing the flabby, bare forearm over the leather. It is said that in the past a good currier was often recognisable by the fact that his forearm was coloured a near-black.

The blacking of waxed goods is done on the flesh side with a mixture of lamp black and oil, applied to the surface with a circular colouring brush. Smuts are removed with an oval smutting brush and the hide is smoothed and brightened with the forearm or by rubbing with a smooth, thick glass sleaker. Leather in which the grain side is blacked is brush dyed and the grain raised by boarding.

There are, of course, numerous variations in the currying of leather. True Morocco leather of goatskin, for example, has to be tanned with sumac, oiled, dried and then grained with a cork board and finally stretched on a frame. Oil or chamois leather is freely impregnated with fish oil, pressed and washed in alkaline solutions, while calf kid is glazed with flour, egg yolk and oil.

The currier's craft is a very ancient one for in prehistoric times primitive man knew all the secrets of treating stiff hides with oils and specialised equipment. Indeed, the technique of currying changed but little in thousands of years and it is only within the last seventy years with the popularity of chrome leather that the techniques of leather dressing have changed to any great extent.

3. The Saddler

Among the large number of country crafts and industries that have been laid low by the march of progress, none has dwindled so alarmingly as the craft of the saddler and harness maker. In the past, when the inhabitants of Britain looked no further than the boundaries of their own localities for the means of life, the wheelwright, the blacksmith and the saddler were essential members of every rural community. From prehistoric times to almost a hundred years ago the means of communication between one community and another depended almost entirely on the craftsmanship of these three important workers.

The demand for horse harness alone was sufficient to warrant the existence of three distinct and specialised leather workers. The saddler made nothing but saddles for draught and riding horses, the collar maker specialised in making the hundreds of different sizes and patterns of horse collar, and the harness maker made the remainder of the horse's gear. Nevertheless, with the rapid disappearance of the horse from the British scene

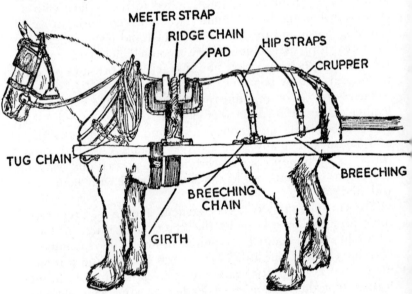

Fig. 46. Cart Harness.

in the late nineteenth and early twentieth centuries, the work for each individual specialist grew less and less. By 1910 those that still remained in the trade had been forced by circumstances to spread their activity over a much wider field, so that one craftsman could undertake all the work that previously had demanded the services of three specialists.

Since 1920 the farm horse has largely disappeared from many districts and the few saddlers that still remain at work, mainly in the market towns, are concerned with repairing all kinds of leather goods, ranging from horse bridles to binder canvases and from brief cases to footballs. It is only in those place such as East Ilsley in Berkshire and Newmarket, which are in close proximity to racing stables, and to a lesser extent in those districts such as mid-Wales which are centres of pony trekking, that the craft bears any resemblance to its past glory. Elsewhere, the true rural saddler, once so common in all parts of Britain is a rarity. In Wales, for example, there were 252 saddlers' shops in 1918. In addition the itinerant craftsman who possessed no workshops, but moved around the country to make and repair horse harness was commonplace. In 1963 there were thirty-two saddlers' shops in Wales, and of those only seventeen were

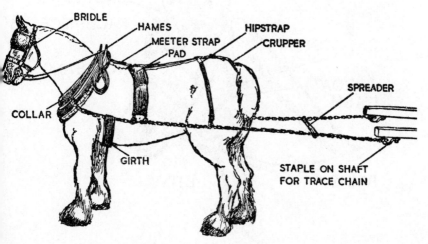

Fig. 47. Trace Harness.

217

occupied by craftsmen working on a full-time basis. In addition only eight of the craftsmen were under the age of sixty, nine being over seventy-five years of age.

Nevertheless, there still exists a considerable demand for the saddler's services, for although horse draught on farms is a thing of the past, horse riding is increasingly popular and repairing belts, canvases and other equipment is a task that constantly needs doing. As in the past, the saddler is still responsible for making all kinds of leather goods, with the exception of boots and shoes.

Saddlery is essentially a hand craft, depending entirely on the craftsman's instinct, dexterity and experience. In the past it took seven years to train a skilled saddler. For the first year the apprentice was given no task apart from waxing hemp threads and stitching neatly. Later, he was taught how to cut out leather for collars, saddles and harness in such a way that the thicker parts of the hide would always form the sections subjected to the hardest wear. But before the apprentice ever tried his hand at making a complete set of harness, these essentials had to be mastered.

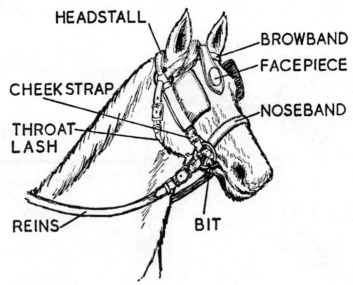

Fig. 48. A Horse Bridle.

One of the most skilled of the saddler's tasks is the making of a horse collar. In the past the design of these varied considerably from one district to the other. Some northern collars had very high peaks, while those of the south had very low peaks at the top, but the method of construction was basically the same in all parts of Britain. As a draught horse works by pushing against the collar, the power being transmitted through the hames and thence to the harness and tugs of the cart or plough, it is essential that the collar is well fitted and smooth.

The saddler's first task in making a collar is to measure the horse carefully, for every collar is made specifically for a particular type and size of animal. The wale or roll of the collar is first made from the tougher variety of leather. This is cut to a size that is always some eight inches longer than double the length of the finished collar. For example, to make a twenty-four-inch collar, the leather must be cut to a length of fifty-six inches to allow for shrinkage. The strip of leather is some seven or eight inches wide and before sewing up into a roll it is thoroughly damped. With an awl and ten-stranded waxed thread the leather is sewn up in such a way that one end of the

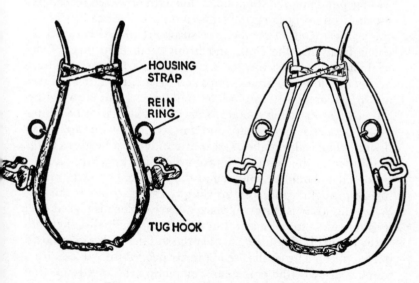

Fig. 49. A Horse Collar and Hames.

seam extends considerably beyond the other. This extension is called the barge and to it the more supple leather of the collar body will be fitted in due course.

The straw used for filling the wale is in most cases the best type of unthreshed rye straw that has been thoroughly combed and dampened. The wale is packed by means of a long iron stuffing-rod, a tool some twenty inches long with a V-shaped notch at the tip. The craftsman places a few strands of rye in this notch and with the bottom of the rod resting on the bench, firmly stuffs the straw into place inside the tube. The strands must overlap and interlock. It is a task that must be completed quickly while the leather is still moist, so that on drying it will shrink evenly upon the straw. The roll itself is continually turned round the craftsman's knee to shape into a semicircle; the two ends are stitched together and the wale is completed. Before it is dried, however, the craftsman must make sure that there are no irregularities in the stuffing.

The body of the collar is made from much thinner, lighter leather to which is attached a length of pure wool, checked cloth. These are stitched to the wale, the craftsman using an awl for punching the stitch holes, a length of waxed thread and a palm iron for pushing the semi-circular collar needle through the leather. Rolls of combed rye straw are placed between the collar body and the cloth and firmly secured in place. Once again the craftsman has to ensure that the leather stuffing is evenly distributed with no lumps and irregularities. The stitches are drawn as tightly as possible, pulling each stitch to tighten the other as in lacing a boot. Next, the straw has to be beaten down between the lacings and this is done with the heavy lignum vitae collar mallet. Great attention must be given to the shaping from the point of view of utility and appearance, for a good collar should be rounded at the bottom, flat at the centre line of draught, gradually growing narrower towards the top. When the straw is firmly in place a layer of flock is placed over it to provide a smooth, soft, but firm cushion. Finally, the cloth of the leather body is strained over the stuffing with a long-nosed pair of pliers. The cloth is temporarily pegged into place with a number of awls, the craftsman completing the task by sewing the cloth to the body with strong waxed thread.

The aristocrat of the leather workers in the past was the saddler himself, who in his work used the best variety of hogskin, silver-plated staples and threads of silk. He had to be proficient in woodwork, too, for a saddle's comfort depends very greatly on the correct shaping of the beech-wood saddle tree which forms the basis of all saddles. In modern saddles, the tree is often of metal. Despite the variation in the design of saddles, the basic method of construction varied little. After preparing the saddle tree, which, in the past, was made by the saddler himself, but which in more recent times could be bought from the large-scale manufacturers of Walsall, lengths of strong webbing are prepared. These are damped and strained across the tree to be nailed in place. As the webbing dries out, it provides a firm, springy surface. Strong linen is then used to cover the webbing and this, in turn, is covered by white serge, both of which are strained over the saddle tree and nailed in place. A small hole is cut in the surface, and in order to prevent the serge from unravelling a little wax is placed around the cut. With a steel tool, some twelve inches long and one inch wide, a tool known as a seat steel, well-carded wool is stuffed into the saddle until it is firm. In a high-grade riding saddle the seat is of the best quality hogskin damped and then nailed to the saddle tree. The skirts, the flaps, the stirrup leathers are of brown leather cut with the half-moon hand knife. In some cases a piece of thin pigskin is glued to its surface to improve its appearance.

A great variety of leathers are used in the saddler's trade, the most common being brown leather obtained from the backs of animals. 'Harness backs' as they are called are of high quality and can be cut into straps of considerable length. For cart horse harness, however, the leather is dyed black and can be greased time and time again without spoiling the colour and in order to maintain its supple quality. The craftsman also uses many types and thicknesses of thread, ranging from simple hemp to fine silk thread for saddles, riding bridles and martingales. Since the saddler requires a great variety of thicknesses of thread for his work, he twists and waxes his own thread. This is twisted by rubbing against the knee and thoroughly waxed by pulling and drawing out. Although beeswax was used in the past for waxing the best quality white thread, the usual wax known as cobbler's or black wax is made from pitch, resin and linseed oil.

Nails are also extensively used by saddlers both for assembling harness and for decoration. For assembling cut nails from five-eighths of an inch to one inch long are preferred, while in saddle making, japanned clout nails are used. For finer work the craftsman may use silver, nickel or brass headed nails. For making a cart saddle with its heavy wooden ridge and black leather, brass nails were traditionally used.

TOOLS AND EQUIPMENT

No craftsman possesses more tools than the saddler and many of those he uses are peculiar to his trade. In the past these tools were made by country blacksmiths, but for many years it is the large-scale manufacturers of Walsall that have held a monopoly in the supply of leather-working tools. Thus the equipment of the country saddler is virtually standardised throughout Britain and few local variations in tool design exist.

(a) Knives

Paring Knife. A knife with a blade no more than three-and-a-half inches long with the end of the blade at an angle of forty-five degrees to the shank. It is used for thinning and paring down the edges of leather.

Hand knife. A general-purpose knife with a blade some six inches long for cutting leather, thread and numerous other processes.

Head knife. A sharply curved, concave knife blade attached to a wooden handle which is used for cutting the holes in buckle tongues and for cutting any circular shapes or holes in leather.

Half moon knife. A knife with the handle in the centre and at right angles to the half circular blade. It is a general purpose tool used for cutting, splicing and thinning leather. Half moon knives can be obtained in different sizes with blades from four-and-a-half inches to seven-and-a-half inches wide.

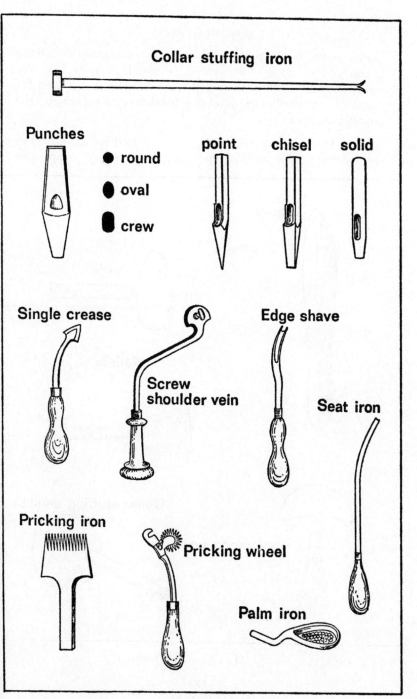

Fig. 50. The Saddler's Tools: I.

Cutting gauge. A tool somewhat similar to a carpenter's marking gauge and is made of box-wood or metal. A knife is firmly screwed to the edge of the ruled stem and the tool is used for cutting a straight line parallel to a fixed margin by moving the adjustable block.

Plough. This is a somewhat more complicated metal version of the cutting gauge and is mainly used for cutting straps and

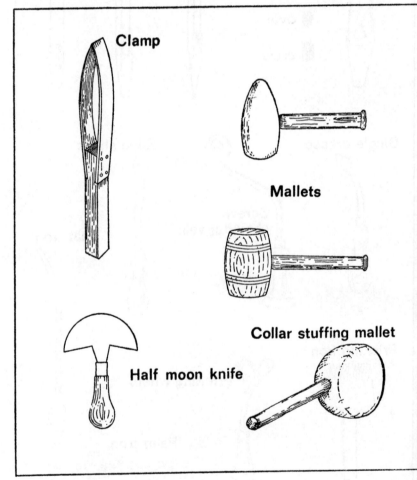

Fig. 51. The Saddler's Tools: II.

belts. Straps from three-quarters of an inch to four inches wide can be cut very quickly by sliding the knife backwards or forwards along the marked gauge.

Spokeshave. The saddler uses this tool, which is similar to those used by woodworkers for thinning down leather, particularly the ends of straps. It is also used to trim traces and other straps. After a trace is stitched, the uneven edges have to be rounded and smoothed with the spokeshave.

Slitting machine. A small tool with an adjustable knife fixed to the saddler's bench. A strap can be drawn through the machine between the knife and the block and rapidly reduced to a half or third of its thickness.

Edge trimmer. A short V-shaped chisel for running along the edges of straps to take off the sharp edge before dyeing.

Washer cutter. A tool with a horizontal inch scale and a knife and pivot at right angles to it for cutting round pieces of leather. Measures some six inches wide.

(b) *Punches*

A saddler possesses a large number of punches of different sizes and shapes, each one known by a standardised number.

Round punches. Numbered 1–16, the smallest being suitable for very narrow straps, the largest for making holes five-eighths of an inch in diameter. The tool is punched with a mallet and the cut piece can be taken out of the punch through the orifice at the front.

Oval punches. Numbered 17–32. Many craftsmen prefer the oval variety to the round for cutting buckle holes in straps, for they do not impair the strength of straps to the same extent.

Crew punches. Numbered 33–43. These cut longer, narrower, parallel sided oval holes than the true oval punches. Again they are mainly used for cutting buckle holes in the wider, thicker variety of strap such as the breeching.

Hand punch. In principle these are somewhat similar to pliers and are fitted with interchangeable round, oval or crew cutting nipples of different sizes. The tool is particularly valuable for punching the thinner variety of leather and for repair work on the farm, for it can be used without removing the harness from the horse.

Scalloping irons. These punches are used for cutting ornamental designs in leather, and there are a vast number of them depending on the saddler's preferences.

Punching lead. To punch leather a piece of lead some one-and-a half inches thick and some twelve inches square is placed on the bench and the leather placed on it. Since lead is soft it will not damage the delicate cutting edges of the punches.

(c) *Mallets and Hammers*

Punching mallet. A round-headed mallet some fourteen inches in length used for beating punches.

Collar mallet. A heavy lignum vitae mallet with a flat, round head for shaping the stuffed bodies of collars.

Hammer. The true saddler's hammer is a light narrow-headed tool with a cross-pein and round face. The head measures some six inches long and the handle is some twelve inches in length. In addition many saddlers use a square-headed wooden mallet and a heavier version of the light hammer for leather work.

(d) *Leather Markers*

Pricking stamp. This punch-like tool is used for stamping lines preparatory to stitching. They vary in width from three teeth, used for marking scalloped work, to twenty-four teeth for straight lines. The teeth on each iron are designed to mark a certain number of stitches per inch from six to sixteen. They are set at a slight angle to the iron to make an impression on the leather and act as a guide to the shape and length of the stitch.

Prick Wheels. A prick wheel consists of a serrated, revolving wheel attached to an iron shank and wooden handle. They are designed for marking stitches ranging from seven to sixteen to the inch. The serrated wheels are interchangeable.

Screw race. An adjustable V-shaped tool used for grooving lines when it is necessary to sink the stitches below the surface of the leather.

Single crease. A wooden-handled tool with a thick triangular tip used for marking leather. For marking thick leather they are heated before use.

Screw crease. A wooden-handled tool with a pair of small, adjustable triangular blades for marking lines along the edge of the leather and for marking the lines for stitching. By means of a screw the points are adjusted, so that the line to be creased can be nearer or further away from the margin. The saddler usually possesses a light and a heavy double crease for marking the different qualities of leather.

Checker. This is a small double crease with fixed points for marking ornamental checked lines on loops. One edge is run along the last line marked and serves as a guide to keep the lines parallel. Checkers again come in different sizes.

Beveller. A tool that is similar in shape to the single crease but the triangular point is much thicker and its sides bevelled. They are used for creasing or marking loops on leather that requires ornamenting and the point of the beveller is thoroughly heated before use.

In addition saddlers have many other specialised creases such as single and double purse creases with square points which can be bought in many different sizes; they have single, double, triple or bevel monkey veins with rectangular blades for decorating harness and a variety of seam turners.

(e) *Perforating Tools*

Awls. The saddler always has a variety of awls, each one fixed to a wooden handle. *Stitching* awls vary in size from one-and-a-quarter inches to three inches long and some should be thick enough to stitch perhaps a ten-threaded cord of hemp, while the smaller should be slender enough to thread silk and cotton threads.

Bent awls are also required for stitching wire in saddle making and for stitching in inaccessible positions.

Needles. A large number of these are required. *Harness needles* numbered 1–6, the lowest number being the coarsest and used for all waxed threads. *Quilting needles,* 2 or 3 inches in size are required for such fine tasks as quilting saddle panels. *Pointed needles* for use with the thimble in stitching linings to saddle panels and other purposes.

Collar needles. Of half-moon shape or straight with bent points ranging in length from three inches to six inches. These are required for collar making. The longest are required for heavy cart horse collars of considerable thickness.

Seat awl. This is used for easing and levelling stuffing in saddles. It can also be used for levelling thread. This is turned once around the awl which is then drawn sharply backwards and forwards, the lumps thus being taken out of the thread.

Palm iron. This is a thimble used on the palm of the hand when driving collar needles through leather. A shallow honeycombed well is formed in the hand part which prevents the needle from slipping. At the point that projects from it a hole is found and this is used to force the needle closer to the leather and for drawing the needle through the leather.

(f) *Miscellaneous Tools and Equipment*

Compasses. Small compasses with straight twin-pointed arms are constantly required by the saddler for such tasks as marking the widths of strap to be cut. Race compasses with a knife point are also used for cutting a small groove or line along the edges. They take off a narrow strip of the grain leaving a faint line.

Clamp. This consists of two springy pieces of wood screwed together for holding the work firmly in position while a piece of leather is sewn. This is held by the saddler at a slant between his knees. In the past two oak barrel staves were often used by country saddlers for making clamps.

Collar stuffing rod. This tool used for stuffing collars is an iron rod some twenty inches long with a V-shaped notch at its tip.

Seat iron. A flat iron rod some twenty inches long with a serrated tip used for putting flock into saddles. Unlike the collar stuffing rod, the seat iron can be bent easily so as not to tear the saddle cover or stretch it.

Loop sticks. These are hardwood strips, usually of box-wood varying from one-and-a-half inches to two inches in width and from one eighth to half an inch in thickness and they are used for shaping leather loops.

Rubber. A piece of hard close-grained wood or even glass some six inches square and V-shaped on one edge. It is used for smoothing stitches on the underside of straps, smoothing down edges or for flattening and levelling any two substances such as leather and linen pasted or stitched together.

There are a number of other tools that are not peculiar to his trade that the saddler requires. For example, his tool chest usually contains a variety of rasps and files, long-nosed pliers, pincers and nail claws.

4. The Bootmaker

Although the rural bootmaker, once so common in all parts of Britain, is a rarity today, hand-made boots and shoes are still in considerable demand. Bespoke boot and shoemakers are still found in most towns, while in the chief centres of the footwear trade in Leicestershire, Northamptonshire, Norfolk and Somerset, the hand bootmaker is still far from rare. He works in a trade where only fashion has changed, for the technique of boot-making has changed but little in hundreds of years. The hand bootmaker differs from his fellow worker in a large factory in that he is responsible for performing every operation from start to finish, while the factory worker is in the main responsible for only one process. It was only at a late stage that the boot-making industry became highly mechanised, for hand work and simple tools tarried much longer in bootmaking than in almost any other trade. Woollen manufacturing, for example, was highly mechanised by the middle of the nineteenth century, but it was only during the first quarter of the present century that factory methods gradually supplanted traditional workmanship in the boot and shoe industry; indeed as hand craftsmen are still employed by large organisations, that process of mechanisation is far from complete.

The bootmaker requires a number of different qualities of leather for his craft. For example, shoe upper leather must be soft and supple, sheepskin or kid may be required for linings, while sole leather must be hard and durable. In addition the quality of leather in the front or vamp of a shoe may be quite different from that used for the back or quarter of a shoe, while that used for the tongue may be different again. Cutting the various sections demands considerable knowledge of leather, for the parts have to be cut in such a way that there is very little wastage of leather. A hide may vary considerably over its surface and the craftsman must know exactly what part must be cut from a particular section of skin. Since boots are made in pairs, the bootmaker must pay attention, not only to the colour of leather, but also to its thickness and stretching qualities so that each boot matches its fellow as nearly as possible in every respect.

The process of cutting the upper parts of a boot or shoe is known as 'clicking'. The equipment of the hand clicker is very simple, for all he requires is a cutting board and a knife. The cutting board is made up of small blocks of wood clamped together so that the knife edge cuts across the grain. In order to prevent the surface from becoming rough, this has to be scraped and smoothed at frequent intervals, for a rough surface hampers the free movement of the knife. The clicking knife is a short-bladed tool and although today clicking knives are fitted with blades that can be changed according to the type of leather that is to be cut, in the past the bootmaker required a series of knives. For example, to cut heavy, thick leather a curved blade was considered best, while for thin leather a straight-bladed

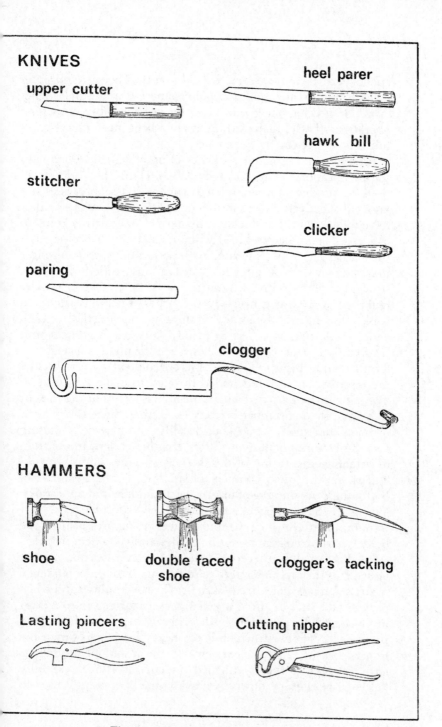

Fig. 52. The Bootmaker's Tools: I.

clicking knife was necessary. In addition the clicker requires an awl of small diameter, with a point some two and a half inches long, for making the guide holes for the assembly or closing operations. The cloth or kid linings of a boot must also be carefully cut to pattern by the clicker.

After clicking come the sequence of processes concerned with the preparation, fitting together and stitching the various sections to produce the completed uppers. These processes are known collectively as 'closing'. Some of the edges of the leather have to be reduced in thickness by paring away with a knife, so that seams may be produced without bulkiness. In some cases the leather has to be decorated with perforations while its edges may be serrated or gimped. The various sections are then stitched together with awl and thread. The craftsman usually makes his own thread from several straws of hemp twisted and waxed together and pointed with stout pig bristles at both ends. With the boot resting firmly between his knees and secured by a strap or piece of rope held firmly down with one foot, stitching begins. The awl pierces the leather, the bristles are inserted, crossed and pulled through to make a lockstitch. The stitches are flattened with a burnisher, irregularities are cut away and the boot upper is ready for lasting. Since the pattern of boots and shoes varies considerably, the process of closing also varies; ornamentation differs greatly, as does the pattern of stitching, the nature of the sections and the linings.

Perhaps the most complex of all the processes is that of bottoming; the shaping of insoles, heels, middle and outer soles. The outer sole and heels, since they receive most wear, are cut from butt leather, while the middle and insides are cut from the lighter portions of the hide, the bellies and shoulders in particular. First of all leather for soles is soaked in water in a narrow vessel. It is then hammered to solidify it and reduce its tendency to stretch. The insoles are tacked in place over a last, and when partially dry two or three wooden pegs are driven in to hold it in place and the tacks removed. With a sharp knife the leather is trimmed. The welt, which is the heavy leather to which the uppers are attached is next sewn to the insole all around its edge, but before this is attached the edge has to be carefully flattened or thinned down. An awl with a bent point is used to perforate the insole at points where the welt is to be stitched. Heels are built up of layers or lifts of belly leather, finished with a single layer of butt leather. They are shaped with flat-headed hammer on a lap stone or lap iron, a smooth surface which is considered essential for the correct shaping and conditioning of sole leather. The middle and outer sole are treated in the same way, cut to shape and channelled with a line parallel to the outline of the sole. While the welt is sewn on with long stitches, averaging four to the inch, the sole is sewn on with very short stitches, possibly eight to the inch. The stitches are completed within the channel and they should have

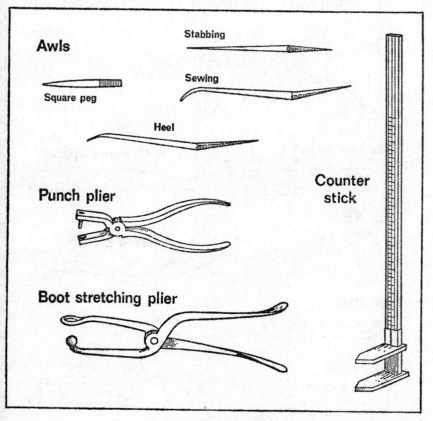

Fig. 53. The Bootmaker's Tools: II.

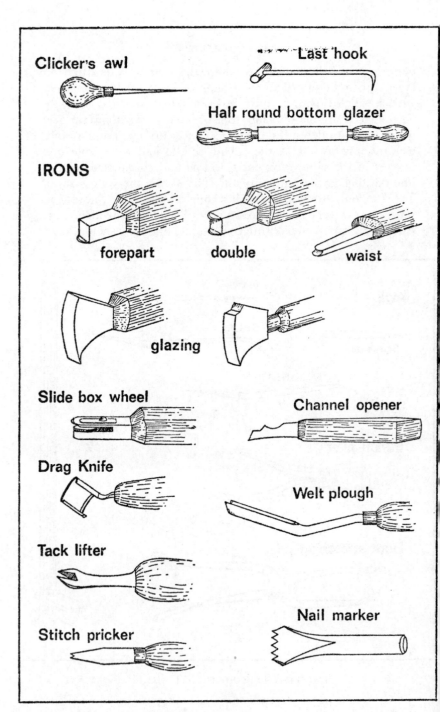

Fig. 54. The Bootmaker's Tools: III.

a regular pattern. Therefore considerable care is necessary in piercing the sole with the awl.

After stitching, the bottom is finished before the heel is put on. The stitch channel is closed by pressing it out towards the edge of the boot and rubbing it down to a smooth surface. The edges of the welt and sole are gently hammered until they are level and the bottom is rubbed with wet pumice stone. The heel is then fixed with wooden pegs and stitched firmly in place.

Finally the boot is lasted. The assembled uppers are strained with pliers over the metal or beechwood last which represents the shape of the customer's foot. The boot is then ready for sewing and the boot is polished and finished with great care. Lace holes are cut, eyelets inserted and all irregularities smoothed down.

5. The Clogmaker

A craft closely related to that of bootmaking is that of clog-making. Indeed in some parts of the country one craftsman was responsible for making both types of footwear. In others, however, the clogmaker was a specialised craftsman, concerned only with making wooden-soled clogs. In addition to itinerant cloggers (pp. 22–5) almost every village and rural locality, particularly in the north and west, had its clogmaker, who made footwear for each individual buyer, measuring the feet and making the clogs to fit those feet. Unlike the clogger, the village craftsmen used a great deal of sycamore. In the past Welsh clogmakers reckoned that a sycamore tree cut from the hedgerow produced far superior soles to those cut from a forest or plantation. The trees are felled and immediately converted into sole blocks, first with beetle and wedge, then with an axe and finally with the large stock knife. The process so far, is similar to that adopted by itinerant cloggers, and a few deft strokes with this guillotine-like stock knife soon reduces the blocks of wood to nearly the correct shape. In the case of the village clogmaker, however, measurements that are more accurate than the cloggers 'men's', 'women's', 'middles' and 'children's' are adopted, for the clogmaker measures the customer's feet accurately and transfers those measurements to a paper pattern. In many clogmaker's workshops, patterns representing the feet of generations of local inhabitants may still be found. After highly skilled work with the stock knife, a similar knife, but in this case with a convex blade some three inches wide is used to shape the top surface. This is the hollowing knife and it is followed by the morticing knife or gripper, whose narrow V-shaped blade cuts a channel for fitting the leather uppers all round the sole. Finally the sole is finished with rasps and short-bladed knives until it is perfectly smooth.

The leather uppers are again cut out in accordance with a paper pattern, the method of working being the same as clicking in bootmaking. Stiffeners are inserted at the heels, lace holes are cut and eyelets fitted and the assembled leather uppers are strained over a wooden last. It is tacked in place, hammered into shape and left in the last for a few hours to be moulded into the correct shape. Unlike a boot, the clog is removed from the last before assembling. Unlike the boot, too, the clog upper is not sewn to the sole, but nailed with short flat-headed nails. A narrow strip of leather is cut and placed over the junction of uppers and sole. Great care has to be taken to ensure that the nails used in assembling point downwards and are in no danger of damaging the wearer's feet. Replaceable grooved irons are nailed to the sole and the heel; a bright copper or brass tip is tacked to the front and the clogs are ready for wear. With constant use and the replacment of irons at regular intervals a pair of clogs may last without resoling for at least twelve years.

Notes

I. Introduction

1 Jenkins, J. G. *The English Farm Wagon*, 2nd ed. 1977.
2 Peate, I. C. *Welsh Folk Crafts and Industries*, 1945, p.x.

II. Woodland Craftsmen

1 Fitzrandolph, H. E. and Hay, M. D. *Rural Industries of England and Wales*, Vol. 2, 1926, p. 101.
2 Edlin, H. L. *Woodland Crafts in Britain*, 1949, p. 78.
3 For a description of the Sussex method see Edlin: ibid., p. 73.
4 Ibid., p. 73.
5 Fitzrandolph & Hay: op. cit., p. 102.
6 Edlin: op. cit., pp. 73–4.
7 For a full discussion of the uses of charcoal in industry see Edlin: op. cit., pp. 161–5.

III. Village Woodcrafts

1 Fitzrandolph and Hay: op. cit., p. 36.
2 Fitzrandolph and Hay: op. cit., Vol. I, p. 99.
3 Ibid.
4 Jenkins, J. G. 'The Cooper's Craft,' *Gwerin*, Vol. 1, No. 4, 1957, pp. 149–60.
5 Jenkins, J. G. and R. A. Salaman: 'Note on Coopering,' *A History of Technology* 1958, Vol. III, p. 128.

237

6 'Stails' or 'Tails' are the straight handles of such tools as rakes, forks and hoes. 'Snaiths' or 'Sneads' are the artificially curved handles of such tools as scythes.
7 Jenkins, J. G., op. cit., 1962.
8 Mayes, L. J. *The History of Chairmaking in High Wycombe*, 1960, p. 10.
9 Ibid., p. 11.
10 Ibid., p. 17.

IV. Metal and Straw Crafts

1 Duddle, R. S. *The Craft of the Metal Worker*, 1951, p. 81.
2 Edward Elwell Ltd., 1962 Catalogue.
3 Rural Industries Bureau. *The Blacksmith's Craft*, 1952, p. 3.
4 The Annual Report of the Rural Industries Bureau, 1959–60, pp. 11–12.
5 Rural Industries Bureau. *The Thatcher's Craft*, 1961, p. 4.
6 Ibid., p. 125.
7 Freeman, C. *Luton and the Straw Hat Industry*, 1953, p. 13.
8 Ibid., p. 13.

V. Stone and Clay Crafts

1 Woods, K. S. *Rural Crafts of England*, 1949, p. 222.
2 Thompson, R. H. G. 'The Medieval Artisan' in *A History of Technology*, Vol. III, 1957, p. 384.
3 Ibid., p. 385.
4 Macdonald, J. (Ed.) *Stephens Book of the Farm*, 1908, Vol. I, p. 105.

VI. Textile Crafts

1 Wymer, N. *English Country Crafts*, 1946, p. 80.
2 Patterson, R. 'Spinning and Weaving' in *A History of Technology*, Vol. II, 1957, p. 193.
3 Lemon, H. 'The Hand Craftsman in the Wool Textile Trade,' *Folk Life*, Vol. I, 1963, pp. 66–76.
4 Evans, H. *The Gorse Glen*, 1948, pp. 87–8.
5 Interview with Herbert Marrison, the last of the Castleton rope makers in April 1964.

6 Fitzrandolph & Hay: op. cit., Vol. I, p. 210.
7 Brayley, E. W. and Britton, J. *Beauties of England and Wales*, Vol. IV, 1801, p. 519.
8 Claridge, J. *General View of the Agriculture . . . of Dorset*, 1793, p. 26.
9 *The Sunday Times*, 7th November 1971, p. 67.

Bibliography

I. GENERAL

ALEXANDER, BRUCE (ed. .), *Crafts and Craftsmen*, 1974.
ARNOLD, JAMES, *The Countryman's Workshop*, 1953.
ARNOLD, JAMES, *The Shell Book of Country Crafts*, 1968.
BLANDFORD, PERCY, *Country Craft Tools*, 1974.
The Book of English Trades, and Library of the Useful Arts, 1827.
DERRICK, FREDA, *Country Craftsmen*, 1947.
——*Country Craftsmen*, 1950.
DERRY, T. K. and WILLIAMS, T. I., *A Short History of Technology: from the Earliest Times to A.D. 1900*, 1960.
EDLIN, H. L., *Woodland Crafts in Britain: an Account of the Traditional Uses of Trees and Timbers in the British Countryside*, 1949.
HARTLEY, DOROTHY R., *The Countryman's England*, 1942–3.
HARTLEY, D. R., *Made in England*, 1939.
HARTLEY, D. R. and ELLIOT, M. M. V., *Life and Work of the People of England: a Pictorial Record from Contemporary Sources*, 3 Vols., 1925–31.
HENNELL, THOMAS, *The Countryman at Work*, 1947.
HOGG, GARRY, *Country Crafts and Craftsmen*, 1959.
HUGHES, G. B., *Living Crafts*, 1953.
JENKINS, J. G., *The Craft Industries*, 1972.
JOBSON, ALLAN, *Household and Country Crafts*, 1953.
JONES, J. L., *Crafts from the Countryside*, 1975.
MASSINGHAM, H. J., *Country Relics*, 1939.
MOXON, JOSEPH, *Mechanick Exercises: or the Doctrine of Handyworks* . . . 1703.
NORWOOD, J. L., *Craftsmen at Work*, 1977.
OXFORD UNIVERSITY. Agricultural Economics Research Institute: *The Rural Industries of England and Wales. A Survey made*

on behalf of the Agricultural Economics Research Institute, Oxford.
Vol. 1. 'Timber and Underwood Industries and some Village Workshops', by H. E. Fitzrandolph and M. D. Hay, 1926.
Vol. 2. 'Osier-growing and Basketry and some Rural Factories', by H. E. Fitzrandolph and M. D. Hay, 1926.
Vol. 3. 'Decorative Crafts and Rural Potteries', by H. E. Fitzrandolph and M. D. Hay, 1927.
Vol. 4. 'Wales', by Anna M. Jones, 1927.
QUENNELL, MARJORIE and C. H. B., *History of Everyday things in England*, 4 vols., 3rd ed. revised, 1950–2.
SALZMAN, L. F., *Building in England down to 1540: a Documentary History, 1952.*
——*English Industries in the Middle Ages, 1913.*
SINGER, C. J. *et al.* (eds.), *A History of Technology.*
Vol. I. 'From Early Times to Fall of Ancient Empires', 1954.
Vol. II. 'The Mediterranean Civilizations and the Middle Ages', 1956.
Vol. III. 'From the Renaissance to the Industrial Revolution, *c.* 1500–*c.* 1700', 1957.
Vol. IV. 'The Industrial Revolution, *c.* 1750–*c.* 1850', 1958.
Vol. V. 'The Late Nineteenth Century, *c.* 1850–*c.* 1900', 1958.
STOWE, E. J., *Crafts of the Countryside*, 1948.
TOMLINSON, C., *Illustrations of useful arts, manufacturers and trade*, n.d.
URE, *Dictionary of Arts, Manufacturers and Mines*, edited by R. Hunt and F. W. Rudler, 4 vols., 1878.
WILLIAMS, W. M., *The Country Craftsman; a study in some rural crafts and the rural industries organisation in England*, 1958.
WOODS, K. S., *Rural Crafts of England: a Study of Skilled Workmanship*, 1949.
—— *The Rural Industries round Oxford:* a survey made on behalf of the Institute for Research into Agricultural Economics, 1921.
WYMER, N. G., *English Country Crafts: a Survey of their Development from Early Times to Present Day*, 1946.
—— *English Town Crafts: a Survey of their Development from Early Times to the Present Day*, 1955.

II. WOODLAND CRAFTSMEN

EDLIN, H. L., *Woodland Crafts in Britain: An Account of the Traditional Uses of Trees and Timbers in the Countryside*, 1949, 1973.
FORESTRY COMMISSION, *The Manufacture of Wood Charcoal*, 1961.

LAMBERT, F., *Tools and Devices for Coppice Crafts*, 1957.
MAYES, L. J., *The History of Chair Making in High Wycombe*, 1960.
MAYES, L. J., *The Windsor Chair Maker's Tools* (A descriptive guide to the collection in the High Wycombe Museum) n.d.
ROE, F. G., *The Windsor Chair*, 1953.
RURAL INDUSTRIES BUREAU, *The Thatcher's Craft*, 1961.
WALTON, JAMES, 'Charcoal Burners' Huts', *Gwerin*, vol. 2, no. 2 (1958), pp. 58–67.

III. VILLAGE WOODCRAFTS

ARNOLD, JAMES, *The Farm Waggons of England and Wales*, 1969.
BAGSHAWE, T. W., 'Rake and Scythe-Handle Making in Bedfordshire and Suffolk', *Gwerin*, vol. 1, no. 1 (1956), pp. 34–57.
BOBART, H. H., *Basket Work through the Ages*, 1936.
COLEMAN, J. C., 'The Craft of Coopering', *Journal of the Cork Historical and Archaeological Society*, vol. 1. XLIX, no. 170 (1944), pp. 1–12.
COLLIER, D., *Basket Making*, 1924.
COVENTON, W., *Woodwork Tools and their Use*, 1953.
ELKINGTON, G., *The Cooper's Company and Craft*, 1933.
FARMER, F. H. (ed.), *Handbook of Hardwoods*, 1972.
FIRTH, J. F., *The Cooper's Company*, 1848.
GOODMAN, W. L., *A History of Woodworking Tools*, 1964.
HANKERSON, F. P., *The Cooperage Handbook*, 1947.
HORNELL, JAMES, *British Coracles and Irish Curraghs*, 1938.
JENKINS, J. G., *Agricultural Transport in Wales*, 1962.
JENKINS, J. G., *The English Farm Wagon*, 1972.
JENKINS, J. G., *Nets and Coracles*, 1974.
JENKINS, J. G., *The Cooper's Craft*, 1972.
JENKINS, J. G., 'Some Country Basket Makers', *Gwerin*, vol. 3, no. 4 (1963), pp. 186–9.
JENKINS, J. G., 'Bowl Turners and Spoon Carvers', *Folk Life*, vol. 1 (1903), pp. 35–42.
KILBY, K., *The Cooper and his Trade*, 1971.
KNOCK, A. J., *Willow Baskets*, 1965.
MERCER, H. C., *Ancient Carpenter's Tools*, 2nd ed., 1951.
OWEN, T. M., *Welsh Folk Customs*, 1959.
PEATE, I. C., 'Some Welsh Woodturners and their Trade', *Studies in Regional Consciousness and Environment* (1930), pp. 175–88.
PEATE, I. C., *Welsh Folk Crafts and Industries*, 1945.
PINTO, E. H., *The Craftsman in Wood*, 1962.
—— *Treen and other Wooden Bygones*, 1969.

ROSS, WALTER, *The Village Carpenter*, 1937.
SALAMAN, R. A., *Dictionary of Tools used in the Woodworking and Allied Trades*, 1975.
STURT, G., *The Wheelwright's Shop*, 1923.
WRIGHT, DOROTHY, *Baskets and Basketry*, 1959.

IV. METAL AND STRAW CRAFTS

AUSTIN, J. G., *The Straw Plaiting and Straw Hat and Bonnet Trade*, 1871.
DONY, J. G., *A History of the Straw Hat Industry*, 1942.
DUDDLE, R. S., *The Craft of the Metal Worker*, 1951.
FREEMAN, C., *Luton and the Hat Industry*, 1953.
GALE, W. K. V., *Iron and Steel*, 1969.
HOGG, G., *Hammer and Tongs*, 1965.
HOLMES, C. M., *The Principles and Practice of Horse Shoeing*, 1928.
INWARDS, H., *Straw Hats, their History and Manufacture*, 1922.
LAMBETH, M., *The Golden Dolly*, 1969.
LISTER, R., *Decorative Wrought Iron work in Great Britain*, 1957.
LISTER, R., *The Craftsman in Metal*, 1966.
NIALL, I., *The Country Blacksmith*, 1966.
RICHARDSON, C., *Practical Farriery*, 1950.
ROBINS, F. W., *The Smith*, 1953.
RURAL INDUSTRIES BUREAU, *The Thatcher's Craft*, 1961.
RURAL INDUSTRIES BUREAU, *The Blacksmith's Craft*, 1952.
RURAL INDUSTRIES BUREAU, *Wrought Iron Work*, 1957.
SANDFORD, L., and P. B. DAVIS, *Decorative Straw Work*, 1964.
SMITH, D., *Metalwork: an Introductory Historical Survey*, 1948.
WEBBER, R., *The Village Blacksmith*, 1971.

V. STONE AND CLAY CRAFTS

BENFIELD, E., *Purbeck Shop: a Stoneworker's Story of Stone*, 1940.
BILLINGTON, D. N., *The Art of the Potter*, 1937.
BILLINGTON, D. N., *The Technique of Pottery*, 1964.
BREARS, P. C. D., *The English Country Pottery – Its History and Techniques*, 1971.
CLARK, K., *Practical Pottery and Ceramics*, 1966.
CLIFTON, TAYLOR A., *The Pattern of English Building*, 1972.
DALTON, W. B., *Craftsmanship and Design in Pottery*, 1957.
DAVEY, NORMAN, *History of Building Materials*, 1961.
DIGBY, G. W., *The work of the Modern Potter in England*, 1952.
DOBSON, C. G., *Roofng Slates and Tiles*, 1952.

DOBSON, E. A., *Rudimentary Treatise on the Manufacture of Bricks and Tiles*, 1850.

FOURNIER, R., *A Handbook of Practical Pottery*, 1973.

GODDEN, G. A., *An Illustrated Encyclopaedia of British Pottery and Porcelain*, 1966.

GOODSON, F. L., *Clay Preparation and Shaping*, 1962.

HAGGER, R. G., *English Country Potters*, 1950.

HONEY, W. B., *The Art of the Potter*, 1946.

KNOOP, D. and G. P. JONES, *The Medieval Mason*, 1933.

MITCHELL, C. F., *Building Construction*, 1902.

NASH, W. G., *Brickwork 1*, 1966.

RAINSFORD-HANNAY, R., *Dry Stone Walling*, 1957.

RHODES, D., *The Complete Book of Pottery Making*, 1959.

—— *Clay and Glazes for the Potter*, 1959.

ROWDEN, E., *The Firing of Bricks*, 1964.

SALZMAN, L. F., *Building in England down to 1540*, 1952.

SOLDNER, P., *Kiln Constructions: Design and Making*, 1965.

THOMAS, J., *The Rise of the Staffordshire Potteries*, 1970.

WALTON, J., 'The English Stone-Slater's Craft', *Folk Life*, vol. 13 (1975), pp. 38–53.

VI. TEXTILE CRAFTS

DAVENPORT, E. G., *Your Hand Spinning*, 1953.

HADERER, A. E., *Ropes and Rope Making*, 1950.

INTERNATIONAL WOOL SECRETARIAT, *The World Book of Wool*, n.d.

—— *Warp and Weft*, n.d.

—— *Woollens and Worsteds*, n.d.

—— *Wool in History*, n.d.

—— *Wool through the Ages*, n.d.

—— *Growing Wool*, n.d.

—— *Science and Wool*, n.d.

—— *Making Wool Fabrics*, n.d.

JENKINS, J. G. (ed.), *The Wool Textile Industry in Great Britain*, 1972.

—— *The Welsh Woollen Industry*, 1969.

LIPSON, E., *The History of the Woollen and Worsted Industries*, 1921.

MARET, E. M., *Vegetable dyes*, 1940.

—— *Handweaving today*, 1939.

PONTING, K. G., *The Wool Trade, Past and Present*, 1961.

SIMPSON, L. E. and WEIR, M., *The Weaver's Craft*, 1932.

WOODHOUSE, T. and KILGOUR, P., *Cordage and Cordage Hemp and Fibres*, n.d.

VII. LEATHER CRAFTS

BORDOLI, E. (ed.), *The Boot and Shoe Maker*, 4 vols. (1935).
CARNELL, H. A., *Leather*, 1950.
HASLUCK, P. N. (ed.), *Saddlery and Harness Making*, 1962.
JENKINS, J. G., *The Rhaeadr Tannery*, 1971.
KEEGAN, T., *The Heavy Horse: its Harness and Harness Decoration*, 1973.
PROCTOR, H. R., *The Making of Leather*, 1914.
STANDAGE, H. C., *The Leather Workers Manual*, 1921.
THORNTON, J. A., *Textbook of Footwear Manufacture*, 1958.
WATERER, J. W., *Leather Craftsmanship*, 1968.
WATERER, J. W., *Leather and Craftsmanship*, 1956.
WATT, A., *The Art of Leather Manufacture*, 1890.

Index

247